LINKIN PARK
AN OPERATOR'S MANUAL

THE ULTIMATE GUIDE BY NEIL DANIELS

Linkin Park: An Operator's Manual
by Neil Daniels

A CHROME DREAMS PUBLICATION
First Edition 2009

Published by Chrome Dreams
PO BOX 230, New Malden, Surrey,
KT3 6YY, UK
books@chromedreams.co.uk
WWW.CHROMEDREAMS.CO.UK

ISBN 978 1 84240 471 3

Edited by   Cathy Johnstone
Cover Design   Sylwia Grzeszczuk
Layout Design   Marek Niedziewicz

LINKIN PARK

AN OPERATOR'S MANUAL

THE ULTIMATE GUIDE BY NEIL DANIELS

*I'd like to thank the following
people for their help with interviews,
research and for their thoughts
and opinions...*

THE ROCK FOLK:
Carl Begai (*BW/BK*), Malcolm Dome
(*Classic Rock/Metal Hammer*), Lonn
Friend (legendary rock writer/ex-*RIP*
editor), Mark Hoaksey (*Powerplay*),
Dave Ling (*Classic Rock/Metal Ham-
mer*), Tamas Madacsy (Piknik Park),
Joel McIver (Author), Anthony Mor-
gan (*Lucem Fero.com*), Jason Ritch-
ie (*Get Ready To Rock.com*) and Ron
"Bumblefoot" Thal (Guns N' Roses).

EVERYBODY ELSE:
Rob Johnstone and all at Chrome
Dreams, Robert McKenna for design-
ing and regularly updating *neildan-
iels.com*, my partner, Emma, and my
family and friends. Apologies if I have
missed out any names.

Acknowledgments ... 4
Introduction ... 6
About The Author ... 10

[ONE] THE STORY OF LINKIN PARK

Chapter 1 One Step Closer
The Early Years (1996-1999) ... 11
Chapter 2 Global Theory
Hybrid Theory & Reanimation (2000-2002) ... 27
Chapter 3 World Domination
Meteora & Collision Course (2003-2005) ... 45
Chapter 4 Hands Held High
Creating Minutes To Midnight (2006-2008) ... 61
Chapter 5 Linkin Park Today (2009) ... 79

[TWO] PERSONNEL & ASSOCIATES

Chapter 6 The Ex-Members Of Linkin Park ... 87
Chapter 7 The Solo Projects ... 91
Chapter 8 The Peers ... 101
Chapter 9 The Associates ... 117
Chapter 10 The Influences ... 133

[THREE] THE MUSIC & LIVE CAREER OF LINKIN PARK

Chapter 11 The Music ... 147
Studio Albums ... 147
Remixes & Collaborations ... 155
CD/DVD Packages ... 161
Live Albums (CD/DVD) ... 163
Demos ... 169
EPs ... 170
DVDs ... 174
Singles ... 176
Music Videos ... 184
10 Most Memorable Linkin Park Songs ... 194
10 Kick-Ass Live Recordings ... 201

Contents

Bootlegs – The Unofficial Linkin Park Recordings . . . **204**
Paying Homage – Linkin Park Tribute Bands . . . **208**
Tribute Albums . . . **210**
Linkin Park Underground – Fan Club Only Releases . . . **213**
Guest Appearances / Featured Vocals . . . **217**
Compilations Featuring Linkin Park . . . **222**
Soundtracks Featuring Linkin Park . . . **223**

Chapter 12 **The Gigs & Tours** . . . **225**
Headlining Tours . . . **225**
Selective List Of Support Bands . . . **236**
Festivals . . . **238**
Charity Concert Appearances . . . **250**
Memorable Gigs / Tours Around The World . . . **252**
Memorable North American Gigs . . . **253**
Memorable UK Gigs . . . **254**
Memorable TV Appearances . . . **256**

[FOUR] BITS & PIECES

Chapter 13 **Bits & Pieces** . . . **259**
Selective List Of Awards . . . **259**
Polls/End Of Year Lists . . . **264**
The Critics Response To Linkin Park's Music . . . **266**
Linkin Park In Their Own Words . . . **273**
Random Trivia . . . **277**
Official Linkin Park Books . . . **280**
Unofficial Linkin Park Books . . . **282**
Unofficial Linkin Park DVDs . . . **283**
Unofficial CD/Audio Books . . . **285**
Websites – Linkin Park In Cyberspace . . . **286**
Linkin Park In Showbiz . . . **290**
Timeline . . . **293**

"We've always been a band that experiments with different sounds. Sometimes the most simple sound works for the song and sometimes it takes a lot of work to make a sound happen."

Mike Shinoda speaking to *nyrock.com*, 2003

In what is essentially a relatively short space of time (2000-2009) Linkin Park have become one of the most successful metal bands of the past decade. They are certainly one of the top groups of their ilk since the controversial grunge era, there's no question about that. Of course there are generic debates about Linkin Park because of their nu-metal roots and heavy use of rap vocals and scratching, but their latest album, *Minutes To Midnight* – which is basically straight-forward yet ballsy metal – is a testament to their strength as a bona fide contemporary metal band. They have graced the covers of possibly every major music magazine in publication (rock, metal and urban) in the UK, America and the rest of the world and have played to packed stadiums worldwide.

However, despite great commercial success, they have never been darlings of the rock critics. *Hybrid Theory* sold in its millions but frequently received mixed or mediocre reviews. The famous American music critic, Robert Christgau famously wrote in *The Village Voice* that *"...the men don't know what the angry boys understand..."* awarding the album only two stars. And Christgau's reluctant review was not the only one to express a dislike for the Southern Californian band. The metal-hating weekly *NME* did not warm to the band's unique style, proclaiming: *"...otherwise damn fine, soaring emo-crunchers like 'With You' and 'A Place For My Head' are pointlessly jazzed up with tokenistic scratching..."* For Linkin Park it has been a case of, you certainly can't please everyone, least of all the critical establishment.

In the author's opinion, Linkin Park's three studio albums, *Hybrid Theory*, *Meteora* and *Minutes To Midnight* have not received the critical attention they deserve, despite enthusiastic record sales and enough awards to fill a recording studio. *Hybrid Theory* is still a fantastic album and *Meteora* has many good spots, despite suffering from the difficult 'second album syndrome' which has plagued many bands – trying maybe too hard to be like its older sibling – and is patchy at best. On the other hand, *Minutes To Midnight* was a welcome surprise and showed critics that the group had, indeed, grown up. It didn't please everyone, but credit should go to the band (and its producer Rick Rubin) for attempting something totally different from the norm.

However, it's those in-between albums that gave Linkin Park their first big missteps: *Reanimation* and *Collision Course*. The live albums *Live In Texas* and *Road To Revolution* are predictable affairs, but nevertheless thoroughly enjoyable. Each member of the band is talented in their own unique way and when they get together as one tight force they can clearly create vibrant, exciting and often unconventional compositions.

There are naysayers who have attacked Linkin Park for being the worst type of corporate rock band in existence; a band that records angst-ridden music simply as a marketing tool, as a means to make money in these post-grunge years. Of course, such misguided statements are erroneous. Linkin Park are not a corporate rock band. Corporate rock is just a generic term the press uses to separate the million-selling rock bands from the arty bands that can't shift any records yet create supposedly awe-inspiring lyrics.

Linkin Park were not conceived by some A&R rep at a major label; their career has not been dictated by their label, well, in no way dissimilar to any other band on a major label. They formed in Southern California in the late nineties; three of the band members (Mike Shinoda, Brad Delson and Rob Bourdon) were High School buddies. Sure, Jeff Blue at Warner Records gave a helping hand, but any band would be grateful to an A&R executive for giving their career a kick-start. How many bands owe the legendary A&R guy Jeff Kalodner (ex-Atlantic and Geffen) a big thank you and a hand shake? In this post-Nirvana/Kurt Cobain world, so many bands have been mocked for having angry lyrics and even angrier vocals; it's as if nobody can be angry because, well, Cobain was a messiah and nobody can speak for a generation of kids the way he did. Chester Bennington certainly had his fair share of inner turmoil and has battled his personal demons, so why can't he justifiably write about his experiences in the song lyrics?

As the title suggests, *The Operator's Manual* is not a biography per se, but rather a guide to the music of Linkin Park. In sum, Part One is a potted history of Linkin Park that quickly takes you through the important parts of the band's story, beginning in the mid-nineties; Part Two offers mini-biographies of the solo/side projects of the individual members as well as the careers of former members of Linkin Park, and even potted biographies of some of their nu-metal peers and influences; Part Three goes in-depth on the music and tours, while Part Four is basically a compilation section detailing awards, websites and unofficial published material on the band as well as lots of other goodies. There are boxes of information situated throughout the book and relevant to each section, which expand the story of Linkin Park.

It's a reference book, similar to my last work, *The Bon Jovi Encyclopaedia* [Chrome Dreams 2009], and as such is perfect for both dipping in and out of or reading from cover to cover – either way it will hopefully prove informative, enlightening and entertaining. There are many different sides to the band, and hopefully this book, with the way it is formatted, will explain all the different facets of a truly groundbreaking and some-

times controversial group. One word that certainly describes them is "unconventional." They like to do things differently.

This is by no means a definitive biography, that's not the point; it's a way of telling the story of the band and examining the music in a way that's not your straight forward biography, it's more of a *reference* book. Many people have helped the band on their road to success and this book will highlight many of those names, some of them familiar, some of them almost unheard of. It's all here: the highs and lows, the wins and loses, from the beginning to now. Bands are funny things...

Neil Daniels
June, 2009

Visit me at *neildaniels.com*

NEIL DANIELS

has written about classic rock and heavy metal for a wide range of magazines, fanzines and websites. He has penned books on Judas Priest, Robert Plant and Bon Jovi and co-authored *Dawn Of The Metal Gods: My Life In Judas Priest & Heavy Metal* with Al Atkins. Neil currently writes for *Fireworks*, *Powerplay* and *Get Ready To Rock.com*, and occasionally contributes to *Rock Sound* and *Record Collector*. His reviews and articles have also appeared in *The Guardian* and *Big Cheese* and on the websites *Drowned In Sound.com*, *Carling.com* and *Unbarred.co.uk* as well as *Planet Sound* on CH4 *Teletext*. Neil has also contributed articles and reviews on films to the academic publication *MediaMagazine* and the popular arts ezine *musicOMH*. More information is obtainable at *neildaniels.com*.

BOOKS BY NEIL DANIELS

The Story Of Judas Priest: Defenders Of The Faith
(Omnibus Press, 2007.)

Robert Plant: Led Zeppelin, Jimmy Page & The Solo Years
(Independent Music Press, 2008.)

The Bon Jovi Encyclopaedia
(Chrome Dreams, 2009.)

Dawn Of The Metal Gods: My Life In Judas Priest & Heavy Metal with Al Atkins
(Iron Pages, 2009.)

PRAISE FOR THE AUTHOR'S PREVIOUS WORKS

"Neil Daniels is great on the early years of Brummie metal legends Judas Priest…"
Classic Rock on *The Story Of Judas Priest: Defenders Of The Faith*

"The book also has a curious appendices exploring – among other things – Percy's interest in folklore and mythology."
Mojo on *Robert Plant: Led Zeppelin, Jimmy Page & The Solo Years*

"If you're a Bon Jovi fan then you're going to find a lot to dive into within these pages."
Record Collector on *The Bon Jovi Encyclopaedia*

CHAPTER 1

ONE STEP CLOSER: THE EARLY YEARS (1996-1999)

"We're just musicians. If people ask me what I do, I tell them that I'm a musician. I don't say that I'm a rock star. Number one, it's not my rock."

Mike Shinoda[1]

The story of Linkin Park can be traced back to the mid-nineties, an unsettling time for fans of metal music. Grunge, the sound of Seattle, had decimated a vast majority of the eighties rock bands and a new breed of rock star was born. Alternative rock/metal became the mainstay in the nineties and Linkin Park would, in years to come, create their own unique brand of alternative music using digital samples, rap vocals and metal guitars.

Mike Shinoda and Brad Delson were High School friends from sunny Southern California, and it was their friendship and shared love of both rap and rock music that led them to form their first united musical endeavour. Shinoda was born Michael Kenji Shi-

noda on 11th February, 1977, the year *Star Wars* was released. The older Shinoda got, the more profound his love of music became: whilst attending Parkman Elementary and Lindero Canyon Middle School, he studied classical piano at the behest of his mother, Kim Shinoda. An artistic child, his tastes in music varied; he never harboured any prejudice towards a particular genre, which is uncommon amongst children who tend to be far more concerned with the current (fickle) trends. As the years progressed, Shinoda met an equally enthusiastic kid named Brad Delson at Agoura High School. By this point, Shinoda had taken to learning the guitar and furthered his passion for music by listening not just to jazz and blues but rock, rap and other types of popular music. Although his Japanese heritage was important to him (his father, Leslie, is of Japanese descent) Shinoda was completely immersed in American pop culture, including movies and com-

Agoura High School

ic books. He was especially interested in computers and art, thus it wasn't just the music that he enjoyed but the record sleeves too. Growing up, his favourite artists included Run DMC, Grandmaster Flash and Public Enemy, amongst lots of others.

Delson was inspired by Shinoda's rapping skills and the pair became immediate friends. This was around the late eighties when rap and rock were beginning to merge together as if it was some weird science experiment. Run DMC and Aerosmith had joined forces for the hit single 'Walk This Way' and The Beastie Boys were already excelling themselves as an extraordinary hybrid rap-rock band.

Brad Delson came from a hospitable family. His parents would arrange charity Christmas dinners and both Brad and his buddy Mike Shinoda would wait tables for those less fortunate than themselves. Brad Delson was born

Bradford Phillip Delson on 1st December, 1977. He started playing guitar after hearing the impact the electric riff had on people, as if it was some magnetic force-field in a science-fiction show like *Star Trek*. Delson eventually met fellow guitarist Rob Bourdon, who was leaning more towards the drum stool than the plectrum, and the pair formed an outfit called Relative Degree. The tale goes that they played one single solitary show and quickly folded. It was their only aim. Nothing less. Nothing more. Just the one show. Delson told Shinoda about his new friend and the trio quickly became friends and let their imagination run free.

When Robert Plant and Jimmy Page got together at Page's boathouse on the River Thames in Pangbourne, Berkshire the singer and guitarist talked about music that was not simply black and white, but had shades of grey and varying textures and tones. They liked Joan Baez's 'Babe I'm Gonna Leave You' and the Muddy Waters tune 'You Shook Me. They wanted to merge the electric guitar with the folk acoustic guitar and send the listener into another realm of consciousness. It was those ideas which formed the basis for Led Zeppelin. Well, the triumvirate of Mike Shinoda, Brad

Brad Delson - School Years

Xero with Jeff Blue

Delson and Rob Bourdon also had plans for a modern style of music that was completely extraordinary for the time. Shinoda brought his love of rap and free-styling to the table while Delson was into rock and on the other side of the coin completely, Bourdon was a keen funk enthusiast. He dug the likes of James Brown – the 'Godfather of Soul' – Stevie Wonder and even Earth, Wind and Fire. Shinoda and Delson also liked the electro pop sounds of Depeche Mode and New Order. What would happen if all those four musical genres were thrown into the one melting pot?

In 1995, the three budding musicians graduated from college and formed their first outfit together, Super Xero, more popularly known as Xero. The line-up of the band would soon be extended when Shinoda enrolled at California's prestigious Art Cen-tre College of Design in Pasadena to study graphic design and illustration. As every prudent person knows, it is always wise to have a back up plan so if either his art career or music career went belly up he'd have one or the other to fall back on. It was at the college where Shinoda met Joseph Hahn, a fellow artistically inclined hip-hop and rap enthusiast. Of Korean descent, Mr. Hahn was born in Glendale, California on 17th March, 1977 and was at the college to pursue a career in the film industry. Hahn was fixated with comic books and big screen Hollywood special effects extravaganzas like *Close Encounters Of The Third Kind* and *Star Wars*. It was his early interest in pictures and music that led him towards video directing. Joe Hahn was the

Mark Wakefield

key ingredient in the band. Neither an extrovert nor a show-off, Hahn was more interested in the mixing side of rap than the actual vocal parts. It was the creation of a piece of music from different instruments which compelled him.

Where as Shinoda's instrument of choice was a microphone, Delson's a guitar and Bourdon's a drum kit, Hahn's tool was a turntable. He was more a DJ than anything else, interested in creating a montage of sounds and creating samples, loops and scratches with his decks.

Next-up to join the fold was bassist Dave "Phoenix" Farrell.

"I actually studied the violin for about eight years," he once said, *"and I've also played a lot of cello. When I got into rock music I switched over to guitar – then I switched to bass in the first real band I was in at high school."*[2]

In his late teens, Brad Delson enrolled at University of California, Los Angeles (UCLA) to take a Bachelor of Arts degree in Communication Studies that concentrated in Business and Administration. A member of Phi Beta Kappa academic society, Delson shared a dorm room with Dave Farrell. Mike Shinoda's childhood friend, singer Mark Wakefield, also became a member of Xero in early 1996 and the initial line-up of the band was cemented. Around this time Joe Hahn quit college to join the film industry in the special effects department, but he continued to jam with Xero and record demos in Shinoda's makeshift studio in his bedroom.

Xero was a fun project and an excuse to cover their favourite artists, usually a hip-hop outfit or a metal band. There was a definite divide in the band in terms of mu-

Brad Delson at University of California

sical inspiration. On the one hand there was Delson, Farrell and Bourdon with their unquenched taste for all things loud, aggressive and electric, hence their eagerness to blast out Metallica tunes. And then there was Shinoda and Hahn who were more interested in Depeche Mode or Public Enemy. It was at this juncture that they decided to focus completely on Xero: they didn't want to be just another band trying to make it big in the City of Angels, a town that is as famous for swallowing and spitting out the talent as it is for furthering one's career. Hell, that's Hollywood as they say.

The mid-nineties saw a vastly evolving musical landscape. Grunge had become a thing of the past after Kurt Cobain's suicide and shrewd industrial metal bands like Nine Inch Nails and the 'God Of Fuck' Marilyn Manson, were making (infamous) names for themselves in the mainstream, while on the other hand a new breed of metal band offered an alternative and even intelligent slant to the genre. The days of Mötley Crüe and Poison were stuck in the past and bands like Korn and Rage Against The Machine blasted their angry music across the nations. As for rap and hip-hop, it would still be some years before – gulp – masses of

white working (and even middle) class music lovers would actually go into a store and buy a controversial Run DMC album. Nevertheless, the 1990's music scene was the perfect breeding ground for a band like Xero. They didn't give a damn about trends; they wanted to create their own.

Xero recorded a demo in Mike Shinoda's bedroom. They had the talent, the enthusiasm, and fortunately, the equipment to record music. The demo in question was a self-titled affair that featured just four tracks: 'Rhinestone', 'Reading My Eyes', 'Fuse' and 'Stick N' Move.' The only member not to be acknowledged in the songwriting credits was Mr. Rob Bourdon. It was this demo that commenced Linkin Park's recording career because 'Rhinestone' was an earlier version of the *Hybrid Theory* track 'Forgotten'; 'Stick N' Move' has a riff that was later repeated in the track 'Forgotten'; the band also recorded a tune called 'Esaul,' an infant version of 'A Place For My Head' which also features on the band's smash-hit debut. Of course any notion of a smash-hit album at that point was exactly that – a notion.

Xero sent out countless copies of their first demo to as many record labels as they could think of. They received no reply and whatever response they did receive was probably a polite rejection, something along the lines of *"Sorry this is not for us. But keep trying, you have potential."*

Frustration came into play and the members, particularly singer Mark

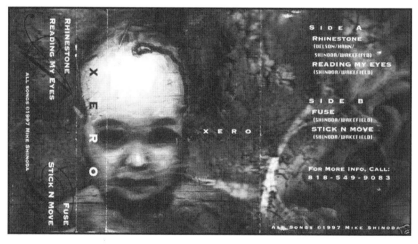

Their debut demo was recorded in 1996 and released the following year with just a limited amount of copies available. The main purpose of the demo, as is always the case with independently released music, was to promote the band to which ever fanbase they appealed to (in this case an alternative crowd) but also as a means to attract potential record deals.

Wakefield, were becoming increasingly annoyed at a lack of success and recognition. They may have been onto something with regards to their distinctive sound, but was it too experimental? Did record executives think Xero's music would be too far from the mainstream? It is a debatable point, but for answers one would have to ask the executives in question. However, there was certainly a market for a band that had a thirst for electric beats, rock guitars and experimental vocals. It worked for Aphex Twin, Tool and Deftones. Yet the suits in the high rise record company office buildings obviously didn't think so.

The timing could not have been more apt. Guitarist Brad Delson

constructive criticism and said he would check them out. An obvious man of his word, he took some of his fellow executives along to see Xero support the rising alternative metal outfit System Of A Down at the iconic club Whiskey A Go-Go in West Hollywood. Ticket sales were not on the high side but there was an aura about the place, and as it was Xero's first major show they were nervous as hell. At the

was doing work experience at Zomba Publishing in Los Angeles. His boss was an A&R man named Jeff Blue, who was previously a successful music journalist, and knew as much about the music itself as the business side of the industry. Delson did the wise thing and handed Blue a copy of Xero's self-titled demo. Blue, liking what he heard, offered some harsh yet

Whiskey, could the band repeat the success that had been afforded to such legendary names as the Rolling Stones, Alice Cooper and The Doors? Everything about the venue bled rock and roll. It was in the air, the paint... and even the sweat. As it happens, Xero gave a good enough performance to win them a publishing deal with Zomba. The band had been working their collective backsides off for the past year, struggling with either college or work (possibly both) as well as trying to make a go of it with the band, and now all the hard work seemed to have paid off. Although a publishing deal was not a record deal, suddenly that big leap did not seem so hard to make. There was something on the horizon and they were getting closer to it.

Speaking some years later about his early relationship with Xero/ Linkin Park, Jeff Blue explained:

WHISKY A GO GO

The world renowned Whisky A Go Go club at 8901 Sunset Boulevard, West Hollywood, has witnessed performances by the true elite of British and American rock acts since it opened its doors in 1964. The Who, Led Zeppelin, Alice Cooper, Cream, Oasis, Nirvana, Roxy Music and Guns N' Roses have all trodden the boards at the Whisky, and it was as support to System Of A Down in 1997 that Xero, an early incarnation of Linkin Park, were first witnessed on the stage of this legendary venue. The audience that evening included executives from Zomba Music, and the band were signed to a publishing deal the next day.

Fast forward to 8th November, 2006, and the three remaining members of The Doors are celebrating their 40th anniversary at the club, fronted by Val Kilmer, the actor who had portrayed Jim Morrison in the Oliver Stone, Doors movie. Later that evening Chester Bennington joins Densmore, Krieger and Manzarek, also as an honorary Lizard King.

"For three and a half years, I spent every day with Linkin Park, also in the development process, and I was able to sign them. So all in all I've been with Linkin Park for a total of six years now. I'm a big believer in the spending-time way of developing."[3]

Jeff Blue

Xero performed more showcase gigs for record labels; it has been reported that they played half-a-dozen such shows during a weekend that preceded Mike Shinoda's final exams at the Art Centre College of Design.

However, Wakefield was finding it hard to be in a band without a record deal and thus any financial backing and as 1998 progressed his mind wondered off to the possibility of other perhaps more lucrative and fulfilling projects. Bassist Dave Farrell was also getting anxious and thinking of other things. *What if the band doesn't make it? What do I do then?* They could have been playing in a group whose success looked more assured. Farrell left to spend more time with other bands and to concentrate on his college studies. Wakefield left too. Depending on the source of information, Wakefield was either forced to leave the band or left on his on volition. Wakefield

would still have a role to play in Linkin Park; he is acknowledged in the songwriting credits on *Hybrid Theory* and the remix opus *Reanimation*. This, of course, left two holes in the band. Which route do they go down now? They could call it a day, feeling somewhat burnt out and unwelcome in the business or they could shop around for a new bassist and singer and give it another go. There was talent there; it just needed to be nurtured.

Cue Kyle Christener, who came in to play bass after Farrell's departure. Finding a singer took a little longer and this is where Jeff Blue, an avid supporter of the band, stepped in and offered his expert opinion. It was in March 1999 when Blue, Vice President of Zomba Music, suggested an Arizona singer named Chester Bennington audition for them – Bennington had actually been name-checked to him by a friend in the business.

The singer was born Chester Charles Bennington on 20th March, 1976 in Phoenix, Arizona. Prior to auditioning for Xero, he had a soul destroying job at Burger King, the fast food chain, whilst also gigging in the post-grunge outfit Grey Daze, which he quit at some point in 1998. Grey Daze was a great training ground for the young Bennington; the job gave him the confidence and ambitions for life that he needed. They'd actually released an album called *No Sun Today* and although

Bennington had gigged in other groups and done some solo stints, Grey Daze is his most well-known pre-Linkin Park outfit.

Bennington had not had an easy life; his parents had divorced when he was just 11 years old and he battled a drug addiction (allegedly to be cocaine and methamphetamine) in his teens; this addiction would fuel some of the anger that is apparent in his vocals and the lyrics to some songs on *Hybrid Theory* and *Meteroa*.

Bennington shared the same law firm as Xero, a company called Miniet, Phelps & Phelps, so it was almost predestined that the two sides would meet somehow. The story goes that Jeff Blue – who at

ZOMBA MUSIC PUBLISHING

Originally founded in London in the mid seventies, Zomba Music launched in the lucrative North American market in 1981, and set up the Jive record label, home to such notables as Britney Spears, Backstreet Boys and N'Sync. Linkin Park has an interesting history with Zomba Music Publishing, which began when UCLA student Brad Delson had an intern stint at the company and handed A&R chief Jeff Blue a demo of his band Xero. Blue first saw Xero live in 1997 at the Whisky A Go Go (supporting System Of A Down) and he signed them to Zomba immediately after the gig. The 1999 EP *Hybrid Theory* (featuring

Chester Bennington, Mike Shinoda, Brad Delson, Joe Hahn, Rob Bourdon and Kyle Christener), was released via Zomba in May 1999. Zomba was sold to the giant Sony/BMG in its entirety in 2001, netting over $3 billion for the owners of what was then the world's biggest independent label.
Visit *zombalabelgroup.com*

Grey Daze

the time was staying in Texas for a music conference – sent Chester Bennington two demo recordings: one tape had the vocals of Mark Wakefield whilst the second was purely instrumental. Blue asked Bennington to record his vocals on the second tape. It was actually Bennington's 23rd birthday on the day he received the tapes and he initially turned Blue down, saying he had personal commitments. However, Blue persuaded Bennington to give it a go and so the singer left his birthday party and travelled to a local studio in Phoenix where he worked on the demo. He played the tapes back to Jeff Blue and the band the next day over the phone and they were blown away by Bennington's vocal strength and power. Blue knew he had the perfect singer for Xero. Bennington then auditioned for them in LA at the behest (and personal fiscal cost) of Jeff Blue and it seemed that he had everything Mike Shinoda was looking for in a singer. He was a strong rock vocalist whose voice would work in unison with Shinoda's rapping and the band's eclectic sound. Other singers had auditioned for Xero but with Chester Bennington it was literally a done deal. Who knows what would have happened for the band if Blue hadn't met his friend at the music conference in Texas and recommended Chester Bennington from Phoenix?

Bennington moved to LA right away and his wife Samantha, whom he married on 31st October,

1996, moved to California just a month thereafter. It was in the Sunny State that stands next to the Pacific Ocean that his life would change forever.

Xero's line-up now looked like this: Chester Bennington (vocals), Mike Shinoda (MC, vocals, keyboards, rhythm guitars), Rob Bourdon (drums), Brad Delson (lead guitar), Kyle Christener (bass) and Joe Hahn (turnta-

sel', 'Technique', 'Step Up', 'And One', 'High Voltage' and 'Part Of Me' as well as a hidden track called 'Ambient' (also known as 'Secrets.') One thing the EP did show positively was how quickly Shinoda embraced Bennington's writing skills. The Phoenix born singer had certainly lived a life and he wanted to convey his emotions and thoughts in the band's lyrics and so he was the co-writ-

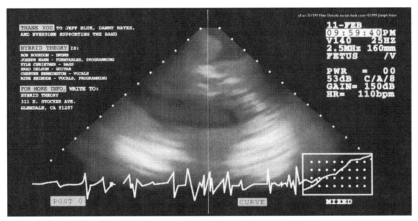

bles and samples.) Another major change came in early 1999 when they changed their name from Xero to Hybrid Theory. Wanting to get noticed with a powerful new singer, the band recorded a self-titled EP in Shinoda's bedroom studio. *Hybrid Theory* features songs that would later be reworked on their mega-selling debut album. Produced by Mike Shinoda, the EP consists of 'Carou-

er of 'Carousel', 'And One' and 'Part Of Me.' While Dave Farrell was temporarily out of the picture, the bass parts were laid down by Christener and Delson. But Christener was the only member who was *not* acknowledged in the songwriting credits.

The artwork and photography for the EP, which was released in May 1999 and limited to just a thousand copies, was designed/

completed by Mike Shinoda, who had gradated from college the previous year with a degree in illustration; he could have quite easily secured a job as a graphic designer had he not chosen to pursue his duties with the band.

"The month I graduated," he explained several years later, *"I had to decide if I should turn*

oda's MC-ing than Mark Wakefield's voice ever did, and Bennington also brought his love of a good melody to the table. He was a huge fan of the British-American melodic rock band Foreigner, whose melodies ('Jukebox Hero' and 'Cold As Ice') are some of the most famous in popular music. Bennington was also said to be a fan of the great Canadian progres-

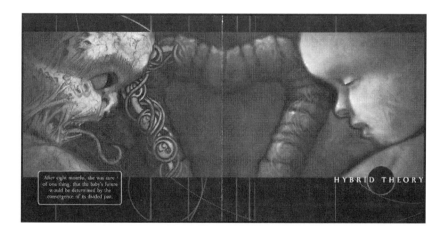

After eight months, she was sure of one thing: that the baby's future would be determined by the convergence of its divided past.

HYBRID THEORY

my focus to the music or stay on course with the art. The band was in a once-in-a-lifetime opportunity, and I decided to take my chances with that." [4]

Joe Hahn was also involved with the design of the cover sleeve.

What the EP did was gel the band into a tight unit. Bennington's more traditional rock voice worked much better with Shin-

sive rock masters Rush and even the lesser known AOR band Loverboy. More in common with other members of the band was Bennington's love of Depeche Mode, the British New Wave band whose iconic brand of electro-synth pop had an indelible impact on Hybrid Theory and consequently their later music as Linkin Park. And as a frontman Bennington learned from seasoned rock stars like Scott Weiland of Stone Temple Pilots and Al Jourgensen of Ministry.

The EP was dished out to as many record labels as possible, including the major players and the independent ones. They had tried it with the *Xero* demo and failed to get any recognition, but with *Hybrid Theory* they had really honed their skills as songwriters, had a better singer and a more commercial sound. It was all well and good being a band with an experimental sound, but there had to be something in the music to grab the listener and possibly infiltrate the mainstream charts. The record company suits were all about commercialism, but Hybrid Theory did not want to sell out, or more accurately, betray their roots. Sure, bands like Tool had a large cult following but for whatever reason record labels would not give Hybrid Theory the big break they needed. Songs like 'Carousel' and 'And One' were specifically aimed at attracting some kind of following. In fact, the successful Hollywood comedian, former child actor and broadcaster Jeff Duran played 'Carousel' on the radio station KIXA 106.5 before any other commercial show picked it up.

The band knew they had to hammer the promotion of *Hybrid The-ory* and whilst pasting posters to walls all around LA, posting copies of the EP to labels, spreading the band's name through word of mouth and plugging the name everywhere possible was all good, it will only take you so far and there was only so much the six of them could do individually and collectively. They knew that, which is why they formed the Street Team. At this point, the World Wide Web was becoming a force to be reckoned with in the computing world and although it would still be a few years before it would become an essential daily tool for the vast majority of people, the band realised that it could be a helpful and possibly essential marketing tool. Basically, via the Internet the band got in touch with groups of people based all over the States and asked them to promote their music. Rob Bourdon elaborated some years later:

"I would assign everyone in the band to go on the Internet and recruit five or six people a day... We'd go into a Korn chat room and say, 'There's this new cool band called Linkin Park, go check out their MP3,' pretending like we weren't in the band."[5]

Each Street Team had a captain and was handed the demo tapes, plus some memorabilia such as posters, badges, stickers, artwork or whatever and the Street Team would promote the band in their area using the things the captain was handed. This is a common marketing scheme, but what made Hybrid Theory's plan stick out was their ingenious use of advanced technology.

The Internet also helped the band spread their name around the ternet and used it to its full advantage, so it was really quite a coup for the up-starting LA band.

Mike Shinoda spoke about the Street Team's dedication to the band in 2003:

"We had these pockets of fans all over the place. They were small but they were so dedicated. We had groups of fans in places like Sweden who would ask for

globe. Over time the Street Team would help the band acquire fans all over the world (even though they didn't play gigs outside of America at that point) which they knew nothing about.

Creating a large fanbase in North America was essential. If indeed the band was due to play in an area where they had a Street Team then the members (or Footsoldiers) would stand outside of the venue and hand out posters and flyers to whoever was around. It would still be some time before the music industry and the artists themselves took note of the power of the In-

stickers and tapes and t-shirts to pass on."[6]

They continued to gig in their local area and record songs in Shinoda's house much to the displeasure of the locals who could hear the band practice until midnight. It's usually the case that band's practice in the garage or back yard, but Shinoda's equipment was based in his bedroom and before they made a name for themselves as a forceful live band they were really a studio band. Hahn and Shinoda were obsessed with computers and recording technol-

ogy and so Hybrid Theory's music was conceived in his home studio as opposed to a cheaply rented rehearsal space. It was that kind of forward thinking that would really be one of the key ingredients for their success a couple of years later.

One of the companies that turned them down was Warner Records and the band had even played three showcase gigs for the A&R executives there but to no avail. They didn't get a record deal and so as 1999 progressed, their career prospects looked glum despite being a regular fixture on the local live circuit, which included several more gigs at the Whiskey A Go Go. It has been suggested that they played over 40 exhaustive showcase gigs for record labels, including one for the music industry figure Mike Galaxy at The Gig club in Melrose, a plush area of Los Angeles. The usual polite but negative replies did not deter the group from pursuing their dream. Indeed they chose to make a go of it and Brad Delson, after having graduated college, had even made the bold decision of forgoing law school to give his full attention to Hybrid Theory. It was at this point that Jeff Blue stepped in and gave the outfit the big push they needed.

CHAPTER 2

GLOBAL BREAKTHROUGH: HYBRID THEORY & REANIMATION (2000-2002)

"I think it would be unfair to completely take the fans' needs out of the picture, so it's partly for our fans and partly for ourselves, because if you're not happy, then you don't have much. You can't make everyone else happy, so at least we should be happy first."
Mike Shinoda[7]

Whilst interning at Zomba Music Publishing Brad Delson had seen A&R chief Jeff Blue sign acts as varied as Macy Gray and Limp Bizkit. Blue knew good music when he heard it and from the thousands of demos he must have been sent on a regular basis, he could tell a talented artist from the get-go. That is why, when he moved to Warner Records in 2000, he took Linkin Park with him. The band had undergone yet another name change but this time the name would stick. They had discovered that there was an elec-

tro band in the UK (from Swansea, Wales, specifically) called Hybrid and to avoid any legal entanglements whenever their debut full-length studio album would be released, they prudently decided to call themselves Linkin Park. A modern popular music legend was born.

With bands like Korn making a name for themselves and having already worked with Limp Bizkit – and knowing that System Of A Down were making headway – Jeff Blue reckoned that there was a niche in the alternative metal market for a band like Linkin Park, but unlike those others and many of the so-called nu-metal outfits, Linkin Park used electro sounds and digital beats that gave them a distinctive edge.

What any band needs, regardless of their talent and ingenuity as a unit, is a top producer, preferably someone who has worked with similar outfits, has lots of experience and an ear for music the way a successful A&R rep does. After shopping around, Jeff Blue got in touch with Pearl Jam producer, Don Gilmore.

"...with Linkin Park we went through a whole selection of producers," Jeff Blue explained, *"and nobody wanted to do it. Don Gilmore was the only one*

who was really interested, he was the only one available, and he ended up being perfect and doing a phenomenal job on it."[8]

The renowned Andy Wallace was hired as the album's mixer. The band was ready to go. They began recording *Hybrid Theory* in March 2000 and spent a couple of months working on the album at NRG Recordings in North Hollywood. Don't forget the group already had over five years worth of material in their archives and it was just a case of re-working certain parts of the songs, mostly the rapping, the guitars and dig-

LINCOLN PARK

After ditching their previous monikers, Xero and Hybrid Theory, the band we know as Linkin Park, took their current name from the idyllic green gardens in Santa Monica known as 'Lincoln Park'. Originally the idea of Chester Bennington, who at the time had just joined the group, the band were forced to marginally change the spelling as the website domain www.lincolnpark.com was already in use and owned by an Illinois real estate company. Lincoln Park was an area often frequented by Chester, and the whole band agreed it would be a cool homage to their community to name the group after a local area. They later discovered that there are parks located all around America with the same name. Since this third and seemingly final name change however, Linkin Park have taken criticism from some quarters of the press, who have derided the name for its lack of imagination.

ital beats. Most of the melodies remained the same but it was the songwriting which took a significant turn. Those songs on *Hybrid Theory* are very angry creations and through his collaboration with Mike Shinoda, Chester Bennington managed to convey his deepest, darkest secrets and feelings about his drug addiction, the divorce of his parents and the inevitable disappointments in life. Perhaps the songs that prominently display those feelings are 'Crawling', 'Papercut' and 'In The End.' Those sentiments are universal, which is one of the reasons the band would be so successful in the following year. Bennington was certainly at his most introspective at that point and he was spending less and less time with his wife because all his energy was going into Linkin Park. Those feelings no doubt led to Bennington's famous line almost one minute into 'One Step Closer': *"Shut up when I'm talking to you..."*

As a six-piece there is a lot of compromising involved. They write the songs together and come to a final consensus on the lyrics and music and especially the choruses, which are a very important part of Linkin Park's music. The beefy metallic choruses are partly responsible for the future success of *Hybrid Theory*. Agreeing

Don Gilmore

on the lyrics and the meaning of the words is important in order to maintain consistency and to avoid loosing the meaning in translation from a thought to a song. It's one of the reasons why they chose to lay out the lyrics in the album's sleeve notes. They wanted their fans to read them and try to create their own meaning from the words.

Besides creating their own unique sound, as with any band that have a degree of knowledge about music, they couldn't help but have their influences filter through into the individual compositions: 'Crawling' has touches of Depeche Mode, while 'In The End' has a Metallica style guitar attack and the lyrical content of 'Papercut' is reminiscent of The Smiths at their most sombre. Other influences that seep through into the album include Deftones, Joy Division, Stone Temple Pilots, Public Enemy and The Roots. With Don Gilmore's help the band had created an accessible album which they may not have been able to do had they not had the fortunate opportunity of hooking up with such a successful and knowledgeable producer. The album needed to sell for the band to make a living from the music. They'd spent most of their adult lives struggling to achieve the clichéd dreams of rock super-stardom and fortune but to achieve that ambition their music had to appeal to a significant amount of people – and that meant having it played on the radio and on TV channels like MTV. The key to the success of *Hybrid Theory* lay, in part, in their knack for creating a thoroughly memorable melody, crunching guitars, hip-hop instrumentals and scratching, atmospheric keys, pounding drums and powerful singing and rapping vocals.

Somewhere along the way Dave Farrell had replaced Kyle Christener in Hybrid Theory when he finished college, but after deciding to spend time with another outfit called The Tasty Snax (aka The Snax), Farrell left again, just before the band re-named themselves for the third and final time. A stand-in bassist by the name of Scott Koziol was hired to play

bass alongside fellow stand-in Ian Hornbeck and guest bassists The Dust Brothers, known for their work with Beck. Of course a full-time permanent bassist would have been a better option, but time was of the essence. The label wanted the album out before the end of the year and Linkin Park had some major touring to do in support of *Hybrid Theory*.

Before the release of the album the band hit the road for some dates, not a specific tour, rather a series of gigs, including some evenings as support to P.O.D. They were mostly club dates but they did get to play the famous Roseland Ballroom in New York and travel to Canada for a show in Toronto.

They were already building up a name for themselves as a studio band but onstage they still had their worth to prove. At that point their image left a lot to be desired. They dressed in what could be termed street clothes: slightly baggy jeans or kakis, t-shirts with a band name or some other sort of symbol or design; one of two of them would wear a baseball cap and Bennington looked a little dorky with a goatee and glasses. And a couple of the guys were a little overweight. They were dressing five years younger than they actually were. It was

The Tasty Snax

Nevertheless, it was the music that was important to them and it would be some time before an image make-over occurred. It's a look they were totally comfortable with and even in their music videos they didn't bother much with high-end fashion, as shown in their first effort 'One Step Closer.'

"Somebody just told me that they heard that most bands don't have a good time shooting their video or they don't like their first video," Shinoda mentioned to one writer during an interview, *"I think we had a blast."*[9]

as if they were just hanging out at the shopping mall, as though they were starring in a Kevin Smith movie (*Mallrats.*) Sometimes they would get slightly annoyed when interviewers would ask them about their image and whether they went out drinking, smoked or whatever. To the band it was the music that was important, not the appearance or the glamour of the social scene. Sure, Chester Bennington had a history with drugs, but it was exactly that, history. To this day they remain totally professional and are the complete opposite of excessive bands like Guns 'N Roses and Aerosmith. The word 'hedonism' doesn't really fit into the story of Linkin Park, and never has. And right from the beginning they never lost their temper with journalists, always being patient and polite, perhaps a little tired or sarcastic but rarely obnoxious.

Nu-metal was in full swing in 2000 with bands like Limp Bizkit, Papa Roach and Staind doing their stuff. Certain similarities (the merging of rap with metal with bits of electronica, for example) between Linkin Park and the nu-metal genre were apparent, but not quite as distinctive as some were led to believe. Linkin Park were a much darker band than, say, Limp Bizkit. It was one of the reasons why it took them a few years to get signed, and although their music had become more melodic in time, there were still elements of the band which their label was unsure of. Of course, there would be some detractors who'd say the group were merely copying their peers and trying to squeeze into the nu-metal market but, hey, these guys had been doing it since 1995, so in actual fact they could justifiably claim to be in some way co-originators of the nu-metal genre. It was the sound of contemporary metal.

Linkin Park made an immediate impact onstage and left any doubters walking away from the venue with a look of shock on their faces. Surprisingly, for a band whose music sounds totally contrived in the studio, they kicked arse during those 2000 dates. Joe Hahn's turntables and scratches sounded much better than one would have thought and Shinoda's rapping, although never great, was a powerful collaboration with Bennington's rock voice. The band took bassist Scott Koziol on the road with them and he proved to be an important member of the Southern Californian unit.

There was simply no time to rest. *Hybrid Theory* was released in the United States on 24th October, 2000; the band had been sitting on the album for a while and were ecstatic that it was finally available in record stores. To drum up support for the record, 'One Step Closer' was released to the radio in August and issued as a single in November. Suddenly, people were starting to talk about

Scott Koziol

this band from the LA area called Linkin Park. The critics were not quite as overwhelmed by the album as the people who bought the CD were; on the whole the reviews were mixed but encouraging nonetheless.

Matt Diehl was dubious about the band and their album in his review in *Rolling Stone*:

"Linkin Park's debut album... is a freaky-deaky fusion that works in spots... They can slice and dice, but just not deep enough."

Writing for *Yahoo! Music*, Mary MacIan noted the band's influences ranged from Metallica to Nine Inch Nails to Rage Against The Machine. In a generally good review, she commented:

"Fortunately their hip hop/ rock melange is very palatable - tracks like opener 'Papercut' and 'Points Of Authority' are sprawling, snarling explosive ca-

tharses, offset by a tune you can actually sing to. What makes it less appetising is a tendency towards (albeit eclectic) radio friendly US pop, when Bennington suddenly starts singing like he's in a boyband."

It could have been much worse for the band. *Hybrid Theory* went into the *Billboard* 200 at number 16 but peaked at number two as sales and promotion increased. Just a couple of years

It was around this time that the press started to mock the band and accuse them of being a 'corporate rock' outfit, created by Lou Pearlman, the former pop manager of Backstreet Boys and 'N Sync (he is currently serving 25 years in prison for fraud.) Of course, those claims were utter nonsense. Sure, it was good timing on the band's behalf, to release their first album around the same time a bunch of other bands were enjoying mainstream success with unique brand

previously the group was struggling to get a record deal, unsure about their future as a band. And now they're feeling on top of the world. But it was hard work; the rigours of the promotional rounds with TV, radio and magazines was draining, and on top of that they had to play some live shows and try and squeeze in a social life somewhere.

of rap and metal. But as we've learned, Linkin Park were making music in some form or another long before the nu-metal phase commenced. It was something that would really bug the band especially as they'd matured as songwriters and were penning powerful lyrics that meant a lot to their fans as well as each other.

Hybrid Theory spawned a further three singles: 'Crawling', 'Papercut' and 'In The End.' They were good choices, representing different facets of the band's musical style. As the touring increased and the group's profile grew, so did the sales of *Hybrid Theory*. In its first five weeks of release in the States it sold enough copies to be certified Gold and by the end of 2001 it had sold almost five million copies, a staggering amount by any band's standards. In 2009, it has been estimated that *Hybrid Theory* is not far off the 30 million mark in terms of global sales.

Fans in the UK were able to buy the album on the 20th January, 2001 and just a week later

'One Step Closer' came out as a CD single. It was not only a top 10 hit in Britain but other countries too, including Austria, Switzerland, Poland, Finland, Australia and New Zealand. It was fortunate for the band that they had Jeff Blue on their side. Imagine what might have been had Brad Delson not worked at Zomba as an intern and thus met Mr. Blue?

2001 was a big year for the band; it would be a whirlwind of activity, awards shows, publicity events, interviews and most importantly touring. They launched their debut headlining tour – dubbed *Street Soldier's Tour* – in January and blitzed through over 20 major North American cities. Any concerns about Linkin Park being a poor live band were immediately quashed. They proved themselves as worthy as the great live acts of their era, and got to play at the famous House of Blues clubs in Las Vegas and Chicago.

A great moment for the band was when they got to support their idols, the alternative metal band the Deftones, in March. They were also joined by the tour's openers Taproot. Touring Europe was a great ride. They were steadily building an eager fanbase and probably making quite a bit of money too from the sales of the album. Writing on the popular website *Drowned In Sound*, one reviewer commented on the show at Glasgow's SECC on the 23rd:

"Their overall sound was much, much better than Taproot. But after a few songs it got really boring. They're a bit too reflective and sentimental..."

Earlier in the year they'd visited Europe on a quick-fire promotional trip and played their first gig in the UK on 11th January at King's College (London) but a full scale tour was in order – and that's exactly what they did. The oddly named *US To Europe* tour kicked off in the band's home town of LA on 16th April and included dates outside of those two continents; they played Australia, New Zealand and Japan before a single date in Denmark on the 30th May and one in London at the Brixton Academy on 4th June. The latter show was reviewed in the British indie music weekly rag, *NME*:

"But while it may be stage-managed with an unnerving attention to detail, this is also a top night out... The boundary between nu-metal and manufactured pop is blurring. But on tonight's evidence, that might not be such a bad thing."

They were invited to play at various festivals because of their rising profile – hence the haphazard nature of the *US To Europe* tour dates. They had nailed down a tight set-list that presented the album in the most positive way. The most startling affect of their live performances was probably the guitar playing of Brad Delson; his riffs sounded incredible.

The success of *Hybrid Theory* granted the band certain privileges such as a tour bus and an expanded personnel of helpers, roadies and assistants, but not enough to give the band huge egos. Like any band they needed help with sound-

Black Sabbath as well as Marilyn Manson, Slipknot, Papa Roach, Disturbed, Crazy Town and Black Label Society. Linkin Park's set wasn't long (there were too many other bands on the bill for each of them to play for over an hour) but the eight or nine songs they did perform each night certainly gave them some kudos amongst the metal elite. What Ozzfest did for Linkin Park was expose them to new audiences. After all, the band had never been on a metal festival before so playing on the same bill as the likes of Marilyn Manson was something they'd never experienced. At the same time they had traits in common with such acts as Crazy Town and Papa Roach. It was a challenge for Linkin Park, especially when it came to playing famous metal holds such as the Mid-West of America, where bands like Iron Maiden, Metallica and Judas Priest have played legendary shows to thousands of fans. It's tough, working class areas that appreciate metal so Linkin Park had a difficult game on their hands; they could either win the fans over to their side or fail.

However, some successful band's, especially in the metal and rap genres, cannot forgo a bit of controversy. In a town called Santee, near San Diego, a teenage boy named Charles Andrew Williams

checks and rehearsals. By now, Dave Farrell had rejoined the fold and the Linkin Park line-up that we have come to know was fixed: Chester Bennington, Mike Shinoda, Joe Hahn, Brad Delson, Rob Bourdon and Dave Farrell.

By the time the summer had arrived, they were asked to play the hugely successful and influential Ozzfest, a touring metal festival that was headlined by Ozzy Osbourne and masterminded by his wife, Sharon, the daughter of the late rock manager Don Arden. The tour (June-August) saw Linkin Park playing to the biggest audiences they'd ever performed for up to that point. They shared the main stage with headliners went to school with a handgun in his bag. It was on 5th March, 2001 when Williams killed two of his school mates and injured 13. He was a Linkin Park fan, and the media, who are forever looking for a scapegoat, decided to blame the band's music for Williams' hideous act. The media scrutinised the words to his favourite songs, like 'Crawling', 'In The End' and 'One Step Closer.' The band issued a press statement which was written with the utmost sincerity.

Of course, it is common for lonely people to seek refugee in art whether it is literature, music or the movies. The film *Taxi Driv-*

Phoenix and Chester - Ozzfest 2001

er and the cult novel *A Clockwork Orange* by Anthony Burgess (and the film adaptation by Stanley Kubrick) have both been criticised for causing people to commit crimes. Even the heavy metal band Judas Priest went to court: two American teenage boys attempted to commit suicide (one of them died instantly, the other died three years later from his injuries) after listening to the Priest song 'Better By You, Better Than Me'. It was argued that the boys heard subliminal messages in those songs. Those kinds of troubled people tend to look for deeper meanings that would otherwise have been missed by the average happy-go-lucky youngster. Speaking to one American journalist, Mike Shinoda commented:

"Yes that kid connected with the lyrics, but so did a million other people, totally different kinds of people."[10]

At the time of Linkin Park's controversy, the massacre at Columbine High School in 1999 was still fresh in the public (thus the media's) consciousness and any incident after that was placed heavily under the microscope, usually rock stars or rappers were to blame. An artist like Marilyn Manson or Eminem would be examined radar and it seemed any crime committed by a young person went back to those iconic pop culture figures. One would certainly not have expected to hear Linkin Park's name used in such media-heavy stories; but then they were burgeoning rock icons, meaning they were in the media spotlight and were being watched. Linkin Park were not connected to the occult or anything devilish or sinister, it's just that Chester Bennington had a history with drugs and had lived quite an unconventional lifestyle for some time, so he had a lot to write about in his lyrics. A lot of young, socially disconnected teenagers could – and still can – connect with that kind of angst.

The one thing the band must be applauded for is their dedication to their fanbase. Before and after gigs they'd chat to fans, sign autographs, hand out memorabilia and through their Street Teams they'd find out their fans opinion on the

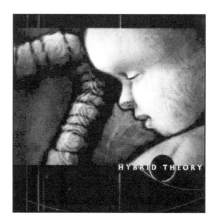
Hybrid Theory EP - fan club edition

performances and set-lists. It was a sturdy relationship. Also, the Internet was playing a significant part of their career and so they created their official website and in addition founded Linkin Park Underground, their official fan club. The first 500 hundred applicants were posted a remastered copy of the *Hybrid Theory* EP. In years to come the fan club would grow into a significant part of the group's career and even help them out with album titles and decision making. Following the release of *Hybrid Theory* and the batch of singles, in order to keep momentum the band released their first DVD *Frat Party At The Pankake Festival* (aka *Frat Party*) in November.

"That name came about because we thought it would be funny,"

Shinoda commented in 2008, *"but, looking back, half of the band thinks it was a stupid idea while half of the band still love it. I think that if we named it today then it would probably not have the same name."[11]*

They also found time throughout the year to make guest appearances on other artist's music and to contribute to soundtracks.

By the end of 2001 Linkin Park had clocked up over 300 live shows for that year alone, a staggering amount by any band's standards. They'd never played so many live gigs in their career. Hell, they'd probably played more shows in 2001 than they had between 1995 and 2000, but that's the way the business worked. They were confident enough to produce top quality material in the studio so after the release of their first album they wanted to hammer the live circuit. They'd had a successful stint round the summer festivals but they were now big enough and confident enough as live performers to headline their own shows in big in-door arenas. But the life of a touring band is not easy: there's an abundance of interviews to do as well soundchecks, rehearsals and travelling on the tour bus, flying from country to country and checking in at hotels can all lead to a burn out. It's often the case that bands are away from their families for long periods of time, and it was this that really got to them. The kind of schedule they lived was incredibly draining even

for a band like Linkin Park; sure, they were young and healthy but they missed their home comforts.

It was a crazy time for the group but all their hard work paid off, even if the mainstream music publications sniggered whenever the name 'Linkin Park' was mentioned. The metal press, on the other hand, were more generous towards them – so much so that they graced the covers of some major metal magazines around the world. They even picked up a gong at the *Kerrang!* Awards in London and were recognised at the MTV Video Music Award's for their excellent music videos.

2002 was approaching, and fast. The band was ready for a break but there was more pressure to tour and work on a sophomore album. The follow-up release is often dubbed 'the difficult second album.' It is even harder if the first album is a monstrous success like *Hybrid Theory*, because that means there is a lot more to live up to, whereas a band like, say, AC/DC, worked for years on a few good (but not great) albums before they hit a creative peak with *Highway To Hell* and *Back In Black*. What ever is in vogue in the music world at the time has a lot to do with the success of an album/band. Linkin Park was obviously pigeon-holed in the nu-metal movement.

What they chose to record next was a really ballsy move that many other bands would never

have attempted. They began collaborating with other artists, including Korn's Jonathan Davis, Staind's Aaron Lewis, The Humble Brothers, The X-Ecutioners and a bunch of underground rappers, on remixes of songs from the *Hybrid Theory* album and EP. The idea alone caused controversy with fans and had critics shaking their heads in disbelief. The metal fans were, of course, pleading for an album of new material, but those who were more interested in urban music were intrigued to hear what the band could conceive with so many guest rappers. It was a big project and the credits list reads like that of a Hollywood movie with so many people involved. Not only were there many guest appearances by other artists, but also a myriad of engineers, mixers and assistants.

The 20 track album, named *Reanimation*, was recorded at several studios whilst the band where on tour during the second half of 2001: they had committed themselves to the Family Values touring festival (with Chester Bennington's heroes Stone Temple Pilots and main act Staind) and a headlining North American tour called *Countdown To Revolution*.

Produced by Mike Shinoda, whose talent in the recording studio was becoming quite clear to critics, *Reanimation* was a top five hit in both the UK and US when it was released in July 2002. According to *Yahoo! Music* the album sold 270,000 in its first week of release.

The critics were seemingly undecided; some of them admired it while some did not take to it all. Writing on the popular and influential Canadian music website *Canoe – Jam Music!*, one reviewer commented:

"Perhaps, if you're a stone Linkin Park fan, you'll want these re-worked versions of 'Crawling' and 'One Step Closer'. As for the rest of it, well, let's just say we spent two weeks listening to this CD one night. Time to reanimate your songwriting chops guys."

In the States, *Entertainment Weekly* said:

"On the one hand, the results are more varied than the monochromatic Hybrid Theory. *On the other hand, the remixes at times obliterate one of the band's most distinctive characteristics – the vocal interplay between singer Chester Bennington and MC Mike Shinoda, a blend that allows their pop tendencies to poke through from time to time."*

To promote the album MTV made videos for each song for *MTV: Playback*, and various editions of the album were released over the course of the following year.

One question that plagued the band was: the song titles are unreadable so how do you play these songs on tour? Given the fact that *Reanimation* was a totally studio conceived album, the band had set themselves a tough task to fulfil.

Linkin Park were certainly not ones to shy away from a challenge and what they did next was either going to become a huge success or a miserable failure. The band organised a festival of their own.

Having played on some festivals in 2001 they saw the huge potential for a bill of their own that was not specifically concentrating on metal but also rap music as well, the two genres that Linkin Park were famous for. They kicked off Projekt Revolution tour one on 29th January and finished in the first week of March. Joining them on the journey around the States was DJ Z-Trip, Cypress Hill and Adema. Although the festival tour would not reach the UK for some time the band flew to Europe in March for a major headlining European tour with dates in England, France and Holland.

The touring schedule for 2002 certainly wasn't as rigorous as it was the previous year but it was still a lot of hard work. Whilst sitting on the tour bus around Europe the band was coming up with ideas for a new album. Of course, it had to be a proper album, not a remix or a live effort, but a full-length studio opus with original songs. If they had released anything different from a studio album their fans would have gone nuts and the critics probably would have dug into them for "milking the cow" that was *Hybrid Theory*. Sure, many had pointed the finger at *Reanimation* for being a filler album, but it did bring the band's love of urban music to the forefront. By now they were financially and commercially successful so the only challenges that could face them would be to create new music.

Whilst playing in Greece they saw the rocky heavens known as Meteora and it was truly inspiring. The area is known for its half-a-dozen monasteries which have been there for centuries. The band got a sense of its history and were in awe of its beauty and the peaceful, tranquil surroundings. When they got back to the States they couldn't get it out of their minds and kept talking about Meteora. There was a profound sense of inspiration and honesty about the place which Linkin Park felt they could convey in their music. After all, hundreds of years ago people had actually built it. Like the great pyramids of Egypt, the Meteora was a significant historical achievement.

By the end of the year the band had even founded an independent record label, Machine Shop Recordings, which would have its music distributed through Warner Records. It was another bold step for the band and as well as releasing their own music they were keen to look elsewhere; they were on the hunt for other similarly minded artists. It was initially a small project headed by Mike Shinoda and Brad Delson but the whole band got involved with Delson heading A&R.

In December, Linkin Park let it be known that they had already begun production of a brand new studio album to follow *Hybrid Theory*. They told their fans that it was inspired by Meteora in Greece and that the songs had already been written; they'd actually begun working on the record in secret in April while they were on a tour of Europe. They hooked up with Don Gilmore for the second time and based themselves in NRG Recordings in Hollywood, where they recorded their first album. With *Meteora*, could they re-create the power and success of *Hybrid Theory*? It was going to be a herculean challenge of the highest order. Only time would tell if they could accomplish it.

MACHINE SHOP RECORDINGS

Founded in 2002 and initially run by Mike Shinoda and Brad Delson, Machine Shop Recordings is a small record label operated by Linkin Park. They deal mostly with rap/hip-hop and rock artists and Shinoda and Delson are the label's A&R men. It was first going to be called The Shinoda Imprint but changed to MSR when the band got involved. It is an imprint of the Warner Music Group, which is Linkin Park's label. Linkin Park releases its own albums through MSR/WMG and has done so since 2003's *Live In Texas*. Fort Minor – Mike Shinoda's side-project – is signed to MSR, while Holly Brook, Styles Of Beyond, Simplistic, The Rosewood Fall and No Warning were previously signed to WSR. The label is currently on hold while Linkin Park concentrate on their own music.
Visit *machineshoprecordings.com*

CHAPTER 3

WORLD DOMINATION: METEORA & COLLISION COURSE (2003-2005)

"...we've been trying to reach out to hip-hop magazines. Because a lot of what we do is hip-hop. Even though initially you'll think of rock."

Mike Shinoda[12]

Meteora was released in March 2003. Did it live up to expectations? Would the music press establishment continue to mock them; criticise them for (wrongly) perceiving the band as a cynical, corporate rock outfit from LA? Would they continue to be labelled as a money-grabbing marketing juggernaut? The debate was on…

Well, in a way the second album did level up to the hype because it attempted to be a carbon copy of *Hybrid Theory,* but on the other hand, because of it's perceived lack of originality and imagination, it was attacked for being below par. The reviews could have been predicted even before its re-

lease, which by the way, was top-secret.

"Well, obviously, the record label feels that's what needs to be done. We can only say how we feel, and that's excited that people are hearing the record," Bennington informed one British journalist.[13]

One critic, writing in the highbrow British newspaper *The Independent,* wrote:

"...the follow-up, Meteora, *is an impressively single-minded assault on the vast (white) American youth-protest market, featuring the same tried-and-tested gripe-hop mix of fuzz-guitar riffs."*

Meanwhile Barry Walter penned a review in *Rolling Stone*:

"Much of Meteora *adheres to the overly familiar rapping template Linkin Park fit themselves into for* Hybrid Theory. *Yet the band manages to squeeze the last remaining life out of this nearly extinct formula."*

Continuing the debate on the merits of the band's second opus, in the *NME*, Andy Capper stated:

"['Breaking The Habit' is] a welcome break from the usual LP formula of wicka wicka scratch, bad rapping and big chorus which dominates 80 per cent of the record. LP could call this 'Hybrid Theory Part Two' and it'd still sell millions. Whether it'll make them bigger than they already are is a debatable thought. Maybe that's a good thing. 7/10."

itself. It desperately wants to be the epitome of a flawless, high-tech, postmodern, 21st Century rock record. Thankfully, it fails in this."

Although many critics jumped on the bandwagon and were eager to deride the band, what many of them missed out of their reviews was the group's thirst for trying new instruments and adding dif-

On the respected website *music-critic.com*, Alex Robbins penned a lengthy but perceptive review in which he states:

"Lyrically, it's competent, and stays just the right side of tortured and embarrassing navel-gazing... the overriding impression is that Meteora *succeeds in spite of*

ferent musical textures to their songs. Sure, on the surface *Meteora* was very similar to *Hybrid Theory*, but appearances can be deceptive.

"We wanted to step outside of the box, so we used some live strings, piano," explained Shinoda during the usual promotional rounds,

"We used a traditional Japanese flute, which is called shakuhachi. We played with time signatures, different tempos. Songs like 'Breaking The Habit' and 'Faint' are faster than any songs we've ever written and 'Easier To Run' is much slower."[14]

It sold a ridiculous amount of copies, estimated to be around the 800,000 units mark in its first week of release in the States, and continued the band's global domination. To date *Meteora* has sold around six million copies in America and has reached a staggering 20 million in worldwide sales. It would go on to win a number of awards and nominations and the instrumental piece 'Session' was nominated for a Grammy under the category of 'Best Rock Instrumental Performance' in 2003. Be- cause of its success it spawned a whole bunch of singles releas- es in the States: 'Somewhere I Be- long', 'Faint', 'Lying From You', 'Breaking The Habit' and 'Numb.' A series of special editions were also released the following year.

Now to the serious business: touring. The band had steadi- ly built up a reputation for being a reliable live act, had proven themselves to their critics and even before the album had hit stores worldwide they had already begun touring. In late February, they commenced a tour of rela- tively small stages around Europe called the *LP Underground Tour*.

The show at Nottingham Rock City in England on 3rd March, 2002 was reviewed on *bbc.co.uk*:

"But ultimately they have energy and once they realised the crowd

was hero-worshipping them the grins appeared and everyone enjoyed themselves."

The band's gig at the Manchester Apollo on 7th March was reviewed in *Powerplay* magazine (and in their rating system was awarded nine powerpoints out of 10):

"With tickets changing hands for up to £50 outside the venue, it was clear that Linkin Park were big business... Kicking off with three new songs (including the single Somewhere I Belong *at number two) was probably a good move; the crowd were typically ape."*

Some of the shows provoked controversy amongst fans who argued that the set, lasting, only a little over an hour, did not justify the ticket price. After all, the band had one studio album out, a remix album and their sophomore release was at that point (in March) only days away. During the set they played 'Don't Stay', 'Somewhere I Belong', 'Lying From You', 'Papercut', 'Points Of Authority', 'Runaway', 'Easier To Run', 'One Step Closer' and 'A Place For My Head.'

The band's official fan club, Linkin Park Underground, was

growing by the day and always ones to appreciate the support of their fans they kicked off 2003's North American live schedule with 10 shows which gave members FREE admission, ditto the previous European dates.

The success of the initial Projekt Revolution tour meant that there would be a follow-up one, so in April Linkin Park headlined a bill that also included Mudvayne, Xzibit and Blindside. It ran from 9th April to the 26th.

The festival shows during the summer of 2003 were an absolute blast for the six guys in Linkin Park: they got to tour with Metallica on the mammoth Summer Sanitarium. The bill also included Linkin Park's nu-metal peers Limp Bizkit, Deftones and Mudvayne. It was a killer tour and although Linkin Park didn't headline, they received a rapturous response during every performance. More shows followed in Europe although some dates had to be rescheduled because Chester Bennington was suffering from back pains; it also meant that whatever proposed video shoots they had planned, had to be rescheduled. Headlining performances at the UK's enormous Leeds and Reading festivals (on 22nd and 23rd August) preceded a UK tour which sold out within hours of tickets going on sale.

Reviewing the band's show at the Glasgow SECC on 20th November, Paul Connolly wrote in *The Times*:

"In Essence, then, Linkin Park are nu-metal's boy band and, as such, they should sink. That they don't is down to some seriously good tunes that really take flight

when live... So – New Kids on the Rock or mighty metal contenders? Linkin Park are neither, really, but they are a jolly night out."

A big surprise for fans (another product for the critics to point their fingers at) was the release of their debut live album, *Live In Texas*. Recorded over two nights at separate shows in Texas in August, the CD/DVD was unleashed in November. Like the *Reanimation* CD, *Live In Texas* was dubbed another filler product. One could hardly blame the sceptics for their opinions; after all, the band had released four CDs in less than four years and a DVD as well. That's a lot of hard earned cash forked out by the fans. It was another busy year for the band who had built up a reputation as one of the hardest working in the business.

"We don't really take that many breaks. On our breaks we work," Bennington told the UK's *Q Magazine.*

2004 began with a massive tour called the *Meteora World Tour.* The band took P.O.D., Hoobastank and Story Of The Year on the road with them and the jaunt took them all round the country playing to packed houses night after night.

Writing for *Jam! Music*, one reviewer said of the show at the massive Air Canada Centre in Toronto on 24th January:

"But when the jumbo curtain and the clean-cut five-piece (sic) *jumped onto the stage, whatever makes Linkin Park special in theory dissolved into a wall of echoing effects noise."*

The set-list ran as follows: 'With You', 'Runaway', 'Papercut', 'Points Of Authority', 'Don't Stay', 'Somewhere I Belong', 'It's Going Down', 'Lying From You', 'Nobody's Listening', 'Breaking The Habit', 'From The Inside', 'Faint' and 'Numb.'

The tour also took them abroad to places like Europe and South America before they finished in Brazil in mid September.

Some of the highlights of 2004 included performances at the Download Festival, held in the legendary outdoor grounds of Castle Donnington (England) and also in Glasgow (Scotland). The band's profile had risen to extreme heights in Europe, especially in the UK where they gave exclusive interviews to some of Britain's major metal publications. More fansites started to appear on the Internet and record sales were as high as that of any other major global artist. Although Linkin Park had many different musical influences they retained a hardcore metal fanbase and any thoughts about the demise of metal had been squashed since the rise of fellow nu-metal bands. The good thing now was that the press started to cover metal, which they hadn't done properly since the eighties, before the explosion of grunge.

Aside from the release of *Meteora,* there were two major events of 2004 which gave the media huge collective smiles. One was the rapidly growing success of Projekt Revolution. The first two tours had been so successful that for the 2004 ride they arranged for two stages to be built. Ozzfest was the biggest metal touring festival in North America, but what made Projekt Revolution stand out was the eclecticism of the list of featured artists. The Revolution Stage was, of course, the main stage where Linkin Park head-lined at every show. Artists they took out on tour with them included Korn, The Used, Funeral For A Friend and Snoop Dogg. Where else would you get that kind of line-up?

The way audiences around the world reacted to Linkin Park's performances certainly differed, as Dave Farrell explained in 2008:

"Like in Europe in general, specifically in the UK, they bounce up and down, where in the US, they pit – lateral movement. Asia is insane, even there it's so different. Japan is crazy to play..."[15]

Obviously the band had some other events to squeeze into their diary, particularly award shows like MTV and the Radio Music Awards *et al*, but the other major event for them in 2004 was their performance with the legendary and highly-revered rapper and producer Jay-Z for MTV's *Ultimate Mash-Ups* show. The special performance was held at The Roxy Theatre in LA on 18th July and the outcome was the CD/DVD collaborative effort, *Collision Course*. It was a simple premise: Linkin park and Jay-Z 'mashed' some of their recordings together hence the title of the MTV programme. It may sound like a ridiculous idea but it gave both artists a number one album in the United States and glorious commercial success all around the globe, even though the vast majority of critics really seemed to loathe it.

Dorian Lynskey annihilated the album in a review in the British broad sheet newspaper *The Guardian*. Giving the album one star out of four, he said:

"...Jay-Z's bulletproof braggadocio finds no point of connection with Linkin Park's grumpy melodrama... The exercise is never more pointless than on the new

version of Jay-Z's '99 Problems', which was actually a perfectly good piece of rap-rock before Linkin Park got their hands on it."

There is a certain pretentiousness about the concept, and it surely did alienate Linkin Park's metal fanbase, but it also opened them up to more of an urban audience. After announcing their intentions

at the Grammy Awards earlier in the year, *Collision Course* was released in November.

Given how much product the band had released in the past four years it did feel as though they were over-egging the pudding, but that didn't stop the ever tireless Mike Shinoda from launching his side-project, Fort Minor, with the help of Jay-Z. The rapper co-produced Fort Minor's debut album *The Rising Tied* that was eventually released to the public in November 2005. Bennington had hooked up with DJ Lethal of Limp Bizkit and Handsome Boy Modelling School for some separate, small projects.

But as 2004 closed its doors there was a genuine feeling and consensus in the band that they were due for a rest. They had nothing left to prove, had sold millions of albums, won a myriad of awards, and had played to thousands of people all around the world. As with Mike Shinoda and Fort Minor, other members of the band were beginning to look elsewhere for other artistic ventures and as with any band, they needed a little rest from touring and everything else. And so they put ideas for a third studio opus on the back burner for the next year.

Although 2005 may have seemed a fairly quiet year for the Linkin

Park, given how much they worked between 2000 and 2004, in actual fact the members were as busy as ever. Shinoda's schedule was full up with Fort Minor activities, of course; Bennington had ventured off working with DJ Z-Trip and even the LA hair metallers, Mötley Crüe; Hahn was busy making a short film; Delson was working as an A&R man for Machine Shop and looked after the band's mer-

CHARITABLE CAUSES

Over the years, Linkin Park have been involved with a number of charitable causes in and outside of the United States. They even formed their own charity Music For Relief, which is detailed in another entry. They've played at various charity events, including Live Earth Japan, Trinitykids Care, Live 8, Tsunami Benefit and a special one-off gig, *A Night For The Vets: An MTV Concert For The Brave.* In 2004, the band provided money to help the victims of Hurricane Charley. During the same year they also donated thousands of dollars to the Special Operations Warrior Foundation. And then in 2005 they gave money to aid the victims of Hurricane Katrina.

Through their extensive charity work Linkin Park have supported the following causes: AIDS, At-Risk/Disadvantaged Youths, Cancer, Children's Causes, Conservation, Creative Arts, Disaster Relief, Domestic and Family Abuse, Environment, Family/Parent Support, Health and Substance Abuse. They have also lent their support to the following charities: American Forests Friends and Helpers Foundation, LIFEbeat, Live Earth, Make-A-Wish Foundation, Music For Relief, Surfrider Foundation and Unite The United. They'd achieved so much with their first two studio albums, as well as other projects, that they felt they should give back to society by using their name to raise money and by donating some of their vast wealth to charitable causes.

MUSIC FOR RELIEF

Music For Relief was founded by Linkin Park in 2005, after the band had offered their support to the victims of the horrific tsunami in South Asia. They decided to create a charity to aid the victims of natural disasters around the world. The organisation also has the support of a number of celebrities, including Chris Rock, The Eagles, Ozzy Osbourne, Jay-Z, Good Charlotte, Will Farrell and Tommy Lee. The charity has raised over two million dollars and helped victims of the Southern California Wildfires, a disaster closer to home for the band. The charity also helps to combat global warming. The home page on the official website says:

WHO WE ARE
MUSIC FOR RELIEF is a grassroots effort comprised of musicians, music industry professionals and fans who believe that together we can create positive change.

OUR MISSION
To respond to natural disasters and help victims recover and rebuild with an emphasis on housing, education programs and resources. MUSIC FOR RELIEF also recognizes the environmental consequences of global warming, which has demonstrated the capability to accelerate and strengthen certain types of natural disasters. Therefore the second goal of MUSIC FOR RELIEF is to prevent and decrease future natural disasters by reducing greenhouse gasses, seeking renewable forms of energy and educating the public about climate change.

In 2009, during the writing of this book, the band was hard at   >>

chandise with his father Donn, whilst Farrell and Bourdon lived relatively low-key lives that year.

The biggest headlines in Linkin Park's inner sanctum during 2005 related to their commitment to numerous charity projects. In the previous year they'd already donated thousands of dollars to various global charities, but in 2005 they worked through their newly-founded charity organisation, Music For Relief. They also played at Live 8 (Philadelphia) on 2nd July, which included a special performance with Jay-Z.

On a personal front the band members were undergoing quite a few changes. It was not a great time for Chester Bennington and his wife. The pair parted ways in 2005 after nine years of marriage. Those days of working together at Burger King in Phoenix seemed

MUSIC FOR RELIEF

<< work helping the victims of the Australian bushfires and the hurricanes which hit Haiti. Dave Farrell told the band's fans and reporters via a PSA which can viewed on YouTube:

"This past August four hurricanes – Hurricanes Fay, Gustav, Hannah and Ike – all hit the Haiti area. Even prior to these hurricanes Haiti was suffering from a food crisis. Music For Relief is partnering with communities in Haiti as they recover from these storms. And helping to ensure that they're better prepared to deal with future hurricanes and floods. In addition to collecting

funds at musicforrelief.org, we're using a site called SocialVibe for the first time to earn money for the food and clean drinking water that the people of Haiti so desperately need.

Social Vibe and Music For Relief are working together. But we really need you to help make this happen. Here's what we're asking you to do: visit SocialVibe.com/musicforrelief and add SocialVibe to your MySpace, Facebook, blog or whatever online profiles that you use. This will enable you to earn donations for Music For Relief's work in Haiti, without even opening your own wallet. Our goal is to earn $25,000 for clean water, food and reforestation of affected areas in Haiti. The member who invites the most friends to join SocialVibe will win a trip to Los Angeles to hang out with me and the rest of the guys and come see us in the studio working on our newest album..."

Visit *musicforrelief.org*

Chester and his first wife Samantha

light years away. Details on the divorce are hazy but it is generally alleged that Bennington's hectic schedule drew the pair apart, as is often the case with rock stars. The couple had one child together named Draven Sebastian, born on 19th April, 2002. Bennington is now married to a former Playboy model named Talinda Bentley and the couple have a child named Tyler Lee (Bentley also has two other children from a past relationship). Fans started to dub the wives of the band members as "Linkin Ladies."

Bennington expressed his thoughts to the press about his divorce and its impact on the band:

"For a number of years before the marriage split up there were times when it wasn't good. It could be very difficult but it never became an issue with the band. They never said 'your f***ing personal life is getting too much for us to take, you need to knock that s**t off.' There was a lot of respect and understanding. I definitely needed those guys to help me get through that time and I can't thank them enough for being so supportive of me."[16]

Meanwhile Rob Bourdon was dating the actress Vanessa Lee Evigan. He kept details of the relationship relatively hush-hush; the pair had been seeing each other since 2001, although they would go their separate ways in

Mr & Mrs: Joe and Karen Hahn, Chester and Talinda Bennington, Mike and Anna Shinoda

WARNER MUSIC GROUP

Along with EMI, Sony/BMG and Universal, Warners is one of the 'Big 4' of the record industry – enormous global record companies who virtually dominate recorded music in the 21st Century. Warner Brothers Records began life in 1958 as an offshoot of Warner films. Over the following 50 years the company has gone through numerous owners and name changes [WEA, Warner Communications, Time Warner] but since 2004 has been known as The Warner Music Group [WMG]. The company owns numerous smaller labels and among its roster today are, Roadrunner, Rhino, Atlantic, Ryko, Reprise, Sire and even Madonna's Maverick label.

Linkin Park signed to Warners in 1999, and renegotiated their contract in 2005 having by then sold in excess of 35million albums, after the huge success of Hybrid Theory and Meteora. In May 2005, during these negotiations, there was a very public spat between Linkin Park and WMG, when the band accused Warners of not having the clout any longer to market and sell their music because of a recently announced $250million cost-cutting exercise following a Public Stock Offering of the company's shares on Wall Street. The group issued the following press statement that month:

"Linkin Park has become increasingly concerned that WMG's diminished resources will leave it unable to compete in today's global music marketplace, resulting in a failure to live up to WMG's fiduciary responsibility to market and promote Linkin Park." >>

2007. Brad Delson was perfectly happy in his marriage to Elisa Borden, whom he married in a Jewish ceremony in September 2003 at the Skirball Cultural Centre in Los Angeles. Joe Hahn had married his girlfriend Karen Benedict in February after dating for two years. Although Dave Farrell is the quiet one, Mike Shinoda was enjoying life with his wife during their days off in 2005. He married the children's author Anna Hillinger on 10th May, 2003 in a quiet ceremony for family and friends.

It had not been a great year for the band's relationship with their record label, Warner; they disagreed with the label over some financial decisions and it was also believed that the band were not that content with issues of financial security and promotion of their music. Thankfully for both parties a new deal was negotiated between Warner, Linkin Park and their management, The Firm in December. It could have gotten uglier but they all came to their senses.

As Christmas approached it was obviously a time to spend with family and loved ones, but, while plans for a new studio album would take centre stage in the New Year, ideas for their third full-length studio recording had already started formulating by November. Loyal supporters were keenly interested in the path the band would take for it.

WARNER MUSIC GROUP

<< Warners retorted:

"We value our relationship with Linkin Park, and we are proud of our work together since signing the band as a developing artist in 1999. While Linkin Park's talent is without question, the band's management is using fictitious numbers and making baseless charges and inflammatory threats in what is clearly a negotiating tactic. Warner Bros. Records has made significant investments in Linkin Park, and they have always been compensated generously for their outstanding worldwide success."

The *"fictitious numbers"* comment refers to a statement Linkin Park's management released on 2nd May, 2005:

"The new owners of the Warner Music Group will be reaping a windfall of $1.4 billion from their $2.6 billion purchase a mere 18 months ago if their planned IPO moves forward. Linkin Park, their biggest act, will get nothing. Of the planned $750 million raised by an IPO, only about $7 million will be put toward

the company's own operations, with no money going to WMG artists."

However, after several months and presumably numerous meetings between Linkin Park's management, The Firm, and Warner executives, on 28th December 2005, the New York Times announced that Linkin Park had signed a new deal with an advance worth an alleged $15 million, for what would be their third studio album. Their royalty rate was also reportedly raised to a staggering 20 per cent.
A statement to the press was issued by Warner and Linkin Park:

"We would like to thank Linkin Park fans worldwide for their continued support. Despite initial concerns after last year's change in ownership, the band is pleased with the direction of the company and in Warner Brothers Records' ability to effectively market their music worldwide under the leadership of Tom Whalley."

The band is still with Warners.

Visit *wmg.com*

After the mis-steps that were *Re-animation* and *Collision Course*, the distinctly average *Live In Texas* and the disappointing but entertaining second studio opus *Meteora,* the band would have to conjure up something truly startling to maintain their world domination. This is a band who had basically come out of nowhere at the end of 2000 and a year later they had sold millions of copies of their first album.

By 2005 nu-metal had faded; nobody was interested in it anymore. Even the metal magazines began to look at the whole scene as something of a passing trend: nothing more, nothing less. It was fun while it lasted but it was basically a long one-night stand. Indeed, the scene brought some great bands to the forefront of the metal scene around the world and caught the attention of the mainstream market; and for good or bad it got people talking about metal again, yet many of the bands were either on a long hiatus or had faded into obscurity.

Urban music had become massively popular and artists like Eminem had got a generation of young white working and middle-class kids interested in rap. A decade previously such a notion would have been inconceivable, but times change.

Would Linkin Park continue to produce metal as in *Hybrid Theory* and *Meteora* or concentrate more on collaborative rap recordings, as in *Reanimation* and *Collision Course*? Such ideas kept fans waiting on tenterhooks.

8.12sat **TOKYO** / **8.13**sun **OSAKA**

TOKYO / OSAKA
MARINE STAGE / OPEN AIR STAGE

DEFTONES
HOOBASTANK
ZEBRAHEAD
AVENGED SEVENFOLD
TAKING BACK SUNDAY
STONE SOUR
HAWTHORNE HEIGHTS

8.12sat **OSAKA** / **8.13**sun **TOKYO**

TOKYO / OSAKA
MARINE STAGE / OPEN AIR STAGE

MUSE
MY CHEMICAL ROMANCE
LOSTPROPHETS
FALL OUT BOY
THE ALL AMERICAN REJECTS
ELLEGARDEN
10YEARS

8.12sat **TOKYO** / **8.13**sun **OSAKA**

MOUNTAIN STAGE

THE CHARLATANS
SCRITTI POLITTI
EDITORS
THE RAPTURE
PHOENIX
m-flo
65DAYSOFSTATIC
JOHNNY BOY

8.12sat **OSAKA** / **8.13**sun **TOKYO**

MOUNTAIN STAGE

MASSIVE ATTACK

DJ SHADOW
FORT MINOR
ARCTIC MONKEYS
THE KOOKS
WE ARE SCIENTISTS
BOOM BOOM SATELLITES
<TOKYO ONLY>
MANDO DIAO *Special Guest*
<OSAKA ONLY>
MUM DJ SET
WHIRLWIND HEAT

CHAPTER 4

HANDS HELD HIGH: CREATING MINUTES TO MIDNIGHT (2006-2008)

"A lot of groups incorporated a certain sound into their music, some of whom you know, may have been influenced by some of the records we made."

Brad Delson[17]

Linkin Park kept themselves busy in the studio for most of 2006 so it came as a relief that they had some live dates planned. One exciting moment for them was performing 'Numb/Encore' with Jay-Z at the Grammy Awards. On 7th July they played Live Earth Japan in Tokyo and they also performed at the Summer Sonic festival, headlined by Metallica, which also featured Muse, My Chemical Romance, Avenged Sevenfold and a selection of other big-named bands.

The biggest problem facing Linkin Park when recording the new album, titled *Minutes To Midnight*, was choosing which songs to include in the track listing from the bewildering number of songs they'd recorded during the early demo stages – by August they'd composed around 50 tunes. For this album they hooked up with the legendary Rick Rubin, who knows just about as much

about rock and rap as anybody else in the business. Andrew Scheps engineered the album and Mike Shinoda co-produced. It has often been thought that Joe Hahn, a quiet but intelligent member of the band, is the brains behind much of Linkin Park's music, but Shinoda is certainly the one who gets involved with the production side of things as well as the songwriting.

The songwriting process in the band has always had input from each member, but with their darker moments one could certainly argue that Chester Bennington has used the lyrics as a forum to exorcise his own demons. The band takes universal themes of love, life and death and puts their own spin on them; they use themes that they, on a personal basis, can relate to, otherwise what would be the point in singing about them? On all of their studio albums to date they've used stories which are based on real life; sometimes it's situations that have happened in their own lives or the lives of their closest friends. As songwriters, they are storytellers and to tell a good story there has to be something people can connect with on a human level.

The songs since *Hybrid Theory* may not be as angry but there are still some very dark moments.

"That's where we feel we're the most honest," Bennington explained in 2007, *"that's where we feel we're the most sincere. Even when we try to write songs that are inspirational in a positive way, they seem to have an underlying dark element. Sometimes days are bright and sunny, and sometimes they're stormy. That's just the way it goes. Mike and I seem to like writing about the stormy days."*[18]

Another change for the band was the recording location: *Minutes To Midnight* was conceived in The Mansion, Laurel Canyon Boulevard, south of Mulholland. It was certainly more pleasurable than the stuffy environs of a corporate studio. And in the past the band had worked on ideas for an album on the road so getting the opportunity to work in a studio such as The Mansion was near perfect.

The recording was a tiring process that lasted longer than they anticipated due to the sheer volume of material they had in their archives. Shinoda said:

"We ended up working on the songs a lot differently than we had, playing instruments that we'd never touched before."[19]

Many of the songs that had made it to the final cut had evolved significantly from their infancy earlier in the year. Naturally, Warner Records were keen to get the album out as quickly as possible; it had been three years since the release of *Meteora* and the music scene had changed dramatically. Would the public still buy a Linkin Park CD? Nu-metal was dead and they were part of that scene whether they liked it or not. The band knew they couldn't go down the nu-metal route again. It was a style of music that was seen as "uncool", out of date; it fitted into a certain timeframe and 2006 was way beyond that time frame. What Rubin and the band did was to work hard in the studio with a variety of songs; most of the recording sessions involved a lot of experimentation. They tried to create diverse sounds that would get them totally different songs. They had basically copied *Hybrid Theory* with *Meteora* so doing it a third time would have been foolish.

The thing with Linkin Park is, as a collective force and as individuals, they really do love music. Ever since they were known as Xero they've spoken to the press about their love of different styles of music; they're not bigoted. What the six of them bring to the recording process is their enthusiasm for music, so with *Minutes To Midnight* they had a go at experimenting with hip-hop, rap, classic rock, metal and even a bit of punk (although it could be argued that punk also influenced the first two albums, certainly in the angry vocal style of Chester Ben-

nington). It has also been said that *Minutes To Midnight* is more melodic than its predecessors. It had always been important for the band to have memorable melodies and choruses because that is obviously how they hook the listener into the song and in so doing, get them to be attentive to the lyrics.

As soon as October arrived they had recorded around 100 songs. As an average album has 10 tracks they had recorded 10 albums worth of material. Of course, some of those songs could have been failures but some progressed into bigger and better versions. They played around with so many different styles of music during the recording process that when it actually came down to choosing the songs for the album they picked what felt right for them as a band. They tried some stuff that wasn't normally their thing but it felt right to play those songs.

"There were definitely a lot of songs there that we had to work with," explained Brad Delson, *"Some of them were good enough to be on the record but there was also a lot of stuff that you know, hopefully no one will ever hear because they were awful. There definitely is a lot of stuff that didn't make the record that may*

come out at some point in the future."[20]

The album was set to hit stores in the summer of 2006 but, of course, they were still in the studio. Release dates were then planned for the autumn and even by early 2007 the album was still not ready. Usually when a record is delayed so many times and the recording takes longer than scheduled it is easy to read between the lines and think: *Will it actually be any good?* or *Maybe they have to remake the album before it's even finished?* Those doubts were squashed the minute the album hit the stores.

However, there was one major blunder: it was leaked on the Internet on 4th March, 2007, just 10 days before its global release. It is the worse case scenario for a band; having worked hard for one whole year, somebody releasing it illegally on the Internet where people can download it for free before its release could potentially have killed the album. The band quickly responded to the issue via the online Linkin Park Message Board. Here's what they posted:

"To all our Linkin Park fans, We heard today that the album leaked... so I guess some of you have had a chance to hear

what we've been so excited about. We're both excited and disappointed that you're hearing it right now. Here's why:

It couldn't be more exciting to give you all new music, especially after all the hard work we put into it. This album was almost a year and a half of experiments, mistakes, inspiration, and careful craftsmanship. We put everything we had into these songs, and want you to hear every second of it. I can't wait for you to absorb all the levels of meaning in the songs, and the layers of music, eventually forming your own ideas about what the songs mean to you.

At the same time, a leak leaves out some very important parts of this piece of work. We put months of creative energy into the ART of the record, in the booklet, special edition, and big book... almost as long as it took to record hybrid theory (sic). The album has amazing photos, lyrics, and notes about how the songs came together – it's the visual half of the record. On the other hand, the super-special-edition book is packed with exclusive images, stories of the making of the songs, gorgeous art, the CD and a DVD that tells the story, showing the actual moments of inspiration caught on camera. For me, it's

almost hard to imagine anyone really experiencing this album without that part of it.

Even the song sequence alone is very important. It's WAY different to hear the songs in a random order than to listen to this record from beginning to end. At the very least, if you've already downloaded the songs, do us a huge favour and listen to them in the right order...it'll be way more rewarding.

...that's all we wanted to say. If any of you want to be patient and hold off on downloading the album, and get the proper experience by checking out the actual piece in your hands, we applaud you for your restraint! And to everyone else who can't wait: we can't help but understand, because we're just as excited about this album coming out as you are. Either way, thanks for listening, and being a fan of our music.

Thanks for supporting the band, see you on tour!

- Mike and LP"

The exact release date of *Minutes To Midnight* differed from territory to territory but it was issued worldwide in the month of May, 2007. The immediate success of the album surprised everybody, especially the band. They were concerned that they wouldn't be relevant to a younger audience anymore but that was shown not to be the case, quite obviously, when the album was released. How many bands can sell over half-a-million units of one album in its first week of release? Over three million copies of *Minutes To Midnight* had been sold around the world. That's enough to make any record label feel ecstatic. Evidently, the critics were divided in their opinion of the record. But like any new release by a major artist they are "critic proof", meaning sales of the album will not be affected by bad reviews simply because the artists in question are too damn popular with the mass public. It was interesting to see how fans reacted to the unexpected sound of the album: Mike Shinoda did a lot less rapping on *Minutes To Midnight* than on previous recordings, and more singing. There are even guitar riffs on there courtesy of Brad Delson; the inclusion of riffs was probably the idea of Rick Rubin, who had previously worked with AC/DC and Slayer, bands known for their love of a good heavy guitar riff. There's also a lot less scratching; it's as if Joe Hahn takes a back seat on *Minutes To Midnight*, but like Mike Shinoda, Hahn is a very technically-minded person and spent time in the studio tinkering with the programming side of things.

It has become a common theme in recent years for record labels to release various editions of one album (usually as a way to make more money if an album looks as though it's either going to sink – thus making the best of a bad job, or if it's going to be massive – there's even more money to be made) and there were several editions of *Minutes To Midnight* to hit the shop shelves.

In a review of *Meteora* for *Entertainment Weekly*, one critic said:

"As on Hybrid Theory, Linkin Park manage to convey their message without profanity, so there's nothing to censor here, sir! (Canny lads, these.)"

Well, *Minutes To Midnight* shows the six boys had grown into men and were not concerned with offending the establishment. (Don't forget, much of their fanbase had grown up too!) There were three versions of the album: the 'clean edition', the 'regular edition' and the 'special edition' – the latter two both being graced with a sticker stating 'Parental Advisory' because some songs contain profanity. It has to be noted that the band were not afraid of using such language in their lyrics, in fact they actually had a plausible reason.

"Well it's harder to write lyrics without covering up your vocabulary with vulgarity," Chester Bennington explained after the release of *Hybrid Theory,* *"Usually when you say somethin' like 'Fuck that' 'cause you're mad at something; well 'Fuck that' is two words describing the entire situation. So we try to talk about that situation and that's another way for us to challenge ourselves creatively..."*[21]

Minutes To Midnight was a monstrous success and received several nominations at various awards ceremonies around the world. It also spawned some hit singles:

Rick Rubin

'What I've Done', 'Bleed It Out', 'Shadow Of The Day', 'Given Up' and 'Leave Out All The Rest.' In fact, Joe Hahn, who is a major *Transformers* fan, was especially psyched that 'What I've Done' was the lead song for the live action movie of the famous eighties cult cartoon.

The influential American music critic and chief pop writer for the *LA Times,* Ann Powers reviewed the album in said newspaper.

"There's a contemplative feel throughout the album," she wrote, *"especially on the pretty, somewhat indistinguishable ballads where Bennington fully takes the lead. This is the kind of music artists make to find out who they'll become next: It reaches toward many influences – notably U2 (some of the songs invoke the Irish rock group almost note-for-note), but also Tool, Evanescence, Nirvana and Coldplay – without committing to anything."*

In *The New York Times,* Kelefa Sanneh commented:

"Maybe Rick Rubin, who helped produce, got the musicians to loosen up, but loose is relative with a band this fastidious. Instead of writing songs during jam sessions, the members

typically share ideas by swapping hard drives. Even on this album just about everything is tweaked to perfection, and there's always an infectious refrain around the corner (provided you can survive the often banal verses)."

Writing in *Rolling Stone,* the legendary rock critic David Fricke was in favour of the album:

"On Minutes To Midnight, *co-produced by Rick Rubin,"* he wrote, *Linkin Park are more of something else – topical – furiously good at it."*

While it may have garnered some typically snotty criticism from the hierarchy of the music press establishment, the fanzines were certainly more enthusiastic in their approach to the record. In an era where the Internet is becoming the main source of news and information there has been a growth in rock related websites and on many of them *Minutes To Midnight* was certainly well received. The album was praised on the popular UK based site *Hard Rock House*:

"Gone is the teen angst nu-metal mayhem of old to be replaced by a more thoughtful, thought provoking approach that

seems to be having a go at the American Idiot himself George Bush amongst others... Clearly there's an intelligence and deep social conscience in the Linkin Park ethos and finally on Minutes To Midnight *we get to hear it. Whether it's rock 'n' roll or not will be up to the individual."*

The band didn't even need to tour to promote the album; they could have sat back and cheerfully gloated as sales of the album shot up like a rising star. But their fans were eager to see them play live again. They hadn't toured since 2004 and hardcore Linkin Park fans were by now getting withdrawal symptoms. A tour of Europe kicked off in April, which included a special show at London's relatively small but legendary venue, the Astoria in Charing Cross. David Whisson reviewed the Astoria gig in the British broadsheet *The Independent,* commenting:

"Linkin Park's great musical strength is in creating tracks that meld rap and rock, samples and guitars, into a single entity... While the two frontmen are all over the stage and on top of the amps, Bennington flailing and posturing magnificently, the rest of the band focus on weaving an ever-changing blanket of noise."

In an otherwise decent review of the aforementioned gig, *The Times'* David Sinclair was critical of the band's music:

"For the most part, however, the group contended themselves with a trawl through the tried and tested, producing tub-thumping versions of hits such as 'Papercut', 'Breaking The Habit' and 'Crawling'."

On selected dates throughout Europe they were supported by Blindside, the Swedish band. Other dates in Europe included some of the continent's biggest festivals, namely, Alive, Pinkpop, Bamboozle, Rock Am Ring/ Rock Im Park (Rock At The Ring and Rock In The Park) and Nova Rock.

"We actually put a lot of attention on our live show this time around," explained Shinoda, *"ever since we came out of the studio, we were really excited about different ways we could keep the show fresh."*[22]

UK fans couldn't get enough of Linkin Park and thousands of punters turned up for the band's headlining set at the hugely successful Download festival on Saturday 9th June. The band played a

killer set-list: 'One Step Closer'; 'Lying From You'; 'Somewhere I Belong'; 'No More Sorrow'; 'Papercut'; 'Points Of Authority'; 'Given Up'; 'Don't Stay'; 'From The Inside'; 'Leave Out All The Rest'; 'Numb'; 'Pushing Me Away'; 'Breaking The Habit'; 'In The End'; 'Crawling'; 'What I've Done' (Encore) 'The Little Things Give You Away'; 'Bleed It Out' and 'Faint'.

The biggest event on 2007's live calendar for the band was invariably the touring festival Projekt Revolution. They'd put it on hold for the past two years so this time around it was going to be big business – and indeed it was. Between July and September Linkin Park were joined by My Chemical Romance, HIM, Taking Back Sunday and Julien-K *et al.* They played to thousands of fans at each gig and in some of America's biggest in-door arenas so it seemed that the over-crowded festival circuit was still a profitable business for all concerned.

The show at the Walnut Creek Amphitheatre on 13th August was reviewed on the website *indyweek.com*. One writer commented:

"United by loud guitars and suburban angst, nu-metal and emo have mostly melded into one cheerfully anguished omni-genre... the only meaningful difference was eyeliner."

The 15th August show in New York at Jones Beach Theatre got a full review in *The New York Times*. Journalist Kelefa Sanneh said about the band:

"Linkin Park has sold millions of albums by being charmless but proficient, and on Wednesday the members underscored both extremes. They look less rock 'n' roll royalty and more like a bunch of technocrats; considering the meticulous way they make music, that might be an apt description."

They finished 2007's touring schedule with a successful road journey around East Asia playing shows in Thailand, China and Japan.

2008 was another busy year for the band. They began the new year by playing a sold out tour of Europe, with a few dates in some of the UK's biggest venues (supported by Biffy Clyro), including two nights at London's massive O2 Arena by the River Thames. *"Leave it to London to build the biggest, baddest venue on the face of the Earth,"* Bennington screamed to the crowd. The set-list included some of the old and the new: 'What I've Done', 'Crawl-

ing', 'Numb', 'Shadow Of The Day', 'Faint', 'Valentine's Day', 'Somewhere I Belong', 'Points Of Authority', 'Hands Held High' and two songs melded together, 'Wake' and 'Given Up' *et al.*

The UK tour was an absolute triumph for the band. They were even taken aback by the sheer amount of interest it garnered from the fans and the critics. The tour was reviewed in many of the national and, wherever relevant, local newspapers as well as the rock press. There was a sense of accomplishment for the six men in Linkin Park. When they'd first visited the British Isles they were young, dressed like dorky yet street-wise teenagers; the mu-

sic they made then was angst-ridden rap-metal and they were viewed with suspicion by much of the mainstream media. This time around they'd grown up, most of them were married and had kids and were living relatively quiet lives back in their California mansions. Their lives could not have changed more drastically. And Linkin Park are all about looking to the future, rather than overdosing themselves with bouts of nostalgia, which is not always healthy, especially if you want your career to continue to flourish. In 2008, Linkin Park were one of the hottest live tickets of the year in Britain; considering it was only January the rest of the acts to grace British stages had a lot to live up to.

"After the onslaught 'No More Sorrow', 'Somewhere I Belong', and 'From The Inside' kept the crowd going," commented one reviewer about the Nottingham Arena show on the 24th, *"and it quickly became evident that the majority of the set was to be made up with material from the recent* Minutes To Midnight *opus."*[23]

Another journalist, writing in Sheffield's *The Star*, said of the Sheffield Arena gig on the 25th:

"Never to be accused of being one-trick ponies, they confirmed their diversity with a stirring piano and vocal-only section, Bennington proving his range..."

Life on the road was not as stressful as it used to be for the band. After all, they were now one of the biggest live acts on earth, commanding some of the world's biggest concert venues, stadiums and arenas of all sizes. Their entourage of assistants and road crew had gotten significantly bigger, as it does with any act of increasing popularity. But also there was no need to worry about the stresses of promoting the music; the music sold itself. They were on the road to please the fans and because they actually enjoyed it.

"We actually fight very rarely," Shinoda explained, *"We don't fight often at all. It surprises a lot of people... There is never a screaming match, it's not how our guys work."*[24]

The band had by now fully embraced the internet and social networking sites like MySpace and Facebook to promote their music and reach a wide audience. It is easy for a young fan to create a Facebook account and become friends with Linkin Park; obvious-ly this is not in a literal sense (only virtual) but what it does mean is that the fans can have some sort of connection to the band. Those that had joined the fan club or signed up to mailing lists would be the first people to receive the latest news about the group's activities. There are also websites dedicated to the individual members of the outfit, both official and unofficial. Years ago, fans would publish printed fanzines, but in a digital age the printed page is becoming less popular with fans that are, instead, opting to create online fanzines – or ezines/webzines – which are dedicated to a particular act. Sometimes they can actually be more detailed than the official site. It had taken some artists a while to accept the change in music marketing, but Linkin Park had been one of the first bands to explore the various uses of the Internet. In the noughties, the Internet has become a major source of news and promotion for all artists. This is something which Linkin Park should be given more credit for as it has become a major force in the music industry.

The band's relationship with the press was still a mixed one: they have been featured in all types of media, but while the high-brow publications treat them with caution, the music press have warmed to them over the years and of course, the rock publications aimed at younger audiences have fully accepted the band. Linkin Park as we know them now have been around for almost a decade and show no signs of disbanding any time soon, so the sceptics should probably think about taking them more seriously.

A tour of North America was planned to precede the European jaunt. With support from the rising progressive metal band Coheed and Cambria, dates were scheduled for all around the vast continent of North America. It was a massive tour that took them through to March.

As always, the summer was going to be something truly special. Another Projekt Revolution was planned but with a twist. They arranged for the festival to be staged outside of America for the first time in its short history. In June the tour, featuring HIM, Pendulum and N*E*R*D amongst others, was taken to Germany for three nights. And with special guest Jay-Z, an evening was staged in Milton Keynes, England. The show in England has become legendary; they recorded it

MILTON KEYNES NATIONAL BOWL

Linkin Park recorded their second live CD/DVD package at this famed outdoor 200,000 capacity venue in Buckinghamshire, England in June 2008. Some of the world's most successful artists have performed at Milton Keynes National Bowl, including AC/DC, Bon Jovi and Queen. Monsters Of Rock festival has been held at the Bowl as has Ozzfest and various other rock festivals.

for a future DVD and CD release, and as well as playing a set of his own, Jay-Z joined Linkin Park for a few songs at the end of their own headlining performance.

"Jumping straight in with 'One Step Closer' was a bold move", wrote one reviewer on the popular UK website *thrashhits.com*, *"but they knew that they had more than enough material to fill their 90-minute headline slot, and they did. Chester Bennington was on firey form while Mike Shinoda did his best to continue the hip-hop based shenanigans."*

And then the Projekt Revolution juggernaut was taken to North America for a tour that lasted from 16th July to 24th August. In the States they were joined by Chris Cornell, Busta Rhymes on selected dates and The Bravery, amongst other artists on the Revolution Stage and the Second Stage. The problem with Projekt Revolution was actually deciding which bands they wanted to take out on the road with them; the tour had become so successful that more and more bands wanted to hit the road under the Projekt Revolution banner.

"When you put together a list of 150 bands or whatever,"

Bennington informed one online writer, *"Finding the ones who are into the idea, finding the ones who will take the right amount of money, finding the ones that are OK with their position on the bill, finding the ones that are available that haven't already made commitments or not in the studio, that's the most time consuming part and that's really difficult."*[25]

A small addition to 2008's Projekt Revolution tour was a digital souvenir package (DSP) which fans were able to buy. It had never been offered on any previous tour and was further proof of Linkin Park's love of digital technology.

"You can basically opt in when you buy your tickets online for the digital souvenir package." explained Bennington to an American journalist, *"What will happen after that is you go to the show, you watch your show, enjoy that, come home, and in your e-mail you'll have a link to the show, to the MP3s of our set from the show you went to."*[26]

Throughout the year they also found time to perform at Rock In Rio in Portugal, Italy's Heineken Jammin' Festival, Festimad in Spain, Festival d'été de Quebec in Canada and Edgefest in Toronto,

PRESENT

PROJEKT REVOLUTION

SUPPORTING BILL TO BE ANNOUNCED

SUNDAY 29TH JUNE 2008

MILTON KEYNES BOWL

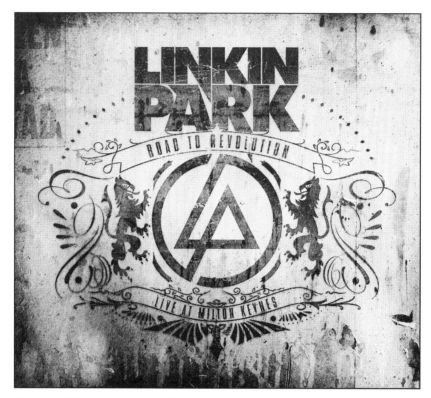

Canada. They had plenty of material to play during a gig; they could chop and change the set-list whenever they liked. The days of having to play the same tracks night after night because they only had one album in record stores was a thing of the past. They also had enough production staff to look after the stage for them, and they no longer had to worry about ticket sales or promotion.

By the end of 2008, the tour had already concluded and it was time to take a break and work on other projects not related to the Linkin Park moniker. However, they spent a significant proportion of time working on a new live CD/DVD package which was recorded at the Milton Keynes show, as previously stated.

On *linkinpark.com* the band gave adult fans the chance to name the CD/DVD in a special contest. The winner was announced on 13th October after the titles were whittled down to the best five: *Linkin Park - Midnight In Milton Keynes*; *Sunset Revolution - Linkin Park Live*

In The UK; *Road To Revolution - Linkin Park Live*; *Revolution In The Iron City - Linkin Park Live* and *Revolution In The UK - Linkin Park Live*. Prior to its official release in November 2008, fans who had actually attended the show were eligible to download it (via the DSP) if they had bought a special code on the day of the event. A far better package than *Live In Texas*, *Road To Revolution* is an excellent illustration of the band's incredible strength as a live act.

Around the time of the release of *Road To Revolution*, the band – in conjunction with their label, Warner Records – promoted the CD/DVD by posting sound clips and videos clips on sites like MySpace, Yahoo! Music and YouTube. The group had previously used YouTube as a means of promotion and had even created a Linkin Park page. However, Warner had fallen into dispute with YouTube (who are owned by Google) about showing their acts on the FREE Internet website. In December, Warner ordered YouTube to remove all its artists from the site; it was alleged that Warner wanted more money from YouTube for allowing them to use its artists. (In 2006, both companies had reached an agreement which stated that YouTube could post videos and audio sound files by artists on the Warner label for free in exchange for advertising revenue.) This meant that all Linkin Park related material on YouTube was pulled, including clips from *Road To Revolution*. In a press statement, Warner Records explained:

"We are working actively to find a resolution with YouTube that would enable the return of our artists' content to the site... Until then, we simply cannot accept terms that fail to appropriately and fairly compensate recording artists, songwriters, labels and publishers for the value they provide."

Finishing a tour and making plans for a break is not always what it seems in a band. In December, they previewed an original instrumental song called 'Lockjaw.' It was made available as a free download to members of the LPU; it was basically the result of a new type of software called Pro Tools 8, which was handed to them by a Californian company called Digidesign.

As 2009 quickly approached, Linkin Park had already begun thinking about their fourth studio album of original material.

CHAPTER 5

LINKIN PARK TODAY (2009)

"I think people are opening up to the idea that we are a band that's not afraid of extending ourselves and spreading our wings and pushing the boundaries of what is acceptable for us. Our fans, they stick with us through this process, and it's pretty awesome."

Chester Bennington[27]

As we've already seen, the six members of Linkin Park are tireless when it comes to new adventures and challenges. Even after a long tour the band were already looking ahead to the future, to making a new album. It is that kind of energy and diligence that has kept them in good stead for the past nine years.

In October of 2008, Linkin Park announced their plans to write and record their first concept album. It was Mike Shinoda who, on his blog, mentioned plans for the new record. Shinoda, Farrell and Hahn began working on some demos at Hahn's personal studio. And then a month later, Chester Bennington – who claimed it was a friend's idea for them to compose a concept album – told MTV:

"For me, you say the words 'concept record,' and the first thing I think of is theatre or the opera or something. There's a story, and everything has to relate to that story. It sounds a little daunting to me, so, I think my confidence level will drop, but when it was presented to us by this friend of ours, we liked the idea. It was an inspiring idea, and it was something we could relate a lot of the things we like to write about to. It couldn't have come strictly from us - an outside source brought it to us in a way that was exciting."

The album was scheduled for release in the middle of 2009 but Bennington was busy with his Dead By Sunrise side-project and so it was assumed that his solo effort would be released first, followed by the new Linkin Park one, possibly taking the album's release into 2010. As is often the case with a new release, the band kept specific details a closely-guarded secret. No producer had yet been named at the time of writing in April 2009.

"We haven't talked about this at length," Shinoda explained, *"Rick [Rubin] was really great. I think we will work with Rick again in the future at some point, but I don't know if this is the record... We're taking care of all our needs at this point."*[28]

Exactly what the 'concept' will be is anybody's guess. Whenever the album is released and whatever the concept proves to be, one thing is for sure: it'll be a huge success and the band will once more commit themselves to a lengthy tour of some of the world's biggest stages.

To keep fans happy and themselves entertained, it was announced in February that they would be included on the bill for the new touring festival named Sonisphere, devised by San Francisco thrashers Metallica. With a different line-up at each show, the tour would take them around Europe. The UK dates were arranged for 1st and 2nd August and the show was planned to be staged in the legendary grounds of Knebworth, once played by such greats as Led Zeppelin and Queen. To clarify the line-up plans, Metallica issued a press statement:

"Summer is around the bend and what would summer be without Metallica playing a few European festival shows? This year we're going to be part of the brand spankin' new Sonisphere festival, the first and only touring European Rock festival which hits six cities for a total of seven shows. We hear that while the usual festival madness will be going on, Sonisphere will have two alternate stages so you don't have to miss a minute of the music. Lamb of God and Mastodon are along for the fun at all the shows and on August 1 Linkin Park will headline the first of the two Knebworth shows (we take the stage for the second one on August 2nd). ...our friends from Slipknot and Die Toten Hosen are hitting a few select cities, with Linkin Park also joining us in Finland..."

The group also continued their exploration of the digital age by teaming up with Warner and Artificial Life for a three year deal to produce games for the iPod Touch and iPhone. The games will include the band's music as the soundtrack.

"We want to offer our fans every opportunity to enjoy our music," said Joe Hahn, *"We're excited to be working with Artificial Life to develop a new and*

unique way for them to experience Linkin Park."[29]

the necessary IP rights for this project."[30]

Eberhard Schoneburg, the CEO of Artificial Life, Inc, said in a press statement in April:

"It is both an honour and privilege to have the opportunity to partner with Linkin Park and Warner Bros. Records. The applications we expect to produce will have exceptional potential in the mobile market. The unique and alternative music style of Linkin Park make them the best fit to be ported into the iPhone platform. We would like to thank Warner Bros. Records for their co-operation to provide us with

There are ways of using digital technology to promote your music, performances and merchandise and of using the Internet as a means to make more money, however, there is a significant amount of people who don't want to buy the music but steal it by illegally downloading albums at no cost to themselves. There is a fierce debate over the impact of illegal, free downloading, and it's argued to be one of the main factors in the decline of CD sales. Record companies are in trouble and are struggling to combat this pandemic.

Mike Shinoda was keen to express his thoughts about downloading:

"I guess I do have a philosophy when it comes to spending money on music. Every dollar you spend on an artist (whether it be on their music, concert tickets, or merchandise) is a statement; it says you want the artist to continue doing what they do. Some people don't think anything about stealing a song from a band that they love, but then they turn around and spend a bunch of money on something that they don't care a lot about... I guess what I'm saying is: I'm not a big fan of the idea of stealing from an artist you love, and then turning around and giving money to a brand or company you don't love."[31]

Despite remaining relatively quiet in the first couple of months of 2009, April delivered yet another piece of exciting news for fans: Mike Shinoda announced via his blog that the band would contribute a new song to the soundtrack of *Transformers 2: Revenge Of The Fallen*. They had obviously contributed 'What I've Done' to the first live action incarnation of the cult classic cartoon, but the second film promised to be an even bigger cinematic experience. Shinoda also confirmed that while the revered film composer Hans Zimmer would be writing most of the music for the movie (with Steve Jablonsky), a song composed by both artists' would be used in the highly-publicised Michael Bay feature. Shinoda said:

"The song we wrote is being used as one of the themes, and we will be writing various interpolations on that theme, and trying out some other thematic ideas as part of the (very large) team scoring the film... We met with Hans last week, and heard some of the incredible things he and his guys have done with our new song. In the next few days, we'll be doing some work with Hans's amazing writing and recording crew."[32]

'New Divide', the lead theme song for the *Transformers 2* movie, got its video premiere on 18th May and it was available to download on iTunes at the end of the month. In a press statement, the film's director Michael Bay enthused:

"I love Linkin Park...This is the second film we've worked on together and the fact that they're huge Transformers *fans makes it all the better. They really*

delivered with 'New Divide' - it's a great song that perfectly matches the film's intensity."[33]

Some critics pointed out the sharp contrast the song has with their earlier work and that it is more aligned with those songs which feature on *Minutes To Midnight*. One reviewer said in the popular online magazine *Entertainment Weekly*:

"So how's the new tune? Not bad, actually, if heavy on a dose of the self-serious. It just features vocals from Chester Bennington though, so those expecting some rhymes might be disappointed. But

midway through there's a robo-riff that will surely melt the faces off of plenty of angsty teens."

If the single is a taster of what to expect from the band on their forthcoming album then they may have a problem on their hands. They'll run the risk of alienating both their metal fanbase and their urban fans. All sorts of questions can be posed: Was *Minutes To Midnight* a one-off? Or will they continue to create more commercial classic rock sounding albums? Will they return to their nu-metal roots and feature rap vocals more prominently in their music?

The story of Linkin Park is about six friends who share a passion for music and an enthusiasm for sharing it with their fans. Now they are in a comfortable financial position, they're just as keen to help other artists with their own music as they are in creating a new album for themselves. As history shows, the music business is constantly evolving; some bands can't keep up with the new trends and consequently, they quickly disappear into the past. But Linkin Park has shown the world that it's a band that can move with the times; they've outlived the nu-metal era and have challenged themselves as artists with various collaborative efforts. Their entire back catalogue – and over the past decade the band have become quite prolific – is surprisingly varied. It shows us that they're not afraid to go against the norm by releasing a remix album, hooking up with the world's greatest rap star or by almost discarding rap completely and making a straight-ahead rock album. And now they're going to do a concept album! One thing is for sure, Linkin Park do not play it safe.

They've made an indelible impression on modern music and that is why they will be remembered for years to come. Looking at pictures of the band from the early years and placing the nu-metal era in an historical perspective, it's easy to see why critics are not friendly toward Linkin Park. However, the Linkin Park of 2009 is a vastly different beast from what it was back in 2001 so why do the critics still dislike them so much? Don't forget, some of the greatest bands in rock history were loathed by critics, but in time, opinions change. And only time will tell if Linkin Park will be accepted as a truly *great band.*

In a way, they seem content with being the outsiders and doing things their own way, enjoying the unconventional approach to making music. It is one of the reasons why they have such a committed fanbase. They enjoy movies, comic books and different styles of music and like to reflect those tastes in their own compositions. With their first two albums and the excessive bouts of touring they showed the world that they can appeal to hardcore metal fans, and upon the release of *Collision Course* they attracted an urban audience. How many other bands could possibly accomplish such a feat? (The answer: not many.)

Maybe with *Minutes To Midnight* they wanted to try their hand at luring the older rock fan to their side. Releasing an album that doesn't follow a particular trend apparent on previous releases can be a dangerous game, but with Linkin Park each record has sold in its millions, so they are doing something right. Do they have an agenda? Who knows.

Ron "Bumblefoot" Thal, the current Guns 'N Roses guitarist, says, perceptively:

"The first time I heard Linkin Park, I thought to myself, THIS is the band that people are gonna recommend 20 years from now, when a young kid wants to discover music from our time. They have it all, ya know? They wrote great songs, made great recordings of them that captured the vibe; they were one of few bands that were able to be musically multi-cultural with integrity. They always came across to me as intelligent, insightful and focused. Much respect for them..."

However, they've yet to have a massive failure, something that inevitably befalls all bands with a long shelf-life, so whenever that will be is anybody's guess. The hardest part is not climbing to the top but staying there...

NOTES

1 Speaking to *shoutweb.com*
2 Speaking to *bassguitarmagazine.com*
3 Speaking to *hitquarters.com*
4 Speaking to *sneakerfreaker.com*
5 Interview with *Time Out*
6 Interview with *The Guardian*
7 Speaking to *nyrock.com*
8 Speaking to *hitquarters.com*
9 Speaking to *shoutweb.com*
10 Interview with *Time Out*
11 Speaking to *planet-loud.com*
12 Speaking to *kronick.com*
13 Interview with *The Guardian*
14 Speaking to *musicOMH.com*
15 Speaking to *smnnews.com*
16 *contactmusic.com*
17 Speaking to *ultimate-guitar.com*
18 Interview with the *Daily Telegraph*
19 Interview with *USA Today*
20 Speaking to *ultimate-guitar.com*
21 Speaking to *kronick.com*
22 Speaking to *thesop.org*
23 Review on *hardrockhouse.com*
24 Speaking to *planet-loud.com*
25 Speaking to *artisanews.com*
26 Speaking to *allaccessmagazine.com*
27 Speaking to *thesop.org*
28 Interview with *Rolling Stone*
29 Press Statement on *business-wire.com*
30 Press Statement on *business-wire.com*
31 Speaking to *freshnerd.com*, March 2009
32 As said on *mikeshinoda.com*, 24th April, 2009
33 As referenced on *blabbermouth.net*

CHAPTER 6

THE EX-MEMBERS OF LINKIN PARK

The band that we know today as Linkin Park is without doubt Mike Shinoda, Joe Hahn, Chester Bennington, Rob Bourdon, Brad Delson and Dave Farrell. However, there were several line-up amendments in the early years.

KYLE CHRISTENER had a very brief stay in Xero/Hybrid Theory. Dave Farrell wanted to return to college to finish his studies and so he quit the band to be briefly replaced by Kyle Christener. Farrell left sometime in late 1998, not long before the future members of Linkin Park changed their band moniker from Xero to Hybrid Theory in early '99. It meant Farrell could not play bass on their first, self-titled EP, released in May 1999 and limited to 1,000 copies. Instead, Christener and Brad Delson took the bass guitar duties on the record. Christener left the fold after Dave Farrell returned yet again, but when Farrell took to some other band, another bassist was hired to pluck the strings on Linkin Park's debut album for Warner. Very little is known about this character and there isn't a website or fansite listed under his name. It has been said that he has since played in a band called NoseDive.

SCOTT KOZIOL was a temporary member of Linkin Park, more of a "stand-in" bassist than anything else. He joined when the band was known as Hybrid Theory and left after Dave Farrell rejoined (again) in early 2001. Koziol played bass on 'One Step Closer' on the album *Hybrid Theory*, released in the States in late 2000 and in the UK in early 2001. He

don and got the job in time for the recording of the album. A virtuoso musician, Koziol already had a worthy list of credits prior to joining the band. His debut came in 1997 when he worked for the Atlanta blues musician Tinsley Ellis on the album (and subsequent tour) *Fire It Up.* He'd previously worked with a number of Southern American blues artists, including Clarence "Gatemouth" Brown, Doc Watson, Robert Lockwood Jr and Johnny Lang, amongst others.

Since his departure from Linkin Park in early 2001, Koziol refuses to give interviews, however, the fansite *linkinparkamerican.com* was granted a rare chat with the former bassist. Asked about his experience in Linkin Park, Koziol replied:

can also be seen in a couple of shots on the video for 'One Step Closer.' Other bassists on the album include The Dust Brothers ('With You'), Ian Hornbeck ('Papercut,' 'A Place For My Head' and 'Forgotten') and it has been acknowledged that Brad Delson also played the instrument on the record. Basically, Dave Farrell was busy with the band Tasty Snax (aka The Snax) after deciding to finish his studies at college and so he chose not to stay in Hybrid Theory/Linkin Park. Koziol also played some live shows with the band throughout 2000.

How did Ohio born Koziol get the job? He was contacted by Barry Squire, the manager of a Los Angeles based musician referral service, about the vacant bassist's slot. Koziol chatted to Rob Bour-

"I was blessed with a unique opportunity to collaborate with the members of Linkin Park. They are innovative artists, musicians, and entrepreneurs. I had only been in LA for about six months when I met the band. They showed me around town, introduced me to a variety of new art, and pushed me in new directions. They work very hard to strive towards perfection musically, visually, and artistically with the greatest respect for their fans. Quality over quantity. It was a

life changing experience that influenced me significantly."

Since leaving Linkin Park, Scott Koziol has played with a number of artists both on stage and in the studio. The list is as long as your arm and includes Kenna, Persephone's Bees, Ima Robot, Katy Rose, Samantha Ronson, Perry Farrell, Revis, Deadsy, 30 Seconds To Mars, 3rd Strike, Michelle Branch, Hanson, Eve 6, The Calling, Powerman 5000, Humble Gods, Kottonmouth Kings, Organic Soul and Hourcast. For a lengthy list of credits pay a visit to his website *basslut.com* and *scottkoziol.com*.

His music took a side step when he began working for Apple Inc. in October 2004 to October 2008. He worked in the capacity of Higher Education Account Executive, which took him to a number of University campuses and Apple stores in the States. He told *linkinparkamerican.com:*

"I was using my artistic skills and playing almost everyday, but my schedule was very busy so I did not take in very many gigs during this time."

In 2008 he received a Bachelor of Music degree from the Boston school Berklee College of Music, on which occasion the British singer Sting was the guest of honour, handing out the degree certificates to the students, including Koziol. He even hooked up with ex-Eagles guitarist Don Felder for some educational music-related projects. Whether or not Koziol will return to music in a full-time capacity remains to be seen; he's not done anything as high-profile as Linkin Park since, and other projects seem to have been more random. There is little Internet activity covering his career and so it has to be a case of watch this space…

MARK WAKEFIELD is probably the most well-known former member of the band Xero, which also included future members of Linkin Park, Mike Shinoda, Brad Delson and Rob Bourdon. Wake-

Mark Wakefield with Taproot in 2000

field hooked up with Xero along with Joe Hahn and Dave Farrell. They independently released a self-titled EP in 1997, which features songwriting contributions from Wakefield. Xero opened for System Of A Down at a show at LA's famous Whisky A Go-Go. Zomba Music executives were present and signed the band to their catalogue of artists. However, a record deal remained elusive. Wakefield grew bored of struggling to get a deal and so he quit the band (or was forced out, depending on the source of information). The exact date of his departure is unclear, but it's widely known that he left just after Dave Farrell in 1998, having joined in '96. It took some time for the band to find a replacement for Wakefield. The plus side for Wakefield is that Linkin Park's debut album *Hybrid Theory* features him in the song credits for 'Runaway', 'A Place For My Head' and 'Forgotten.' Consequently, Wakefield is also listed in the song credits for the band's remix album *Reanimation*. Wakefield's post-Linkin Park projects include, most popularly, being manager for the nu-metal outfit Taproot, who scored a hit album with *Welcome* in 2002 on the Atlantic label.

Club Tattoo

IN CELEBRATION OF CLUB TATTOO'S GRAND OPENING AT MIRACLE MILE SHOPS IN PLANET HOLLYWOOD LAS VEGAS

Chester Bennington (of Linkin Park) Live with a special **FREE** Acoustic performance with his new band

DEAD ▼ SUNRISE

Saturday, July 4th 10:30PM *at* **Steve Wyrick Theater** *located in* **Miracle Mile Shops** *at* **Planet Hollywood Resort and Casino**

▶ **2:00-4:00 PM**
In Store autograph session by **Chester** *and the members of* **Dead By Sunrise** *at* **Club Tattoo**

▶ **8:30 PM**
Death Drop *stunt featuring* **Chester Bennington** *and* **Magician Steve Wyrick**
(on the Miracle Mile Shops/Planet Hollywood parking garage)
(complimentary tickets available at Club Tattoo)

▶ **10:30 PM**
Free Special acoustic performance by
Dead By Sunrise *at* **Steve Wyrick Theater**, *Miracle Mile Shops*
(tickets available at Club Tattoo Shop starting at 2:30PM)

▶ **11:30-4:00 AM**
Party at **Privé Las Vegas** *at* **Planet Hollywood**
(open to the public)

CHAPTER 7

THE SOLO PROJECTS

Not every member of Linkin Park has enjoyed a side-project or a solo career outside of the camp. In fact, it seems that most of them prefer either to concentrate specifically on the band or to non-music related endeavours; it's primarily Chester Bennington and Mike Shinoda who have been pro-active musically outside of Linkin Park. Here's a potted history of the side-projects some of the members have been immersed in.

CHESTER BENNINGTON's solo work is mostly made up of odds and ends without consistent focus. As a guest singer he's appeared on a number of tracks by a myriad of artists (Limp Bizkit, Mötley Crüe, Young Buck, Busta Rhymes, Korn, Stone Temple Pilots, Cyclefly and DJ-Z Trip), but it's his side-project Dead By Sunrise that will inevitably give him some real kudos. The seeds for Dead By Sunrise were sown way back in 2005 when Bennington sang the original song 'Let Down' with Julien-K at the 2005 benefit concert ReAct Now: Music

For Relief. Julien-K was formed by Orgy guitarists Amir Derakh and Ryan Shuck, who were later joined by Brandon Belsky and Anthony 'Fu' Valcic. Bennington hooked up with the four-piece to record 'Morning After', a song that features exclusively on the *Underworld: Evolution* soundtrack. They also collaborated together on a remix of Mindless Self Indulgence's 'What Do They Know?': the track was labeled 'What Do They Know?' (Mindless Self Indulgence vs. Julien-K & Chester Bennington) and features on the CD *Another Mindless Rip Off*. Even on stage Bennington has shown his fondness for working with the band, once replacing singer Ryan Shuck for a gig in Chicago during the Projekt Revolution tour so Shuck could make it to his brother's wedding.

Messrs Chester Bennington, Amir Derakh, Ryan Shuck, Anthony "Fu" Valcic, Brandon Belsky and Elias Andra have an obvi-

Julien-K

Dead By Sunrise

ous musical chemistry and share similar visions for new compositions. So much so that Julien-K and Bennington created Dead By Sunrise, known initially as Snow White Tan, the latter name apparently coming from David Bowie's vintage 1972 song, 'Ziggy Stardust'. Although what exactly Dead By Sunrise means is anybody's guess; it is, however, a memorable name for a band, especially one that purports to be as dark and atmospheric as these guys. Dead By Sunrise is primarily Bennington's solo endeavor with his cohorts taking care of production, programming and any added work. Bennington will apparently play guitars and keyboards on the forthcoming album as well as obviously taking care of the vocal duties. The pro-

posed record has been slated for release a number of times, but due to Linkin Park's hectic schedule it has had to be delayed. Right through to mid 2009 there was a massive amount of speculation on the Internet about its release date but nothing was confirmed.

The band previewed three songs live on 10th May, 2008 to celebrate the 13th Anniversary of the Club Tattoo in Arizona. The songs they played were 'Morning After', 'My Suffering' and 'Walking In Circles.' Another track that will feature on the album is the aforementioned 'Let Down.'

Speaking to *Rolling Stone* in 2008, Bennington confessed:

"I wouldn't call it a side project... We're a full, ready-to-go band and so this is something we take very seriously... We're not

planning on releasing a record this year. We don't know when it's going to come out... I want to make sure the record gets the chance to do what it can do."

Mike Shinoda has made some positive comments on his blog about the album, prompting fans to wonder how radically different it will be from Linkin Park's hard-edged rap-metal. Some have suggested it draws inspiration from the likes of Depeche Mode, Trent Reznor, The Cure, The Cult, early Bowie and Bauhaus.

In September 2008, Bennington was interviewed by the US magazine *Entertainment Weekly*. He said:

"It's going to kick ass. I started working on it in 2005 when we took a seven month break. I wanted to do something creative in that time off and I had songs that I knew weren't Linkin Park songs, but I thought were good. Then we started working on Minutes To Midnight *and that's all I've been doing for the last two years. Now that we're done, I've got this body of work that is strong – very moody, very dark and melodic."*

On 8th April, 2009 Bennington joined Julien-K onstage at The Roxy Theatre in West Hollywood to play 'Maestro' and 'Technical Difficulties'. As well as working with them on the Dead By Sunrise project, Bennington took time out from working with Linkin Park to executive produce Julien-K's debut full-length studio album *Death To Analog* (mixed by the revered Tim Palmer), released on 10th March in the States.

In a press statement circulated on the Internet, Ryan Shuck explained:

"We are trying to say something, we are trying to change things, we are trying to take performance to another level, we are trying to integrate technology in a way that no one ever has, we are trying to continue to write great songs, we are trying to write hooks and have great choruses, we are trying to talk about real life, our lives, situations, things that people can actually identify with, real life, love, relationships, all the things that I used to love in music... We are trying to keep passion in music."

BRAD DELSON may be one of the least well-known members of Linkin Park (to the mainstream), but that doesn't mean his reluctance for fame has put him off any side-projects. Sure, Linkin Park keeps him very busy, as it does with his colleagues, but he has committed himself to some important and worthwhile musical causes. The most prominent role he has is that of A&R representative for Machine Shop Recordings, the band's independently run label which is part of the Warner Music Group. The label was set-up in 2002 by Delson and Mike Shinoda, but since then the rest of the band have become involved in its organisation and promotion.

Delson also produced a remix of the Fort Minor song 'Where'd You Go' which features on the single release and is dubbed the 'BBB Remix' and was issued by Machine Shop. That happened in 2006, fast forward to 2008 and he co-wrote and played guitars on the Busta Rhymes single 'We Made It' (which also features Linkin Park.)

JOE HAHN has been busy on his own projects despite keeping a relatively low-key life outside of Linkin Park. Whereas Chester Bennington and Mike Shinoda's projects are mostly music related, Joe Hahn has been working in the film industry and displaying his talents as a director. We already know about his work as a music video director on some of the Linkin Park videos, but Hahn has also directed a short film called *The Seed*. It was made during 2005 prior to the recording of *Minutes To Midnight*; the band were on a brief break from the rigours of touring and used the opportunity to try their hands at other things. The making of the film ran into 2006 and was eventually unveiled at the 11th annual Pusan International Film Festival in the same year. *The Seed* went through the global festival circuit where it won 'Outstanding Cinematography' in 2007 at the Veneration Film Festival in Newport News and the 'Best Short Film' at the Festivus Film Festival in Denver (2008). Hahn also entered the film at the San Francisco International Asian American Film Festival, the Malibu Film Festival, the Beverly Hills Film Festival, the Los Angeles United Film Festival and the Swansea Bay Film Festival in the UK.

The Seed stars the actor Will Yun Lee and uses a couple of untitled Fort Minor recordings in the soundtrack. It has a deep premise; basically, Yun Lee plays Sung, a homeless person living on the banks of the famous LA River. The viewer is taken into his world but what is reality and what is his dream state? Surrealist filmic techniques are used as the nightmare unfolds.

FILIP ENGSTROM

Engstrom is a Swedish born director who made a short film (four minutes in length) called *Little Pony*, which features a cameo by Joe Hahn. It was created in 2005 for the Sony Dreams series. Another short film in the series is *Max*, directed by Samuel Bayer. In 2001, Engstorn directed, produced and wrote a six minute Swedish film called *Bruno*, starring Johan Syangren and Paula McManus.

Hahn had an epiphany when he saw a real life situation concerning a vagabond:

"I saw a homeless guy having an argument with someone," he is reported to have said at a film festival, *"who clearly wasn't there. I wondered what it would look like to see the fight through his eyes. What if what he was seeing was real? Who does he think is out to get him?"*

Hahn is rumoured to be working on a couple of other short film ventures, namely *Kung Fu High School* and *King Rat*.

What else has Hahn accomplished? Well, aside from setting up a business store in LA called Suru, his passion for the process of film-making has never diminished. He has directed videos for Alkaline Trio, Static-X, Story Of The Year, Xzibit and X-Ecutioners. Hahn spoke to *punktv.ca* about his side career:

"I don't always have a great idea for a video," he said, *"Whenever that happens, I'll pass on the project. That then opens it up to other directors. There are a lot of directors that I admire and would love to work with. Sometimes the*

Suru

guys in the band and label make it difficult to do your job. That is when I start to regret taking on a project."

As a musician he hooked up with his pal Mike Shinoda and worked on a couple of tracks with Fort Minor: 'Slip Out The Back' that features on Fort Minor's debut album *The Rising Tied* and a B-side called 'Move On.' Hahn also remixed the track 'Where'd You Go' and renamed it 'Where'd You Joe.' As a turntablist, Hahn can be heard on The X-Ecutioners track 'It's Goin' Down' and he is even featured in the video (as are other members of Linkin Park.) The 2008 collection *Greatest Remixes* by Good Charlotte features a track called 'The Young & The Hopeless' which Hahn worked on.

MIKE SHINODA has had by far the most interesting career away from Linkin Park. Before we get to his main side-project Fort Minor, it's worth reiterating some of his production credits. He has worked with an array of artists, including Depeche Mode, Styles Of Beyond, The X-Ecutioners, Julien-K, Busta Rhymes and Lupe Fiasco.

Shinoda's love of painting (and his obvious talent for it) led to Fort Minor's first album because in 2004 he created 10 paintings, which ended up being used on the packaging for *The Rising Tied*. It was toward the end of the year when Shinoda formed his side-project Fort Minor.

Shinoda spoke to *rapmusic.com* in 2005:

HOLLY BROOK

Born in 1986 in Wisconsin, Holly Brook moved to LA in 2003 to pursue her career as a professional singer-songwriter. It was in the so-called City of Angels that she hooked up with producer Jon Ingoldsby and songwriters Rob Hoffman and Heather Holley. Together she produced a demo in the hope of catching somebody's eye in the record industry. Of course this is a clichéd story. However, Linkin Park guitarist Brad Delson was fortunately handed a copy of her demo and was so in awe of her music that he signed her to Linkin Park's newly-formed label, Machine Shop Recordings, in 2004. Her 2006 debut opus, *Like Blood Like Honey* was released by MSR and distributed through Warner. In May 2008 her request to be released from her contract with MSR was completed. Her sophomore album was set to be released in the second half of 2009. In between the two, Brook contributed to the debut record of Mike Shinoda's side-project, Fort Minor: she sang on the tracks 'Where'd You Go' and 'Be Somebody.' Speaking in 2006 to *staticmultimedia.com* about her growing success and her support slots for some Fort Minor gigs, she said:

"The touring thing is different though; touring with my mom, we went in a van and [we'd] take our guitars and play for kids at schools or whatever. And now this tour is actually on a bus, the Fort Minor part of it, which is totally new for me, I've never done that before. My shows in between are small, the Fort Minor ones are gigantic... You know, what's funny is after doing a couple of these Fort Minor shows and having a lot of fans from that, it's really cool to see people so into the music but I get really nervous when kids come up to me wanting my autograph and stuff."

Visit *hollybrookmusic.com*

"I was a producer and rapper before Linkin Park. Once the band took off, it was the centre of my focus. A couple of years ago, I started missing doing straight-up hip-hop, and that's when Fort Minor began. I started messing around with a couple of songs, and one by one, other rappers started getting on the songs."

Various ideas have been flung around as to the exact significance of the name 'Fort Minor', but the general speculation is that the word 'Fort' stands for something

BUSTA RHYMES

Brooklyn born rapper Busta Rhymes' career stretches back to 1996 and his debut album *The Coming*. Prior to his solo career he was in the New York hip-hop/rap group, Leaders Of The New School, who released two albums: 1991's *A Future Without A Past* and 1993's *T.I.M.E.*

His hit UK and US singles include 'Woo Hah! Got You All In Check', 'What's It Gonna Be?' (with Janet Jackson), 'Break Ya Neck' and 'I know What You Want' (with Mariah Carey). He has also collaborated with P. Diddy and Pharrell, amongst others. Rhymes has appeared in a number of films, including *Shaft*, *Finding Forester*, *Narc* and *Halloween: Resurrection*. He is a controversial figure who was banned from entering the UK in September 2008 because of his convictions in the US, some of which allegedly include assault and anger issues. >>

sturdy and aggressive while the word 'Minor' (as a minor key on a piano) stands for something sombre, and that Shinoda wanted to merge the two emotions. He was also inspired to form Fort Minor because of groups like Public Enemy, N.W.A, Boogie Down Productions, Run DMC and Rakim.

Shinoda hooked up with Jay-Z, who executive produced *The Rising Tied*, which was recorded at The Stockroom and NRG Studios in LA in late 2004. Although the idea of Fort Minor had been formulating in Shinoda's mind for some time and he'd spent about a year working on demos and writing ideas down, the album came together pretty quickly in the studio.

Shinoda penned all the lyrics, sang and even played all the instruments (except for the strings and percussion) on the album. It spawned the singles 'Petrified', 'Believe Me', 'Remember The Name' and 'Where'd You Go.' For the music videos Shinoda got to work with directors Robert Hales, Kimo Proudfoot, Laurent Briet and Philip Andelman. Unquestionably, the most personal track on the album is 'Kenji' which tells the story of Shinoda's family during the Japanese-American Internment (the moving of Japanese nationals to War Relocation Camps) during World War II. Shinoda's Japanese heritage has always been extremely important to him and his art. Shinoda informed *antimusic.com*:

"After the bombing of Pearl Harbour, the US government began a period of racial profiling. They put all the Japanese-Americans (and some other Asian-Americans) in secluded camps for the duration of the war. My dad was three years old, and had 12 brothers and sisters. My oldest aunt was in her twenties, and had four kids. Her youngest was born in camp. Her husband died in camp. They stayed there for the duration of the war, captive. Once they were released, they returned to vandalized

BUSTA RHYMES

<< In 2007, Rhymes teamed up with Linkin Park for the single 'We Made It', produced by Cool & Dre and featuring on Rhymes 2008 album *Back On My B.S.* It was released in the US on 29th April and in the UK on 30th June, 2008. It was not a massive commercial success: it struggled in the US *Billboard* Hot 100, only making it to number 65, but in the UK it achieved healthier sales peaking at number 10. Interestingly, 'We Made It' contains samples from the Linkin Park track 'Papercut,' Fort Minor's 'Remember The Name' and even 'Thriller', one of Michael Jackson's signature songs. Another interesting connection to Linkin Park's history is that the warehouse which features in the video for the single was also the place where the cover for *Meteora*

was shot. Busta Rhymes and Linkin Park performed the song live for the first time on 25th May, 2008 at the Third Encore rehearsal studio; they were watched by 14 surprised Linkin Park fan club members. The single release contains different edits of the song:

1. 'We Made It' *(Album Version)*
2. 'We Made It' *(A Capella Edit)*
3. 'We Made It' *(Instrumental)*
4. 'We Made It' *(Video)*
5. 'We Made It' *(Explicit)*

In mid-2008 Busta Rhymes joined Linkin Park on the band's Projekt Revolution North American tour, but after an alleged spat with Mike Shinoda, Rhymes left the tour after just 11 shows.
Visit *bustarhymes.com*

homes and racial tension. That's what the song 'Kenji' is about."

The album features guest appearances by Styles Of Beyond, DJ Black, Thought of The Roots and John Legend as well as more obscure names like Holly Brook, Jonah Matranga, Common, Bobo, Kenna and Celph Titled. There was also a bunch of extra songs recorded which were used as B-sides and for the Special Edition release: 'Move On' (featuring Joe Hahn), 'Do What We Did' (featuring Styles Of Beyond), 'Tools Of The Trade' (featuring Styles Of Beyond and Celph Titled), '100 Degrees' (featuring Green Lantern), 'Cover And Duck', 'Strange Things', 'Start It All Up' and 'Be Somebody' (featuring, Lupe Fiasco, Tak and Holly Brook.)

Produced and mixed by Shinoda, *The Rising Tied* was released via Machine Shop Recordings in November 2005. The album's title is yet another play on words similarly to Fort Minor: 'Rising' basically refers to 'rising in the music business' while 'Tied' means 'as musicians they are tied together'. It sold almost half-a-million copies worldwide, with a good chunk of those sales coming from America. Fort Minor even played live in August 2006 at the Summer Sonic Festival in Japan (which also featured Linkin Park.) Shinoda has since announced that Fort Minor is on a sabbatical because he wants to give his full dedication to Linkin Park.

LUPE FIASCO

As of 2009, Fiasco is a revered rapper with three albums under his belt and whose fans include Jay-Z. Originally from Chicago, Fiasco has collaborated with the iconic American hip-hop star Kanye West. Fiasco features on Fort Minor's *The Rising Tied* as well as two tracks on the *We Major* mixtape. Mike Shinoda has also worked with Fiasco as a producer: he produced 'The Instrumental', which features on the rapper's 2006 debut album *Lupe Fiasco's Food & Liquor*.
Visit *lupefiasco.com*

CHAPTER 8

THE PEERS

Linkin Park have transcended the nu-metal genre, which dominated the rock and metal scene at the turn of the millennium. It was derided by the mainstream music press, laughed at by some of the more serious metal scribes and approached with caution by veteran metal enthusiasts, but a whole new generation of metal fans could not get enough. Over the years individual members of Linkin Park have lost weight, changed their image, created their own projects outside of the band and generally grown up. As a band they've grown out of the nu-metal trend (at least that's what Minutes To Midnight *tells us) and moved towards a more classic/alternative rock sound. In 2009, nu-metal is redundant and it's nothing but a distant memory, with many of the band's struggling to make ends meet. On the other hand, Linkin Park's career is flourishing like never before.*
However, it's interesting to note what some of Linkin Park's peers are up to and how their careers have changed since 2000. The following offers potted histories of some nu-metal heavyweights, as well as one or two bands that are not strictly nu-metal but are nevertheless important to the band's story and could still be termed peers. In sum, they're post-grunge/alternative metal bands; many of them played on the 2001 Ozzfest jaunt. Also, all of these bands had breakthrough albums around the same time-frame (roughly 1999-2002) as Linkin Park's initial bout of success with* Hybrid Theory *in 2000/01.*

AMERICAN HEAD CHARGE

American Head Charge's breakthrough album was 2001's *The Art Of War*, produced by Rick Rubin and released through his label American Recordings. Their debut record *Trepanation*, was independently released in 1999. Al-

though they're often touted as an industrial metal outfit some argue they fell into the nu-metal mould after touring with the likes of Coal Chamber and Mudvayne. They've toured/shared the bill with a number of other high-profile metal bands, including Hatebreed, System Of A Down, Ministry, Static-X and Biohazard, among others, and also played on the 2001 Ozzfest with Linkin Park and others. Formed in Minneapolis in 1997, the band have had their fair share of inner turmoil, mostly due to alleged drug abuse. They were released from their record deal with Rubin's label and their third album, *The Feeding*, was issued in 2005 through DRT Entertainment/Nitrus. Guitarist Bryan Ottoson died in 2005, aged just 27; it was alleged that his death was caused by an accidental drug overdose (the drugs were medically prescribed.) Things have been quiet with the band since the release of 2007's live CD/DVD set *Can't Stop The Machine* and they have yet to release their third studio opus. There have been a number of line-up changes in AHC, as they are affectionately known to fans, but the 2009 version is: singer Cameron Heacock, bassist Chad Hanks, keyboardist Justin Fowler, guitarists Karma

Singh Cheema and Benji Helberg and drummer Dane Tuders.

Visit *headcharge.com*

COAL CHAMBER

One of the better known nu-metal bands, Coal Chamber released their self-titled debut album through Roadrunner Records in 1997. Linkin Park video director Nathan "Karma" Cox directed Coal Chamber's debut video 'Loco.' Coal Chamber was formed in 1994 in Los Angeles by former She's In Pain members Dez Fafara and Meegs Rascon (Mike Cox, who replaced John Thor, joined as drummer and Rayna Foss as bassist thereafter). Similarly to Linkin Park, Coal Chamber played a number of high-profile music venues in the LA area such as the iconic Roxy Theatre and The Whisky A Go-Go. After playing Ozzfest in 1996 the band were signed to Sharon Osbourne's

management and played the festival in 1997 and 1998. However, they parted company with Sharon Osbourne's organisation not long after the release of their breakthrough album *Chamber Music* in 1999. Apparently due to inner band conflicts, Coal Chamber split up after the release of their third opus *Dark Days* in 2002. That signal of the end of many a band's career, a *Best Of* album, was released in 2004.

Visit *myspace.com/coalchambermusic*

CRAZY TOWN

Crazy Town's 1999 debut album *The Gift Of Game* spawned the number one *Billboard* Hot 100 single 'Butterfly.' However, that particular song would cause fans at the 2001 Ozzfest to mock them during their set, shouting *"The Butterfly Boys."* The song features the Red Hot Chili Peppers whom Crazy Town had supported on a tour immediately after the release of their debut album. The band was formed in 1995 in Los Angeles by Epic (Bret) Mazur and Shifty Shellshock and gigged hard and fast in the LA area until a record deal was signed with Columbia for their first CD. Both Crazy Town and Linkin Park played on the Main Stage on the

2001 Ozzfest. But their success would not last. They had fallen victim to the fickle nature of the nu-metal trend and called it a day in 2003 after the disappointing sales of their second album *Dark House*. However, the band reformed in 2007 and announced plans for a new studio album (unimaginatively titled *Crazy Town Is Back*) and a possible tour to accompany its release.

DISTURBED

The band we now know as Disturbed has been in action since 1996, previously they were called Brawl. Disturbed's debut album *The Sickness* was released in 2000 on Giant Records. An immediate success with the alternative rock/nu-metal crowd, Disturbed played on the 2001 Ozzfest with Linkin Park and Coal Chamber, amongst many other bands. Furthermore their sophomore release *Believe*

(Reprise) was a number one hit in the US *Billboard* 200. Their third album *Ten Thousand Fists* (Reprise) was also a number one hit. The band issued their third studio opus *Indestructible* in 2008. There's been little controversy in their career; the most high-profiled piece of news was when the video for the single 'Prayer' was banned from many TV stations because of its vivid imagery, which is similar to the 11th September (2001) attacks in America. Still popular, the band continues to tour in 2009 and like Linkin Park their music has changed. *Indestructible* is by far their most sombre and menacing record to date.

Visit *distrubed1.com*

DROWNING POOL

Formed in the country music lovin' city of Dallas in Texas, Drowning Pool, like Linkin Park, have only release three studio albums since 2001. And like Linkin Park their music has evolved from nu-metal to a more alternative rock/metal sound. They played on the 2001 Ozzfest (as did Linkin Park) to promote their debut album *Sinner*. But on 14th August of that year lead singer Dave Williams died in his sleep due to an alleged defective heart muscle, possibly caused by a disease. Singer Jason 'Gong' Jones joined the band in 2003 for their second album *Desensitized* (2004.) However, Jones soon left and was replaced by former SOiL singer Ryan McCombs, who was first heard on 2007's *Full Circle*. Drowning Pool are still working on new music and are set to release their fourth opus at some point in the future. Their first live album *Loudest Common Denominator* was released in 2009. While many of their nu-metal peers have descended into oblivion, the members of Drowning Pool have done well to continue their careers.

Visit *drowningpool.com*

GODSMACK

Godsmack are another band which do not, strictly speaking, fit into the nu-metal category, but after touring on Ozzfest and with the success of their second album *Awake* in 2000, the band have often been often lumped into the genre. Touring with Limp Bizkit in Europe certainly didn't help them move away from this generic tag which critics love to use.

Nevertheless they are still Linkin Park's peers. Having formed in 1995 in Boston they rose to fame during their late 1990s. Their independently released debut album *All Wound Up* was remastered and re-released in 1998 through Universal/Republic Records. *Faceless* and *IV* followed in 2003 and 2006, respectively. There've been some personnel changes in the band: guitarist Lee Richards and drummer Joe D'acro both left in 1997, followed by drummer Tommy Stewart, who left, came back again and then left again. But for sometime now the line-up has been steady with Sully Erna on vocals, Tony Rombola on lead guitar, Robbie Merrill on bass guitar and Shannon Larkin on drums. After a lengthy break, Godsmack announced plans for a brand new studio album to be released in 2010.

Visit *godsmack.com*

HOOBASTANK

Formed in 1994, the Californian band Hoobastank actually go way back with Linkin Park. They're not a nu-metal band but are definitely Linkin Park's peers. Formed in Agoura Hills in sunny California, some of the original band members went to Agoura High School, also attended by Mike Shinoda, Rob Bourdon and Brad Delson.

Hoobastank have gone through several members over the years; the 2009 line-up is: Doug Robb (vocals/rhythm guitar), Dan Estrin

(lead guitar), Chris Hesse (drums/percussion) and Jesse Charland (bass.) They released their debut and sophomore albums, *Muffins* and *They Sure Don't Make Basketball Shorts Like They Used To*, (both self-produced) in 1997 and 1998, respectively. Their third self-produced album went unreleased and they finally made it in 2001 with their eponymous album, which was released through Island and hit number 25 in the US *Billboard* 200. They have a small but loyal following in the UK. Their latest record, 2009's *For(N)ever*, peaked at number 26 in the *Billboard* 200.

The paths of Linkin Park and Hoobastank crossed many times in the Southern California music scene. They've also helped each other out when needed. Hoobastank supported Linkin Park (along with P.O.D. and Story Of The Year) around North America in early 2004; Linkin Park were on the road in support of *Meteora*. Previously, both Hoobastank and Linkin Park had played the famous Colbalt Café where Incubus and Avenged Sevenfold also started their careers.

They look likely to always be on the fringes of mainstream popularity, although the support of a label like Island will certainly aid their career. They've sold around five million albums; Linkin Park have sold over 60 million.

Visit *hoobastank.com*

ILL NINO

Founded in 1998 in New Jersey, the Latin-American nu-metal outfit Ill Nino released their debut album *Revolution Revolucion* in 2001 via Roadrunner Records. It was a success in the United States shifting over a quarter of a million units. In between albums there were some notable changes in the line-up (guitarist Marc Rizzo and percussionist Roger Vasquez moved on), so by the time their second album *Confession* (2003) was released, former Machine Head guitarist Ahrue Luster had joined the fold. *Confession* was not as commercially successful as its predecessor but it was more critically acclaimed. As nu-metal started to lose its appeal, bands like Ill Nino suffered from significantly poorer sales than seen in

previous years. Their third opus, *One Nation Underground*, was a commercial flop (only reaching number 101 in the US *Billboard* 200) and the band left Roadrunner to join a new label. A *Best Of* collection was issued in 2006. Yet the band keeps going: they released a new studio album in 2007 called *Enigma*. It was far from being a commercial success.

Visit *illnino.com*

LIMP BIZKIT

Of all the nu-metal bands at the time, Limp Bizkit was by far the most high-profile and also the most heavily mocked (mostly due to the arrogant nature of lead singer Fred Durst.) The band was formed in 1995 in Florida and released their debut CD two years later: *Three Dollar Bill, Yall$* was not a success. Limp Bizkit made themselves stand out from other bands of their ilk through their showmanship and individual personalities. Their breakthrough came with the number one US album *Significant Other* in 1999 and followed it up with *Chocolate Starfish And The Hot Dog Flavoured Water*, which sold millions. *Results May Vary* (the first record not to feature guitarist Wes Borland) was self-explanatory; critics offered mixed opin-

ions as did the band's fans. An EP (*The Unquestionable Truth: Part 1*) was released and saw the return of Wes Borland, but then, after some live dates, the band laid low. Guitarist Wes Borland left again but returned in 2009 for what was heavily promoted as a "comeback" for the band. Whereas Linkin Park have sort of become accepted by music's critical establishment and have attained a degree of reverence, Limp Bizkit seemed to be the complete opposite, and after the nu-metal phase was over the band lost their appeal. As well as coming across each other at various festivals, Linkin Park and Limp Bizkit both played on the 2003 Summer Sanitarium tour with Metallica headlining.

Visit *limpbizkit.com*

MUDVAYNE

Formed in Illinois in 1996, Mudvayne signed a record contract with Epic in 1998 and released

their debut CD *L.D.50* in 2000. It got some good reviews and obviously helped take the band in the right direction. Their style of metal was more alternative and intelligent (they're influenced by progressive rock/metal) than many of their nu-metal peers. By the time their second album (*The End Of All Things To Come*) was released in 2002 they had changed their stage names and wore makeup while performing. The band hit the road in 2003 for the Summer Sanitarium tour with Linkin Park, Limp Bizkit and headliners Metallica. Previously, Mudvayne and Linkin Park had toured on the 2001 Ozzfest jaunt. They've never been a massively successful band but the success they've had has been constant, obviously aided by a very loyal fan base. Studio albums were released in 2005 (*Lost And Found*) and 2008 (*The New Game.*)

Visit *mudvayne.com*

PAPA ROACH

Formed at Vacaville High School in California in the mid-nineties, Papa Roach signed a record deal with Dreamworks in 1999 and released their breakthrough album *Infest* the following year. (Previously, they had released *Old Friends From Young Years* on an independent label.) *Infest* was a significant top 10 hit in both the US and the UK, going Platinum three times, and the band quickly became one of the major players on the alternative metal/nu-metal scene. They appeared on the Main Stage on the 2001 Ozzfest with Linkin Park and also hit the stages of other major metal festivals around the globe. Drummer and co-founder Dave Buckner left in 2007; Tony Palermo replaced him on the drum stool,

making him a fully-fledged member with singer Jacoby Shaddix, guitarist Jerry Horton and bassist Tobin Esperance. As the nu-metal scene faded around 2002-2003, the band's sound changed somewhat and their record sales dipped: they released albums in 2002 (*Loveheattragedy*), 2004 (*Getting Away With Murder*) and 2006 (*The Paramour Murders*). In 2009, the band are still working hard and released their new studio opus *Metamorphosis,* which as the title suggests, sounds musically different from past releases. Nu-metal may be dead but of the bands that remain, Papa Roach is surely one of the hardest working.

Visit *paparoach.com*

P.O.D.

P.O.D. stands for Payable On Death. The group formed in 1992 in San Diego, California and their breakthrough album came with 1999's *The Fundamental Elements Of Southdown*. The band, who are Christians, with their faith often playing a role in their music, released their fourth record *Satellite* on 11th September, 2001. The album was another commercial success and earned them a Grammy nomination ('Best Metal Performance') for the song 'Portrait.' P.O.D. became one of the more

popular nu-metal bands. 2003's *Payable On Death* caused controversy with fellow Christians because of its occult themed cover, and although it made the top 10 in the *Billboard* 200, sales were not as high as expected, typical for nu-metal bands at the time, as the genre was rapidly slipping in popularity. P.O.D. toured hard on the festival circuit and they (along with Hoobastank and Story Of The Year) supported Linkin Park on the 2004 North American

leg of their *Meteora* world tour. (Previously, Linkin Park had supported P.O.D. prior to the release of *Hybrid Theory*.) 2006's *Testify* marked a change in sound and it was also the last album to feature guitarist Jason Truby. Similarly to many bands of their ilk, they left a major label (in their case Atlantic) and joined a much smaller one (Rhino) and a *Best Of* album was released thereafter. In 2008, they released *When Angels & Serpents Dance*, and although sales were not as high as those achieved during their peak, the album still made it into the top 10 in the *Billboard* 200.

Visit *payableondeath.com*

PUDDLE OF MUDD

Despite putting out two albums in the nineties (*Stuck* and *Abrasive*), it was not until a deal was signed with Geffen (and their subdivision label Flawless Records, owned by Limp Bizkit's Fred Durst) and *Come Clean* was released in 2001 that they achieved mainstream recognition and success. Sales of the album and consequently the band's profile were aided by the hit singles 'Control', 'Blurry', 'Drift And Die' and 'She Hates Me'. The band hit the road with Linkin Park for the 2001 Family Values Tour. As nu-met-

al was on the slide the band's next big Geffen release, *Life On Display* in 2003, didn't shift nearly as many copies as its predecessor. Since releasing *Famous* in 2007, they seem to have slipped off the radar.

Visit *puddleofmudd.com*

SLIPKNOT

Controversial alternative metal band Slipknot formed in Des Moines, Iowa back in the mid-nineties. Prior to the release

of their debut album they went through several line-up amendments, but managed to hit the studio in 1998 and their self-titled debut album, released in 1999, was a huge hit. They played on that year's Ozzfest (as well as in 2001 with Linkin Park) and became a metal phenomenon in what seemed like an instant. Each member of the band wears a unique mask on stage (copied from their idols

KISS, GWAR and Mudvayne) and like many nu-metal and alternative metal outfits, they've had their fair share of criticism and have been constantly mocked in some quarters of the rock music press. Their sophomore album *Iowa* was an even bigger success than its predecessor and won huge acclaim from some major rock publications, including a positive review in *Rolling Stone* by David Fricke. Lead singer Corey Taylor has also enjoyed success as the vocalist in the metal band Stone Sour whose debut CD was unleashed in 2002. Slipknot worked with producer Rick Rubin on their third album, *Vol.3: (The Subliminal Verses)*, which hit number two in the *Billboard* 200. From the nu-metal era Slipknot have emerged as by far one of the most successful bands; they constantly sell-out some of the world's biggest venues and headline major metal festivals all around the globe. Their fourth album *All Hope Is Gone* was released in 2008. In 2009, the group remains a nine-piece with Sid Wilson (turntables), Joey Jordison (drums), Paul Gray (bass), Chris Fehn (percussion and backing vocals), James Root (guitars), Craig Jones (samples), Shawn "Clown" Crahan (percussion and backing vocals), Mick Thomson (guitars) and Corey Taylor (lead vocals).

Visit *slipknot1.com*

SOULFLY

This band was formed in 1997 by ex-Sepultura frontman Max Cavalera. Although they were often pigeon-holed into the nu-metal genre, there is much more to their music; they use all sorts of tribal and South American influences inspired by Cavalera's native Brazil. Their self-titled debut album (1998) was not a huge commercial success but it gave the band some kudos and in the same year they played the mega successful Ozzfest. *Primitive* was a bigger seller and their most nu-metal sounding album. Released in 2000, it features appearances from members of Stone Sour, Slayer, Deftones and Will Haven. Conversely, with *Prophecy* Cavalera used a differ-

ent line-up of musicians and produced a totally different sounding album, taking it as far away from nu-metal as he could get, and using more world music influences. More studios albums followed in 2005 (*Dark Ages*) and 2008 (*Conquer*) and Cavalera remains busy with his side-project Cavalera Conspiracy, which was launched in 2007.

Visit *soulflyweb.com*

SPINESHANK

Nu-metal band Spineshank formed in 1996 and released their debut album *Strictly Diesel* in 1998 via Roadrunner Records, but neither that nor their second release, *The Height Of Callousness,* were immediate commercial hits. The group toured as special guests with some pretty big metal outfits such as Coal Chamber, Soufly, Danzig and Sepultura and played on the 2001 Ozzfest, as did Linkin Park. Their breakthrough album came with 2003's

Self-Destructive Pattern: the song 'Smothered' was nominated for a prestigious Grammy Award for 'Best Metal Performance.' However, their success seemed short lived because singer Jonny Santos left in 2004, and despite attempts to reignite the band with a new vocalist, they announced they were to fold and a *Best Of* was issued. In 2008, Spineshank and Santos reunited and announced plans for a new studio album; but whether anybody cares, now the nu-metal era is in the past, remains to be seen.

STAIND

Staind hail from Massachusetts, New England and formed in 1995. They've never been one of the major players but have been consistently hard-working and creative. Their independently released debut album *Tormented* was first issued in 1996 and is famous for its very controversial cover (which even offended Limp Bizkit's Fred Durst). Initially only a few thousand copies were made available, but due to demand it was reissued by the band. Staind have more in common with their post-grunge heroes (Tool, Rage Against The Machine and Korn) than any of the nu-metal lot. Despite Durst's initial response, he

Park on the 2001 Family Values tour in North America. Albums followed in 2003 (*14 Shades Of Grey*), and 2005 (*Chapter V*). Despite the flagging careers of many of the post-grunge and nu-metal bands, Staind's sixth album, 2008's *The Illusion Of Progress* peaked at number three in the *Billboard* 200.

Visit *staind.com*

became friends with the band and even signed them to his label, Flip. Staind's first success came with 1999's *Dysfunction* (Elektra/Flip) which spawned the singles 'Home', 'Just Go' and 'Mudshovel.' They toured on most of the major metal festivals and released their biggest success (*Break The Cycle*) in 2001; it was a critical and commercial triumph, hitting number one in both the UK and US. Staind toured with Linkin

STATIC-X

Formed in 1994 in LA, Static-X signed to the Warner label in 1998 and released their debut album *Wisconsin Death Trip* a year later. The band has more of an industrial metal style than any other, although there is definitely a nu-metal influence in the melting pot. They have released a total of six studio albums; *Cult Of Static*

THE X-ECUTIONERS

A hip-hop turntablist outfit, The X-Ecutioners formed in New York in 1989. Mike Shinoda produced the track 'It's Goin' Down', which features on the band's 2002 debut *Built From Scratch*. Members of Linkin Park also appear in the video. The group had previously released two compilation albums: 1997's *X-Pressions* and 98's *Japan X-Clusive*. Members of the group formed a side-project called Ill-Insanity in 2007 and released an album called *Ground Zero* the following year.

came out in 2009. They accompanied headliners Linkin Park on the 2001 North American Family Values tour and the bands have remained friends. Guitarist and singer Wayne Static and Linkin Park's Rob Bourdon (on drums) and Dave Farrell (on bass) appear in the music video (Brad Delson, Mike Shinoda and Chester Bennington also make appearances) to The X-Ecutioners 'It's Goin' Down,' which features the turntable skills of Joe Hahn (who has also directed videos for the band). The line-up has changed over the years, using session musicians and different performers on stage. In 2009, the band is Wayne Static (lead vocals, guitars and keyboards), Koichi Fukuda (lead guitars), Tony Campos (bass) and Nick Oshiro (drums).

Visit *static-x.com*

STORY OF THE YEAR

Joe Hahn directed the video for 'Anthem Of Our Dying Day', taken from Story Of The Year's 2003 debut album *Page Avenue*. A post-grunge band, Story Of The Year formed in the mid-nineties in St. Louis and were originally called Big Blue Monkey but changed their name to Story Of The Year in 2002, which is also the title of their EP. The band scored their first big break when they signed to Madonna's label Maverick Records in 2002. They supported Linkin Park (with P.O.D. and Hoobastank) in 2004 during the band's *Meteora* North America road jaunt. They're not exactly what you'd call prolific, having only released three albums: *In The Wake Of Determination* came out in 2005 and *The Black Swan* hit the shelves in 2008.

Visit *storyoftheyear.net*

SYSTEM OF A DOWN

Politically inclined, the music of System Of A Down is famous for being very experimental and also for the subject matter of the lyrics (politics, religion, social issues). The band formed in 1994 in Glendale, California and went on to become one of metal's biggest acts in the new millennium. They're a

hard band to pigeon hole; suffice it to say their music is certainly alternative with touches of nu-metal and prog rock. The band decided to lay low from 2006 and have been on a sabbatical ever since. Their self-titled debut opus was released in 1998 and a further four studio albums followed: 2001's *Toxicity*, 2002's *Steal This Album*, and the two-part work *Mezmerize* and *Hypnotize*, released in 2005.

Visit *systemofadown.com*

TAPROOT

Michigan nu-metal Taproot formed in 1997, and by 2000 they'd signed a record deal with Atlantic Records despite some interest from Limp Bizkit's Fred Durst. After three independently produced and issued albums, their first major release came in 2000 with *Gift*, but it was *Welcome* which was a breakthrough, making it to number 17 in the US *Billboard* 100. Always on the look out for new bands, Jack Osbourne, Ozzy's son, became a fan of Taproot and got them a slot on the second stage at the 2000 and 2001 Ozzfests. Singer Stephen Richards made a guest appearance on the track 'P5hng Me A*wy' which features on *Reanimation*. Also, another link to Linkin Park is that ex-Xero singer Mark Wakefield became Taproot's manager. They never became one of the major players on the nu-metal circuit but they're consistent: in 2005 they released *Blue-Sky Research* and followed it with *One Long Road Home* in 2008. The original line-up of the band is singer Stephen Richards, guitarist Mike DeWolf, bassist Phil Lipscomb and drummer Jarrod Montague.

Visit *taprootmusic.com*

JONATHAN DAVIS

Korn's lead singer Jonathan Davis has one of the most distinctive voices in metal. The band's most popular albums include *Life Is Peachy*, *Issues* and *Take A Look In The Mirror*, which was the final album to feature the original line-up. Davis released a solo CD/DVD (live acoustic) set in 2007 called *Alone I Play* and is set to put out his debut solo album in 2009. He's done a spot of acting and made cameo appearances in some music videos (Ice Cube and Limp Bizkit, among others) and the films *Queen Of The Damned* and *See Other People*. In 2008, he played some solo dates at various festivals – including Download and Ozzfest – with his backing band The Simply Fuckin' Amazings. Korn took part in the 2004 Projekt Revolution, playing second headliners next to Linkin Park. Speaking about the experience, Jonathan Davis said to *livedaily.com* in the States:

"We toured with Snoop Dogg on Lollapalooza in '97, and we played a show with Linkin Park in Mexico City. They're managed by our same manager, and they're really cool guys. It's awesome to have them ask us to come out and be on their tour, because it's fun sometimes not to headline – you don't have all the headaches. We'll play right before Linkin Park; it's all good with us."

The Humble Brothers track, '1stp Klosr' on *Reanimation* features Davis, and the *Queen Of The Damned* soundtrack includes songs written by Davis but sung by other artists, including Chester Bennington on 'System.'
Visit *korn.com*

CHAPTER 9

THE ASSOCIATES

A number of important figures have helped Linkin Park on their journey to global success; directors, producers, engineers and A&R reps, among others. Being in a band and aiming for a record deal and a number one album is not easy, and some help from outside of their inner circle is needed. Here is a list of some of the more significant characters associated with Linkin Park over the past decade.

MICHAEL BAY

Linkin Park fan Michael Bay is the director of the live action incarnations of *Transformers*, which both feature original music by Linkin Park. Bay attended the Art

Centre of Design in Pasadena and went on to direct music videos for Tina Turner, Aerosmith and Meat Loaf and others. His first feature film was 1995's *Bad Boys* and he has since become one of the world's most commercially successful film directors, although he is hardly a favourite of the critics. His others films include *The Rock*, *The Island*, *Armageddon* and *Pearl Habour*.

BLUE LEACH

Despite the slightly cryptic name, Blue Leach is a director of concerts and music videos whose notable back catalogue consists of Pet Shop Boys, The Cure, REM, Snow Patrol, Beck and Depeche Mode. He is a four times winner of the Total Production International (TPI) award for 'Video Director Of The Year.' He directed Linkin Park's 2008 live DVD *Road To Revolution: Live At Milton Keynes*.

On *splinterfilms.com* he is quoted as saying:

"I am passionate about live music, and driven to create adventurous and stimulating performance films. I want every song to look as different as it sounds, to take you deep into the drama and emotion of the performance. My point

being that if the sound of each song in a two hour set carries subjectively an independent message and feeling then clearly the pictures should do the same. To augment the experience. A symbiosis with the music."

JEFF BLUE

Jeff Blue is absolutely integral to the story of Linkin Park. A trained lawyer, Blue turned to music journalism writing for *Billboard*, *Hits*, *Entertainment Weekly* and *Music Connection* before moving more directly into the music industry. In the mid-nineties he landed at job as an A&R rep at Zomba Music Publishing and quickly worked his way up to become the Vice President of A&R. It was at Zomba where he met Brad Delson, whom he hired as an intern from UCLA in the late 1990s. At the time Delson was in a group called Xero, and Blue liked them so much he gave the band a publishing deal with Zomba (he also signed Limp Bizkit and Korn) after seeing them support System Of A Down at the famous LA club The Whisky A Go-Go in 1997. Soon after (1998), Xero were on the look out for a new singer after the departure of Mark Wakefield and the revered A&R man gave them a helping hand. Blue had the

band audition Chester Bennington, formally of the Arizona band Grey Daze. Bennington and his family left Arizona for the glamour of Southern California and Bennington became the lead singer of Xero in early 1999.

They changed the band moniker to Hybrid Theory and released a self-titled demo in May 1999. They changed their name again to Linkin Park later in the year and approached some major labels, including Warner, but had no luck in securing a record deal. After three years of working and forming a professional friendship with Mike Shinoda and his cohorts in Xero and Hybrid Theory, when Jeff Blue became the Vice President of Warner (in 2000) he immediately signed Linkin Park after they had told him of their difficulty in finding a record deal. The rest is history, as they say.

Speaking to *hitquaters.com* before the release of *Minutes To Midnight*, Jeff Blue reminisced about meeting the young Brad Delson:

"He was a very talkative kid, very self-assured. He told me that he was starting a band and that it was going to be bigger than any of my other bands. He was like a kid brother to me. He gave me some early songs, and I gave him a hard time about them."

In addition Jeff Blue has worked for Sony BMG, Virgin, Interscope and RCA. He signed Macy Gray, Limp Bizkit and the Connecticut rock band The Last Goodnight. He is also a musician and a songwriter.

MARK CALTABIANO

Caltabiano is a music video and DVD producer who worked with the band during their *Meteora* era (2003.) He is the producer of the CD/DVD package *Live In Texas* as well as the *Breaking The Habit* DVD. He's also produced some music videos for the band, including 'From The Inside.'

NATHAN COX

Cox started directing music videos in the late nineties working with Coal Chamber ('Loco') and System Of A Down ('Sugar').

Over the years he's also worked with Megadeth, Machine Head, The Rasmus, Coheed and Cambria, Lacuna Coil, Disturbed and most recently Airbourne ('Runnin' Wild'). In 2001, he co-directed 'Papercut', 'Points Of Authority' and 'In The End' with Joe Hahn. For the latter video the pair won an MTV award for 'Best Rock Video.'

GREGORY DARK

Gregory Dark is a director whose credits stretch back to the early eighties and has also worked as a writer, producer, director and actor. He has been credited as Gregory Brown, The Dark Brothers and Alexander Hippolyte. A notable music video director/producer, he has worked on over 60 videos, including those for artists Stone Sour, Britney Spears, Xzibit, Drowning Pool, The Calling,

The Cult, Everlast and Disturbed. His first feature film as director was the 2006 WWE (Worldwide Wrestling Entertainment) film *See No Evil*, which was critically bashed. Dark is the director of 'One Step Closer.'

THE DUST BROTHERS

E.Z. Mike and King Gizmo, otherwise known as The Dust Brothers, have been in the music industry since the mid-eighties. They've worked with such eclectic artists as Beck (*Odelay*), Vince Neil (*Carved In Stone*) and Carlos Santana (*Supernatural*). They've also work with Korn, the Rolling Stones, Tenacious D and most famously the Beastie Boys (*Paul's Boutique*), as well as composing the soundtrack for the cult film *Fight Club*, directed by David Fincher and starring Brad Pitt. The Dust Brothers collaborated with Linkin Park on the track

'With You' from *Hybrid Theory*, playing 'additional beats'.

Visit *dustbrothers.com*

JOHN EWING JR.

Having worked in the capacity of assistant engineer and mixing engineer, John Ewing Jr. is a successful recording engineer who has worked with some of the loudest bands in the music industry. Mostly based at NRG Studios in Southern California, Ewing Jr. has worked with Limp- Bizkit, Korn and Slayer. He engineered 2003's *Meteora* and 2004's *Collision Course*.

MARK FIORE

Mark Fiore has had a close relationship with Linkin Park for some time. He directed the 2008 music video 'Given Up' and the track features on *Minutes To Midnight*. He also directed the *Minutes To Midnight* documentary which is included on the CD/DVD package of said title. He is the band's official videographer and was once in a band called Tasty Snax (later shortened to Snax) with bassist Dave "Phoenix" Farrell before Farrell joined Linkin Park (he had previously been in Xero.) Little else is known about him.

DON GILMORE

Don Gilmore has had quite an eclectic career as an engineer and producer having worked with Duran Duran, Dashboard Confessional, Avril Lavigne and Good Charlotte. In early 2009, it was announced that Gilmore would produce the fifth album, *Shallow Life* by the Italian metal band Lacuna Coil.

Gilmore is a very important figure in Linkin Park's career. In fact it can be argued that if it wasn't for Gilmore the band's first album

STYLES OF BEYOND

Styles Of Beyond (also known as SOB) have a closer connection to Mike Shinoda than to Linkin Park, although they did make an appearance in the video for the Busta Ryhmes/Linkin Park collaboration 'We Made It.' Formed in Los Angeles in 1994, they're an underground hip-hop group featuring Takbir Bashir (Tak), Ryan Patrick Maginn (Ryu), Colton Fisher (DJ Cheapshot) and Jason Rabinowitz (Vin Skully). They were signed to Linkin Park's label Machine Shop Records, but were released from their contract in 2008 for unknown reasons; they planned to release their third album *Reseda Beach* (which purportedly features Shinoda and is executive produced by him) through MSR, but left the label with full control of the album. No release date was scheduled in early 2009. The previous year (2007) they were included on the bill for the Projeckt Revolution tour. Also, the cover for their second album *Megadef* (2003, SpyTech Records) was actually designed by Mike Shinoda. Another connection to Shinoda is that Styles Of Beyond made a number of appearances on Fort Minor's debut album *The Rising Tied* (2005). The song 'Second To None', which was used on the big-screen adaptation of *Transformers*, features vocals by Shinoda. Styles Of Beyond have also collaborated with a number of other artists, including The Crystal Method, Lexicon and Sandman. Visit *myspace.com/stylesofbeyond-music.com*

may have sounded somewhat different. After shopping around for a committed producer, Don Gilmore agreed to work with Linkin Park who'd previously struggled to get a record deal. Gilmore produced and engineered their debut album *Hybrid Theory*, which compiled tracks the band had already recorded as demos, so Gilmore and the band re-recorded those tracks at NRG Recordings Studio in LA. Gilmore returned to produce their sophomore release *Meteora*.

MARK KICZULA

Experienced recording engineer and mixer, Mark Kiczula's credits include Dashboard Confessional, Hollywood Undead, Creed, Kids Scaring Kids and The Crash Motive. Although known mostly as an engineer (he is a Grammy Award winner), Kiczula has also produced some albums, including Hangface's *Metamorphosis*. For a while he was Don Gilmore's personal engineer – of course, Gilmore produced (and engineered) Linkin Park's first two albums. Along with Mike Shinoda and John Ewing Jr he is credited as engineer on *Collision Course*, Linkin Park's 2004 collaboration with Jay-Z.

ETHAN MATES

Successful recording mixer, engineer and producer, Ethan Mates has worked on albums as varied as Mötley Crüe's *New Tattoo*, Red Hot Chili Pepper's *Live At Slane Castle* (as well as other Chili Pepper's releases) and albums by Black Eyed Peas, Cypress Hill and Lionel Ritchie. Further credits include Pussycat Dolls, Tupac Shakur, Sting, Slipknot and Good Charlotte.

Mates co-engineered *Minutes To Midnight* with Andrew Scheps and Dana Nielsen. He is also credited on Linkin Park's *Songs From The Underground Vol 6.0.*, as it features two previously unreleased tracks which he mixed.

Speaking to the music software company *IK Multimedia*, Mates said:

"I probably use the Ampeg SVX more than anything else, mostly while mixing, either directly on the DI track or blending it in with the dry direct track. Recently, I used it to mix the Korn track 'Haze', the title track for a video game. I also have used it to mix a live CD for Linkin Park, the debut album for Burn Halo (Warner Bros), an EP I produced for Rude Buddha (Opus), and

most recently, a collection of iTunes originals for Staind."

Visit *ethanmates.com*

KAZUTO NAKAZAWA

To Western audiences and fans of pop culture, perhaps Kazuto Nakazawa is best known as the director of the animie sequence in Quentin Tarantino's *Kill Bill: Volume 1*. His talent spans different aspects of the animation business, including directing and character design. Nakazawa's credits include *Tales Of Legendia, Parasite Dolls, The Animatrix's, Genius Party Beyond, Ashita No Nadja* and *Samurai Champloo*. Born in Japan in 1968, he has had a life-long love affair with animation and is a central figure in Japanese anime. He recently worked on the animated film *Musashi: The Dream Of The Last Samurai* (2009), directed by Mizuho

Nishikubo, and has worked on a number of video games.

Nakazawa co-directed the 2004 music video 'Breaking The Habit' with Joe Hahn. It won the 'Viewer's Choice Award' at the 2004 MTV Video Music Awards; and it was also nominated for the 'Best Rock Video' at the 2004 MTV Asia Award.

DANA NIELSEN

New Orleans native Nielsen moved to Los Angeles in 2000 to pursue a career in the music recording business. After working freelance as a technical consultant in various studios (equipped with Pro-Tools etc.), he earned a reputation as one of the best consultants in the business. Since 2003, he has worked on albums by some major artists, including Justin Timberlake, Red Hot Chili Peppers, Audioslave, System Of A Down, Sheryl Crow, Jay-Z and even Neil Diamond on his 2006 album *12 Songs*, produced by Rick Rubin.

He co-engineered (with Andrew Scheps and Ethan Mates) 2007's hugely successful album *Minutes To Midnight*, produced by the highly revered Rick Rubin.

EMER PATTEN

Emer Patten is an experienced concert producer whose credits date back to 1999 with REM's *Uptake*. Her Curriculum Vitae reads like a list of some of the most notable acts of the past decade: Morrissey, The Corrs, Red Hot Chili Peppers, Foo Fighters, Depeche Mode, The Cure, Black Eyed Peas, Beyonce and Shakira. She is originally from Dublin but moved to London and got a job working at MTV where she had close ties with War Child, a music charity. Her occupation at MTV was initially in the factual programming and multi-camera performance films and documentaries department. In 1997, she co-founded Splinter (with Nick Wickham), which represents music video directors and producers and creates high-quality performance and concert films. Patten is listed as a producer on Linkin Park's 2008 CD/DVD release *Road To Revolution: Live At Milton Keynes*.

Visit *splinterfilms.com*

KIMO PROUDFOOT

A familiar name with some Linkin Park fans, Proudfoot directed the concert film *Live In Texas* which was recorded on 2nd August, 2003 at the Reliant Stadium in Houston, Texas and on 3rd August, 2003 at the Texas Stadium in Irving, Texas. He then hooked up with the band to direct the concert film *Collision Course*, recorded on 18th July, 2004 at The Roxy Theatre in LA. The performance of 'Numb/Encore' was released as a promo video for the single. Proudfoot also directed the video for the second (lesser known) single 'Breaking The Habit.' Keeping in the Linkin Park camp, he directed Fort Minor's 'Remember The Name' video, which featured Styles Of Beyond. He's also worked with other artists in the capacity of director: No Warning's 'Bad Timing' and Soulfly's 'Roots, Bloody Roots'.

MARK ROMANEK

Romanek is an award winning Chicago born music video director who has worked with a broad range of artists from rock to pop to hip-hop and metal. His credentials include Red Hot Chili Peppers, Janet Jackson, Mick Jagger, REM, Michael Jackson and Keith Richards. His first film as a feature director was the excellent 2002 Robin Williams film *One Hour Photo*, his second being the 2009 re-make *The Wolf-Man*.

He has won three Grammys, three Billboard Music awards and over 20 MTV Music Video Awards. In fact, his contribution to the industry is held in such high esteem that in 1997 he was awarded the 'Video Vangaurd Award' by MTV. Previously it had been handed to the likes of Michael Jackson, Madonna and David Bowie, making him the first filmmaker to receive it. There is a DVD available of his work, simply called *The Work Of Director Mark Romanek*. The special features section has a documentary, which includes interviews with some of the artists he has worked with. Perhaps his most famous video is Johnny Cash's 'Hurt' – a remarkably emotional piece of work. Some other mem-

orable ones include Audioslave's 'Cochise', Nine Inch Nails' 'The Perfect Drug', Madonna's 'Rain', Lenny Kravitz's 'Are You Gonna Go My Way' and Coldplay's 'Speed Of Sound', released in 2005. Romanek directed the 2003 Linkin Park video 'Faint', which won 'Best Video' at the 2004 Fuse Rockzilla Awards.

Visit *markromanek.com*

RICK RUBIN

Rick Rubin is an incredibly successful producer who is notable for resurrecting the careers of Neil Diamond and the late Johnny Cash. But of course there is much more to Rubin's body of work than these two major achievements. He co-founded Def Jam Records (with Russell Simmons) in 1984 in his dorm room at New York University. Two of their most notable acts were Public Enemy and Slayer and Rubin is said to be an early creator of 'rap-rock' (later nu-metal) because it was his idea to have Run DMC and Aerosmith collaborate on the single 'Walk This Way'. Rubin was also the first DJ for the hip-hop/funk-rock group the Beastie Boys: he produced their debut album *Licensed To Ill*, released in 1986.

Rubin once confessed to Germany's *Shark Magazine*:

"I probably am attracted to bizarre things. I'd like to call them progressive things. If you look historically at the biggest bands in the world, they've always been progressive and new. I mean, even The Beatles were a punk rock band; you know, The Beatles used to play with toilet seats around their necks..."

In the 1990s, Rubin mostly concentrated on metal bands after leaving Def Jam and forming his own company Def American Records. This meant a move from New York to Los Angeles. Acts like the aforementioned Slayer, the Midlands based metal band Wolfsbane (with future one-time Iron Maiden singer Blaze Bayley), Danzig, Masters Of Reality, System Of A Down and The Black Crowes were on Def American's roster of artists. He is possibly most well-known for working with Johnny Cash, whose first project with Rubin was 1994's

American Recordings; the pair recorded a total of five albums in the American Recordings series (the fifth was released after Cash's death in 2003). Indeed, in the mid-nineties Rubin seemed to have created a niche for himself by working with veteran artists such as Mick Jagger, Tom Petty and Donovan. Most recently he produced Metallica's "comeback" album *Death Magnetic*, arguably the band's best since the mega-selling *Metallica* in 1991. 2009 sees the release of new albums by ZZ Top and Slayer, produced by Rubin. He's won every major award imaginable, including a staggering 10 Grammys.

Certainly within the past 10 to 15 years Rick Rubin has emerged

as probably the most famous producer in the world; it's also interesting that he refuses to stick to one genre of music, dipping in and out of rap, rock, metal, pop, R&B and country. It's no wonder that in 2007 the revered US publication *Time Magazine* named him as one of the '100 Most Influential People In The World'.

After the success of both *Hybrid Theory* and *Meteora*, it was a wise idea for the band to work with a different producer and record a totally different sounding album, hence *Minutes To Midnight*. It was recorded at Rubin's studio – a very famous place known as The Mansion in Southern California – over the course of 12 months (February 2006 to February 2007). They recorded so many songs (allegedly 150) that the band and their label were forced to delay the release of the album four times before it was finally unleashed in May 2007.

Brad Delson told *Entertainment Weekly*:

"It's really a departure for us. In one of the first meetings we had with Rick, he challenged us [by saying] there were no creative boundaries on what we could experiment with. We really pushed ourselves to try writing songs in a completely new way."

The album was a total departure for the band, which saw them ditching their previous nu-metal traits. There's no doubt that Rick Rubin had a say in this.

Chester Bennington told *All Access Magazine*:

"...with Minutes To Midnight *really, I think the most important part of that process in my eyes was really the fact that we kind of opened our minds up to writing music that just felt right. We went more towards how the songs themselves made us feel and how we responded to them rather than what we thought we should create, what we thought our fans would want us to make.*

In doing that, we wrote a lot of different styles of songs, and we worked on a lot of songs that maybe were a little off the task for us. It really encouraged us and it opened our minds. Songs like 'In Between' and 'In Pieces', and 'Little Things Give You Away', songs that probably we would have thought were cool, but we weren't sure if we could pull them off. I think it opened up that door for us."

Rubin has emerged as somebody who is very important to the Linkin Park story. *Minutes To Midnight*, despite getting only mixed reviews, was a huge seller and cemented the band's position as one of the most important artists of the past decade.

ANDREW SCHEPS

Famed recording engineer and mixer, Andrew Scheps has worked with Audioslave, Green Day, Rolling Stones, Limp Bizkit, Red Hit

Chili Peppers, U2 and Justin Timberlake amongst others. Prior to becoming one of the most sought after engineers and mixers in the American recording industry, Scheps studied at the University of Miami's Music School, before touring with the legendary soul singer Stevie Wonder as his keyboard player. He also worked with Michael Jackson as his mixing engineer before he was headhunted by some top class producers (Rick Rubin, Don Was and Rob Cavallo) as their mixing engineer. He has since worked full-time in the recording side of the industry. Scheps co-engineered *Minutes To Midnight* with Ethan Mates and Dana Nielsen, produced by Rick Rubin and Mike Shinoda.

BROTHERS STRAUSE

Most recently, directing duo Brothers Strause (Greg and Colin) have become known for directing the critically annihilated *Alien Vs. Predator: Requiem*, arguably the worst film in both the Aliens and Predator franchises. They have directed a host of acclaimed music videos, including 50 Cent's 'Get Up', Usher's 'Moving Mountains' and 'Love In This Club' as well as videos for Nickelback, Disturbed, Staind and A Perfect Circle. They own a special effects

company called Hydraulx, which has been involved in such films as *The Day After Tomorrow, Terminator 3: Rise Of The Machines* and *X Men 3: The Last Stand*. Prior to owning their own company and video directing, they worked on special effects for *The X-Files* TV show as well as a number of Hollywood films, including *Volcano*. Born in Chicago, the brothers moved to the City of Angels in the mid-1990s to pursue their Hollywood dream – and it paid off. Not only have they worked in films and the music industry but they have directed advertisements for corporate companies such as Coca-Cola, Ford Motor Company and even the United States Marine Core. They directed the band's second video 'Crawling', taken from *Hybrid Theory* and released in 2001. 'Crawling' was nominated in 2001 for 'Best Direction In A Video' and 'Best Rock Video.'
Visit *brothersstrause.com*

ANDY WALLACE

One of the reasons why Andy Wallace was chosen to mix Linkin Park's first two albums (*Hybrid Theory* and *Meteora*), may have been to do with the fact that Wallace was involved with the production of the legendary Run DMC/ Aerosmith collaboration 'Walk This Way', which was a milestone in the relationship between hard rock and rap.

Asked if he reckoned *Hybrid Theory* would be such a big success, Wallace told *Mix* magazine:

"No. And I would say the same thing holds true for Nevermind. *We knew we liked it as an album. We knew that it was a particularly strong record. But given that there was no track record for that kind of music on a major label*

and you only had indie sales to go by, 50,000 looked good!
And so we all thought, 'Wow. Maybe it'll go Gold.' In fact, I remember I recorded the band live at the Paramount Theatre in Seattle on Halloween, and we'd just gotten word that night that the album had gone Gold, and we were all like, 'Yeah!' – totally naive to the fact that it had gone Gold in about three days. So this indicated something was up. But you never know. Because when a record sells multi-millions, it's a combination of so many different things that led to it."

A Grammy award winner, his discography goes right back to 1986 when he engineered and mixed Slayer's thrash metal masterpiece *Reign In Blood*. He has since worked on dozens of albums that have sold a combined figure of 80 million units – a huge amount by any standard. As engineer, mixer or producer he has worked on such classic albums as Rage Against The Machine's self-titled record (1992), Jeff Buckley's *Grace* (1994), Silverchair's *Freak Show* (1997), System Of A Down's *Toxicity* (2001), Korn's *Untouchable* (2002), Blink-182's self-titled album (2003) and Airbourne's *Runnin' Wild* (2007).

JAY-Z

Probably the most famous rapper and hip-hop producer in the world, Jay-Z has become a cultural icon in the past decade. Born in Brooklyn, New York at the tail end of the sixties, Jay-Z's real name is Shawn Corey Carter. Aside from his musical output, Jay-Z is incredibly rich: he used to be the CEO of Def Jam Recordings and co-founded and co-runs Roc-A-Fella Recordings. In 2008, he co-founded the label StarRoc with Norwegians Mikkel S. Eriksen and Tor Erik Hermansen. He co-owns the sports bar The 40/40 Club and also has a financial stake in the New Jersey Nets football team. His debut album *Reasonable Doubt* was released in 1996 and he followed it up with a series of successful solo records and collaborations (the most famous being 2003's *The Black Album*), until he "retired" in 2003. However, he released his comeback album *Kingdom Come* in 2006, has since released his tenth album *American Gangster* (2007) and made a controversial although hugely-acclaimed headlining performance at the English music festival Glastonbury in 2008.

In 2004, Jay-Z hooked up with Linkin Park for MTV's *Ultimate Mash Ups* show; the premise be-

ing that selected songs from both Jay-Z and Linkin Park's back catalogue would be 'mashed up.' Shinoda revealed their intentions to collaborate at the 2004 Grammy Awards in LA. They recorded their performance for MTV on 18th July, 2004 at the Roxy Theatre in California. A CD/DVD set, *Collision Course* was released in November 2004. The UK newspaper *The Guardian* gave it one star out of five, in fact the majority of critics attacked the album for messing up what are considered perfectly good songs. It spawned the successful single 'Numb/Encore' and the radio track 'Points Of Authority/99 Problems/One Step Closer.' In 2005, he executively produced Fort Minor's debut *The Rising Tied*, recorded at The Stockroom and NRG Studios in LA.

Speaking about his working relationship with Jay-Z, Mike Shinoda told *antimusic.com*:

"When MTV went to Jay about doing the mash-up project, they asked him who he wanted to do it with. He said 'Linkin Park', so I assume he's a fan. Fast-forward to today, it was good to have Jay on board as executive producer on the Fort Minor album. People ask if he wrote any lyrics or music, and the answer is no. But he did something that was very important – he helped me pick through my songs and decide which ones we should put on the album, which we should not, and which had potential, but needed work."

Visit *jayzonline.com*

MARILYN MANSON

Possibly the most controversial figure in popular culture of the 1990's, Marilyn Manson derived his stage name from the actress/icon Marilyn Monroe and the serial killer Charles Manson. Marilyn Manson & The Spooky Kids was formed in Florida in 1989, each member taking their first name from a famous sex kitten/actress and their surname from a serial killer. (Manson's real name is Brian Warner.) Like his idol Alice Cooper, Manson's band shares his name – although through various line-up changes they have been known as Marilyn Manson and the Spooky Kids and the Marilyn Manson Band – yet it remains something of a misconception that Marilyn Manson is actually a solo artist.

The band released their debut album *Portrait Of An American Family* in 1994, although it is credited as a Marilyn Manson record, as are all subsequent releases. They followed that up with an underwhelming EP called *Smells Like Children*, which is known for its cover of the Eurythmics classic 'Sweet Dreams (Are Made Of This)'. 1996's *Antichrist Superstar*, produced by Trent Reznor, was a huge commercial and critical success and the band became major players in the music business. The great metal guitarist John 5 was an important figure in the band after replacing Zim Zum in 1998, but

after some alleged disagreements with the mainman, 2003's poorly received *The Golden Age Of Grotesque* was the last album to feature John 5. At the time of writing in spring 2009 Marilyn Manson's seventh album *The High End Of Low* had just been released.

A fiercely intelligent and well-read man, Manson is an artist who has also made the odd cameo in American films, including David Lynch's *Lost Highway* (1997.)

Manson remixed the Linkin Park song 'By Myself' (re-named 'Buy Myself'); the original version is on the band's debut album *Hybrid Theory*. The 2001 Ozzfest also featured both artists, as did the 2007 Nova Rock Festival in Austria.

Speaking about the Ozzfest experience, Mike Shinoda told *Kronick Magazine* (*kronick.com*):

"…the kids who came to see us were being exposed to Marilyn Manson and those types of things. So all around it was just people checking out some new music. And that's important to us because I want kids that listen to us to learn about these different things that are out there anyway."

Their most high-profile festival was the three-day 2007 Download festival. Linkin Park headlined on Saturday 9th June with Manson as second headliners. On the same day the bill also featured such metal titans as Slayer and Machine Head as well as Bowling For Soup, 30 Seconds To Mars, Aiden, Shadows Fall, HELLYEAH and Turisas. My Chemical Romance headlined the first day with Iron Maiden on the top spot for the final night.

Visit *marilynmanson.com*

CHAPTER 10

THE INFLUENCES

As individuals there are obviously many artists (not exclusively in the music industry) who have had a profound impact on the guys in Linkin Park, but there are also specific bands and singers who have directly influenced Linkin Park's music. Suffice it to say, if it wasn't for the following artists, maybe the style of music Linkin Park have created would be completely different?

APHEX TWIN

Real name Richard David James, Aphex Twin has had a varied career but is widely recognised as a hugely influential electronic musician. It's not hard to see why he has influenced Linkin Park, in partic-

ular Joe Hahn and Mike Shinoda. There's an incredible use of digital beats and programming effects in Aphex Twin's music, which gives him a distinctive edge.

Born in Cornwall (England), Aphex Twin released his first complete studio album in 1992 after a series of EPs. The album is called *Selected Ambient Works 85-92* and launched Aphex Twin into the mainstream; it gained rave reviews from major music publications and was later re-released in 2008. More EPs followed and in 1994 he released *Selected Ambient Works Volume II*. He issued albums in 1995 (*I Care Because You Do*), 1996 (*Richard D. James*) and in 2001 with *Drukqs*. Up until around 2005-2006, he was consistent with the release of singles and compilations and his label, Warp Records, announced a new album release for 2009/10. He has also influenced Tangerine Dream, Brian Eno and Kraftwerk. Some of his music videos are iconic, such as 'Come To Daddy' and 'Nannou'.

DEFTONES

Deftones are an alternative metal band from Southern California that influenced many of the nu-metal bands of the late 1990s. Their debut album *Adrenaline*

was released in 1995 (via Maverick and Warner) and was produced by Ross Robinson who, during his career, has worked with Limp Bizkit, Machine Head and Slipknot. The band toured rigorously throughout the nineties, working hard on the festival circuit, as well as doing the usual rounds with the media. *Around The Fur* was released in 1997 and was a top 30 hit in the States. It recognised the band as a significant player in the metal world. Perhaps it's the more experimental album *White Pony* (2000) that influenced Linkin Park; the band used various styles of music such as trip-hop and digital electronic sounds known as glitch. The record peaked at number three in the *Billboard* 200 and number 13 in the UK. Linkin Park supported Deftones in March, 2001 on a European tour. A self-titled album was released in 2003, *Saturday Night Wrist* came out in 2006 and in 2009 the band promised to release their sixth studio record,

Eros. Within their music you can hear progressive rock, heavy metal, grunge and avant-garde rock and with that kind of experimental sound Linkin Park have been no doubt inspired by the integrity of Deftones.

Visit *deftones.com*

DEPECHE MODE

Depeche Mode emerged from the New Wave scene of the early eighties in the UK. Originally from Essex, their music is electronic, synth-based pop. The initial line-up featured Dave Gahan, Martin Gore, Andrew Fletcher and Vince Clarke. Clarke left the band in the early eighties and was replaced by Alan Wilder who quit in the mid-nineties. Gahan, Gore and Fletcher now work as a trio. Depeche Mode have been a huge influence on many modern bands, including Linkin Park. Chester Bennington told *Rolling Stone* in 2005:

"We took nineties rock, mixed it with eighties pop like Depeche Mode, The Cure and Bauhaus and smashed them together. It's fuckin' driving beats and walls of guitars."

Depeche Mode are also said to have influenced Chester Bennington's highly-anticipated solo album and Julien-K's debut *Death To Analog*, executive produced by Bennington. Mike Shinoda even remixed and produced the track 'Enjoy The Silence'; the original version was released in 1989 and the various remixes came out in 2004. Shinoda told *nyrock.com*: *"I like Depeche Mode, I do."*

Depeche Mode released their first album *Speak & Spell* in 1981 during the New Romantics and New Wave era. A top 10 hit, it launched the band into the mainstream consciousness. They issued 10 more studio albums leading up to 2005 and *Sounds Of The Universe* came out in 2009. Their music videos have a reputation of their own; Depeche Mode has worked with some of the most revered music video directors in the business, including Julian Temple, Tamra Davis, Anton Corbijn, Blue Leach and Uwe Flade. Indeed, their visually alluring music videos have also had a profound influence on Linkin Park.

Visit *depechemode.com*

GUNS N' ROSES

It has been argued that Guns N' Roses are the most overrated band

CAMP FREDDY

Featuring lead guitarist Dave Navarro, rhythm guitarist Billy Morrison, drummer Matt Sorum, bassist Chris Chaney and singer Donovan Leitch Jr., Camp Freddy is a covers band that has been active since 2003. The group previously featured Scott Weiland and Scott Ford. They perform famous rock songs at gigs around America and invite other successful and famous musicians to play with them, including Linkin Park's Chester Bennington, who features on three cover songs released by the band: 'Paradise City' by Guns N' Roses, 'Highway To Hell' by AC/DC and 'Mountain Song' by Jane's Addiction. Visit *campfreddy.net*

of the past 20 years. But on the other side of the coin, it can also be claimed that they are one of the most influential of the modern era. Their debut album *Appetite For Destruction* set a new benchmark for hard rock. The punk aggression and classic rock riffs gave them a huge audience and significant mainstream exposure. They didn't shy away from controversy, especially with an erratic yet venerable frontman – Axl Rose and the arrogant yet hugely talented guitarist, Slash. After the release of the massively overblown albums *Use Your Illusion I* and *II* in 1991, the band's creative output has been patchy and there have been a number of line-up changes. Ex-members have always denied a reunion but considering the amount of money they could make, messrs Rose, Slash, Duff McKagan, Izzy Stradlin and Steve Adler are bound to reform at some point in the future. Linkin Park are one of a number of high-profile acts that have been inspired by Guns N' Roses. Singer Chester Bennington is a friend of Slash and the band has performed Gun 'N Roses songs on stage, including the iconic single 'Sweet Child O' Mine.' Bennington also appears on a cover single of 'Paradise City' by the all-star covers band Camp Freddy.

Visit *gunsnroses.com*

MAYNARD JAMES KEENAN

Iconic alternative rock singer Maynard James Keenan fronts the progressive metal band Tool. He also formed A Perfect Circle with the guitarist Billy Howerdel. Tool's creative output is not prolific (four albums between 1993 and 2006), but their influence on a generation of bands is undeniable and Kennan's lyrical output, although controversial, is certainly thought provoking. His onstage act is, to say the least, unconventional; he rarely has the spotlight

on him and mostly faces the stage backdrop rather than the audience. His distinctive look (bare-chested, Mohawk hairstyle and body paint) makes him unique, like no other rock star. Kennan has also enjoyed stints as a stand-up comedian (inspired by his friend, the late comedian Bill Hicks) and has made guest vocal appearances on a number of tracks by other artists, including Deftones ('Passenger'), Rage Against The Machine ('Know Your Enemy') and Jubilee ('I Don't Have An Excuse, I Just Need Help').

Visit *toolband.com* and *aperfectcircle.com*

ICE CUBE

From Los Angeles, Ice Cube was one of the major stars of the rap world in the 1980s. He was a member of the group N.W.A. (Niggaz With Attitude), which also featured Dr. Dre. Their explicit lyrics provoked massive amounts of controversy but they have remained one of the most revered rap acts of all-time. Their second album, *Straight Out Of Compton* is hailed as a masterpiece in the genre. Ice Cube left the group in 1988 over royalty issues. His debut solo album *AmeriKKKa's Most Wanted* was a huge success when it was released in 1990 and like

N.W.A.'s music, Cube tackled politics, racial and sociological issues in his lyrics. He has since released seven more solo records, the latest being 2008's *Raw Footage*. Ice Cube is also an accomplished actor whose credits include, *Boys 'N The Hood*, *Trespass*, *Three Kings* and *Are We There Yet?* It's not hard to see why Mike Shinoda and Joe Hahn were influenced by Ice Cube; anybody with even the remotest interest in classic rap usually starts with the music of N.W.A. and the Public Enemy.

Visit *icecube.com*

ICE T

Ice T is one of the originators of the genre commonly referred to as Gangsta Rap. Although he is mostly known as an actor these days (he has a prominent role in *Law And Order: SVU*), Ice T has a highly-respected body of work. In 1987,

his debut album, *Rhyme Pays* was released, and although it was not a significant success, it showed him to be a rising star in the genre. The record was also criticised for its controversial lyrics. 1988's sophomore album *Power* won huge critical praise and *The Iceberg/Freedom Of Speech... Just Watch What You Say* went several steps further in terms of producing a darker and more alternative sound. It was probably this album that influenced members of Linkin Park; it contains samples from songs by Black Sabbath, Public Enemy and James Brown to name a few. Ice T's eighth album, *Gangsta Rap* was released in 2006. He is also in a heavy metal band called Body Count, whose 1992 song 'Cop Killer' caused a huge stir over censorship issues. Like Linkin Park, Body Count merges various musical styles together, including, heavy metal, rap and punk. Mike Shinoda is said to

have been a Body Count fan right from the beginning. Their first two albums, *Body Count* (1992) and *Body Dead* (1994), certainly paved the way for nu-metal. Body Count isn't a prolific band and they've had their fair share of line-up troubles, but they're still active. Led by Ice T and guitarist Ernie C, a fourth album, *Murder 4 Hire* was released in 2006.

Visit *icet.net*

AL JOURGENSEN

The great frontman and founder of Ministry has been a huge inspiration for Chester Bennington, not only as a live performer but also as a songwriter. Jourgensen has had a history of drug addiction and was sentenced to five years probation in the mid-nineties for drug possession. Ministry was formed in 1981 and released their debut album *With Sympathy* two years later. They went on to become one of the most revered industrial metal acts of all time. They were one of the earliest pioneers of digital sampling in popular music, which undoubtedly influenced bands such as Linkin Park. Between 1983 and 2007 they released 12 studio albums. Their farewell tour in 2008 was dubbed *C-U-LaTour*.

Visit *ministrymusic.org*

METALLICA

There's a definite Metallica influence in Brad Delson's riffs on *Minutes To Midnight*. Previously his riffs have been accused of being "fuzzy", and it's known that he does not like doing guitar solos. Even on *Hybrid Theory* and *Meteora,* Metallica have some influence in the metal sound of those albums. Linkin Park even went on the road with Metallica on the 2003 North American Summer Sanitarium tour and in 2009 on the Sonisphere touring festival of Europe. Metallica are undeniably one of the greatest metal bands of all time. Whereas many of the hair metal groups of Southern California were interested in the "scene", Metallica were obsessed with music, particularly British and European metal. Their superlative debut album *Kill 'Em All* could have been recorded by one of the New Wave Of British Heavy Metal Bands of the late seventies and early eighties. Metallica's biggest commercial success came with 1991's *Metallica* (aka *The Black Album*) but their releases since then have been below par. 2008's *Death Magnetic*, produced by Rick Rubin after he hooked up with Linkin Park for *Minutes To Midnight*, was better than expected and a huge commercial success. As a live band, they are one of the best you're ever likely to witness. Despite some patchy studio work, Metallica are still relevant.

Visit *metallica.com*

NINE INCH NAILS

The brainchild of Trent Reznor, Nine Inch Nails is perhaps the most influential industrial metal acts of all time (although NIN, as they are commonly known, is a one-man band with Reznor only hiring musicians for the road).

The 2009 live version of the group is Trent Reznor with Robin Finck, Justin Meldal-Johnsen and Ilan Rubin. NIN's breakthrough album was 1994's *The Downward Spiral*, which was recorded in a specially built studio in the house in Beverly Hills where the Sharon Tate murders were committed by Charles Manson's hideous cronies. A further five studio albums were released, the latest being 2008's *The Slip*. Reznor has also worked with Marilyn Manson and Rob Halford, as well as scoring the soundtrack to the David Lynch film *Lost Highway* and remixing songs by Megadeth, David Bowie, U2, Peter Gabriel and allegedly Queen. The electronic beats, digital programming, heavy guitars, experimental sounds and distinctive remixes, apparent in the work of NIN and Reznor's other output, have without doubt inspired Linkin Park. Both Nine Inch Nails and Linkin Park were announced to play the 2009 Summer Sonic Festival in Tokyo and Osaka in Japan.

Visit *nin.com*

PUBLIC ENEMY

In the eighties when hip-hop and rap had social meaning and wasn't all about bling and how many millions are being made, Public Enemy were at the forefront of the scene. Back then, rap groups were conscious of politics, religion and race. The group was formed in 1982 in Long Island, New York and was eventually signed to Def Jam Recordings, a label co-founded by future Linkin Park producer Rick Rubin. *Yo! Bush Rush The Show,* their debut album, came out in 1987, but it was the release of their sophomore opus, *It Takes A Nation Of Millions To Hold Us Back*, that saw the group recognised as serious artists tackling issues of race and politics. The album contains the song 'Being The Noise' which was later re-recorded (in 1991) with the thrash metal

band Anthrax. The collaboration between rap and metal led to nu-metal later in the decade. Without question the song influenced Linkin Park and many bands of their ilk. As a kid, Mike Shinoda was a huge fan and it was their music that inspired him to create his other musical outfit, Fort Minor.

Visit *publicenemy.com*

RAGE AGAINST THE MACHINE

Hailed as one of the great bands of alternative metal, RATM are a politically-minded group, know for their powerful lyrics and very angry music. The cover to their self-titled debut album is the famous photograph of a Buddhist monk burning himself to death in Saigon in 1963 in protest to his government's regime. That 1992 recording is often called one of the greatest albums of all time. In a sense they certainly led the way for nu-metal, and bands like Linkin Park owe a debt to RATM, merging rap, funk, heavy metal and punk into their distinctive melting pot. Their third album, *The Battle Of Los Angeles*, was released in 1999 and like the first album it won huge critical praise and strong sales. RATM are also known as a powerful live

act and after splitting up they reformed in 2007 to play festivals around the world. During the break, drummer Brad Wilk, bassist Tom Commerford and guitarist Tom Morello formed the now defunct alt-rock band Soundgarden with Chris Cornell. Members of RATM have taken part in political activities and rallies.

Visit *ratm.com*

RED HOT CHILI PEPPERS

"I have been listening to Run DMC and Aerosmith and Red Hot Chili Peppers since their first album," Mike Shinoda once told *shoutweb.com*, *"When we first started this band, those things were the only checkpoints in the mixture of these different elements of music."*

The Red Hot Chili Peppers, one of the most successful, revered and distinctive rock bands in popular music, formed in California in 1983. After four albums between 1984 and 1989 their breakthrough came with *Blood Sugar*

CHRIS CORNELL

Chris Cornell is probably one of the most distinctive American rock vocalists of the past three decades. Born in Seattle in 1964, Cornell was the founder and frontman of the alternative rock band Temple Of The Dog, which was a tribute to Andrew Wood, the deceased lead singer of Mother Love Bone; they released one self-titled album in 1991. He is more popularly known as singer of the groundbreaking grunge band Soundgarden, which he co-formed in 1985. They split up in 1997 after five albums, the most famous ones being *Badmotorfinger* (1991) and *Superunknown* (1994.) Around 2001 he formed an alternative Led Zeppelin-inspired rock band called Audioslave with Rage Against The Machine guitarist Tom Morello, bassist Tim Commerford and drummer Brad Wilk. They released three albums: *Audioslave* (2002), *Out Of Exile* (2005) and *Revelations* (2006). Now a solo singer, Chris Cornell released his third studio album *Scream*, in 2009, produced by the rapper Timbaland. It followed 1999's *Euphoria Morning* and *Carry On* from 2007.

In October 2007, Chris Cornell supported Linkin Park on a tour of Australia, which included one date in New Zealand.

Cornell took part in the line-up for the 2008 North American Projectkt Revolution, which also featured Ashes Divide and The Bravery *et al.* Speaking about the tour, Cornell told reporters (*artisannews.com*):

"It's something that fans will see and it's the only time they are going to see it. They are not going to see that line-up all at the same show together again ever. So, that's one of the ways that makes it special and they take that away and they see Busta and Linkin Park doing a song together or they see me come up and sing with someone else's set or something, that's the only time it's going to happen."

The 2008 Linkin Park EP collection *Songs From The Underground* features a version of the Temple Of The Dog song 'Hunger Strike' (written by Cornell), which has Chester Bennington and Chris Cornell on vocals. The bonus track is a live version of 'Crawling', which also has Chris Cornell on vocals. Both tracks were recorded on the Projekt Revolution tour.

Visit *chriscornell.com*

Sex Magik in 1991. Produced by Rick Rubin, it contains some of their most famous songs, including 'Under The Bridge' and 'Give It Away.' The band has set a new benchmark for funk rock. After a disappointing follow-up called *One Hot Minute* in 1995, they returned at the end of the decade with the classic *Californication*. A more spiritual album, *Californication* features some of the best songs in the bands cannon, namely, 'Scar Tissue', 'Around The World' and the title-track. 2002's *By The Way* was another huge commercial success, receiving mostly good reviews, and they excelled themselves creatively with the double-album *Stadium Arcadium* in 2006. After a tour to support the record the band took a long break from the business. The line-up is singer Anthony Kiedis, guitarist John Frusciante, bassist Flea and drummer Chad Smith. What has blatantly influenced Linkin Park is Red Hot Chili Peppers' refusal to do it the normal way; throughout their career they have merged all kinds of musical styles into the one melting pot: heavy metal, hard rock, and funk, rap, punk and psychedelic. Both bands share similarly themed lyrics that detail drug addiction, love, death, life and sociological and political issues.

Visit *redhotchilipeppers.com*

THE ROOTS

A hip-hop band originally from Philadelphia (Philly to the locals), The Roots released their mainstream debut album *Do You Want More?!!!??!*, which followed on from the independently issued *Organix*. The band has since influenced a wealth of alternative acts through their experimental approach to music, a blend of hip-hop, jazz and digital sounds. It's their honest and unconventional approach to recording that has influenced Linkin Park. 1999's *Things Fall Apart* took them in to

the mainstream; it made the top 10 in the American *Billboard* 200 and sold half-a-million units. After releasing two more albums on Geffen, they signed to Def Jam for the release of *Game Theory* in 2006. *Rising Down* also came out via Def Jam in 2008.

MC Black Thought was asked by Linkin Park to collaborate on a song that features on the remix album *Reanimation*. They cooked up 'X-Ecutioner Style' which does not appear in its original form on any other release.

Mike Shinoda confessed to *MTV. com*:

"I don't think he knows how nervous I was when I called him up. A friend of mine told me that he wanted to link us up 'cause he knows one of my favourite groups is The Roots. We're all big fans, and that was something that was kind of a goal of ours as far as the album goes, to get groups that we really admire to participate."

Visit *theroots.com*

RUN DMC

The Run DMC and Aerosmith collaboration 'Walk This Way' was a hugely successful single and sowed the seeds for what was to become known as rap-rock and

nu-metal. It undoubtedly inspired the Public Enemy/Anthrax classic 'Bring The Noise.' Run DMC and Aerosmith even toured together after the release of *Crown Royal* in 2001. So bands like Linkin Park owe a credit to the original trio. The group was formed in Queens, a working class borough of New York, in 1982 by Joseph "DJ Run" Simmons, Darryl "D.M.C." McDaniels and Jason "Jam-Master Jay" Mizell. Jam-Master Jay was shot and killed in Queens, in 2002. The group's last album together while Jam-Master Jay was alive was *Crown Royal*; the previous album being 1993's *Down With The King*. Despite the success of *Crown Royal,* it was heavily criticised for DMC's lack of involvement, yet the band roped in some big names, including Method Man, Fred Durst, Prodigy and Kid Rock. Run DMC went their separate ways following the death of their band-mate and committed themselves to separate projects. Run DMC was announced as one of the five acts to be inducted into the prestigious Rock and Roll Hall of Fame in the United States and was certainly one of the bands that most inspired Mike Shinoda to create Fort Minor.

Visit *rundmc.com*

SCOTT WEILAND

The former lead singer of Stone Temple Pilots and Velvet Revolver is one of Chester Bennington's musical heroes. The pair briefly met backstage at a festival before Bennington collaborated with STP on the track 'Wonderful' from the 2001 album *Shangri-La Dee Da*. Weiland has famously battled heroin addiction and has had stints in jail for drugs and alcohol related incidents. STP released a greatest hits set in 2003 after five studio albums. Although the band were criticised for be-

ing a below-par grunge knock-off, their debut record *Core* was a big commercial success back in 1992. Over time critics have warmed to them and they are now considered one of the great alternative rock bands of all time. They played a reunion tour in 2008 after Weiland famously left Velvet Revolver, which features former members of Guns N' Roses, including guitarist Slash. The band released two albums and Weiland's departure caused both sides to enter into a slinging match in the full glare of the media spotlight. Curiously, in early 2008 it was rumoured that Chester Bennington was set to replace Weiland in Velvet Revolver, but those rumours were quickly stomped on as mere gossip. Bennington informed *Kerrang!*:

"I'm friends with all the guys in Velvet Revolver and have played with all of them before. I'm friends with Scott too. I think the rumour that I was going to join Velvet Revolver started because Slash asked me if I'd come play a show with them in Vegas right around the time that Scott left the band. Timing-wise, it didn't work out for me, though. Maybe people assumed that invitation meant I was joining the band."

He continued:

"If I wasn't in Linkin Park anymore and I didn't know Scott, though, I'd say yes. Who wouldn't? The music is great and it would be a really cool opportunity."

Visit *scottweiland.com*

A FINAL NOTE ON INFLUENCES:

There are other influences, but the ones detailed above are those that Linkin Park seem to name-check in interviews. Of course, there are whole musical genres, as well as individual artists, that have inspired the band: metal, rap, and hip-hop, East Coast hip-hop, a bit of funk and the odd dose of classic rock. Finally, other bands and individuals who have had an impact on members of the band include an eclectic bunch of artists: Alice In Chains, Grandmaster Flash, The Cult, The Cure, Foreigner, Loverboy, Rush, New Order, Joy Division, James Brown, Stevie Wonder, Earth, Wind and Fire, U2, Beastie Boys, Soundgarden, Wu Tang, Mobb Deep, Latyrix and Freestyle Fellowship.

CHAPTER 11

THE MUSIC OF LINKIN PARK

STUDIO ALBUMS

Although Linkin Park may seem like a prolific band with a significant output since their debut was released in the US and UK (2000 and 2001, respectively) they have actually only made three full studio albums in nine years.

HYBRID THEORY

Year Of Release: 2000 *(US)* 2001 *(UK)*.
Track Listing: 'Papercut' / 'One Step Closer' / 'With You' / 'Points Of Authority' / 'Crawling' / 'Runaway' / 'By Myself" / 'In The End' / 'A Place For My Head' / 'Forgotten' / 'A Cure For The Itch' / 'Pushing Me Away'.
Label: Warner.
Producer(s): Don Gilmore.
Engineer(s): Don Gilmore.
Recording Details: Recorded at NRG Studios, North Hollywood, CA.
Songwriters: Linkin Park and Mark Wakefield.
Length: 37:50.
UK Chart Position: Number four.
US Chart Position: Number two.

Special Editions: A Special Edition was issued in Japan in 2002 which includes live versions of 'Papercut',' Points Of Authority' and 'A Place For My Head', previously unreleased tracks 'High Voltage' and 'My December' and an enhanced video of 'One Step Closer.'

Trivia
The album includes additional musicians on bass: The Dust Brothers ('With You'), Ian Hornbeck ('Papercut,' 'A Place For My Head' and 'Forgotten') and Scott Koziol ('One Step Closer'). It has also been reported that Brad Delson played bass on the album because Dave Farrell was busy with the band Tasty Snax.

Reviews
Andrew Lynch
entertainment.ie
"Their angry blend of heavy metal and rap has already won them many fans and it's easy to see why:

they look good, they have plenty to say for themselves and they write loud, insanely catchy songs... It's still a very worthy debut but Linkin Park need to broaden their horizons a little if they're going to make a lasting impact."

Stephanie Dickson
popmatters.com
"The scratchy loops and mix of samples are expertly engineered by Don Gilmore. The eddy of sounds swirling through headphones is mesmerising and proves that this is a far more complex and talented group than the hard rock boy bands of late."

Mike Ross
jam.canoe.ca
"There's a lot happening on Linkin Park's debut CD and it shouldn't take long before you realise this is no Korn klone. 'Hybrid' is a good term... They can actually crank out a ferocious, head-banging groove. They can write introspective lyrics with intelligence. It adds up to one of the finest new rap metal bands I've ever heard."

Notes
Linkin Park's debut album is an angry monster that refuses to stop roaring until the very end. At the time of its release they were a mod-

ALBUM SLEEVES

Linkin Park isn't only famous for its unconventional music but also its distinctive album sleeves. *Hybrid Theory*'s cover is probably the most memorable of the bunch. The soldier on the cover was sketched by Mike Shinoda and the drawings on the inside of the sleeve were created by Shinoda and Joe Hahn; with photography by James Minchin III and art direction and design by Frank Maddock (aka The Flem). The art direction and design for *Reanimation* was done by Mike Shinoda and The Flem, but the actual art was drawn by Shinoda and Joe Hahn. The triumvirate of The Flem, Shinoda and Hahn also took care of the artwork for *Meteora*, with photography by James Minchin III. The Flem took charge of the artwork for *Live In Texas* too, although Shinoda is co-credited under the title of 'Creative Direction'. The Flem and Shinoda are also credited with art direction on the album sleeve for *Collision Course,* but there were other personnel involved in conceiving the illustrations. The album sleeve for *Minutes To Midnight* consists of mostly photographs, some of which were taken by Joe Hahn and Mike Shinoda as well as Ethan Mates and James Minchin III. The photos in the album sleeve for *Road To Revolution* were taken by James Lemiere and the designs were done by The Flem. It's interesting to learn how much involvement the band members have in the look of their album sleeves; there's certainly an edge to some of the earlier illustrations.

ern band with a modern sound. Nu-metal was, well, new; it added a much needed twist to the metal scene in those difficult post-grunge years. Even the album sleeve represented something new, fresh and vibrant; it could well have been some graffiti by the London artist Banksy.

Hybrid Theory opens with the digital beats of 'Papercut' and it becomes immediately obvious that this will be a heavily-produced album. Admittedly, Mike Shinoda's rapping isn't great and Chester Bennington's vocals do grate at times, but the anger is honest and heartfelt when you place the lyrics (drug abuse, divorce, paranoia, social isolation, acrophobia and general angst) into perspective. A dark and sombre song like 'With You' shows an influence that stems from bands like Depeche Mode, Nine Inch Nails and even Stone Temple Pilots. Public Enemy – often hailed as the greatest rap band of all time – were also a source of inspiration for the band when making this record. Indeed, it is a complex album which has not always been given due credit by some quarters of the music press. In hindsight, it's much clearer that *Hybrid Theory* was (still is) far more imaginative and creative than the work of some of their peers, notably Limp Bizkit. The choices of singles were wise

ones: 'One Step Closer', 'Crawling,' 'Runaway', 'Papercut' and 'In The End' are exciting and edgy yet catchy. Perhaps a song like 'Points Of Authority' is just too over-baked even by Linkin Park's standards; there's too much repetition and needless rapping. *Hybrid Theory* is often touted as one of the best metal albums of the past decade and over the years it has grown in stature. It's debatable as to whether the band will come up with something better but that's part of the fun of Linkin Park.

METEORA
Year Of Release: 2003.
Track Listing: 'Foreword' / 'Don't Say' / 'Somewhere I Belong' / 'Lying From You' / 'Hit The Floor' / 'Easier To Run' / 'Faint' / 'Figure.09' / 'Breaking The Habit' / 'From The Inside' / 'Nobody's Listening' / 'Session' / 'Numb'.
Label: Warner.

Producer(s): Don Gilmore and Linkin Park.
Engineer(s): John Ewing, Jr. *Recording Details:* Recorded at NRG Studios, North Hollywood, CA.
Songwriters: Linkin Park.
Length: 36:43.
UK Chart Position: Number one.
US Chart Position: Number one.
Special Editions: A CD/DVD package was released in 2003 and a two-disc Tour Edition (with music videos for 'Somewhere I Belong', 'Faint', 'Numb' and 'Breaking The Habit') was issued in 2004. The iTunes release included several bonus tracks (live versions of 'Lying From You', 'From The Inside' and 'Easier To Run'.)

Trivia
Hit number one in Italy and New Zealand.

Reviews
Nick Reynolds
bbc.co.uk
"It's therefore no surprise that Meteora *doesn't live up to its predecessor. The riffs, hooks and shouting are all present and correct. But the first four songs all sound the same and the guitars don't cut through as they should."*

Tom Sinclair
ew.com
"Not surprisingly, it sticks close to the Hybrid Theory *template, offering music that's by turns petty, bludgeoning, and rhythmic... Linkin Park and producer Don Gilmore have constructed a thunderously hooky album that seamlessly blends the group's disparate sonic elements into radio-friendly perfection."*

Talia Soghomonian
musicOMH.com
"They've locked themselves in the mould they created for themselves. They better be careful and evolve on their next album..."

Notes
The band's second album is almost a clone of *Hybrid Theory*; in fact they make good companions. It is true that they had created this new sound that was unique and different, but following up their "different" first album with something that is almost identical but also below par was not a good plan. *Meteora* has some good tracks but the common feeling amongst fans and critics is that it was an attempt at a carbon-copy. It has been attacked for being simply a marketing ploy to gain as much publicity as possible on the back of their debut opus. It is certainly not a great album and the band could have spent more time on it, but some of the criticism at the time of its release was slightly too cynical.

Meteora opens with the 13 seconds long 'Foreword' which is merely some sound effects before the lead riff to 'Don't Stay' kicks in. There are some good riffs on this album and Linkin Park are more than capable of coming up with some memorable chords. This album has more of a radio sound than *Hybrid Theory*; it's more polished and crowd pleasing with a slight twist. There are backing vocals, violas, cellos, violins, strings and even a flute on 'Nobody's Listening'. However, because *Hybrid Theory* is so familiar, *Meteora* feels less imaginative despite the band's attempt to make it an individual piece of work. 'Somewhere I Belong' is a sing-along metal track and the closing track 'Numb' is another standout composition. 'Hit The Floor' lacks charisma and 'Figure.09' is a standard nu-metal offering. 'Breaking The Habit' is an odd track; it's almost eerie in its production effects. It is, however, a much heavier album than expected. *Meteora* is hit and miss; there are some memorable songs here but at the same time you can almost hear and feel the band trying to compete with its mega-selling predecessor.

MINUTES TO MIDNIGHT
Year Of Release: 2007.
Track Listing: 'Given Up' / 'Leave Out All The Rest' / 'Bleed It Out' / 'Shadow Of The Day' / 'What I've Done' / 'Hands Held High' / 'No More Sorrow' / 'Valentine's Day' / 'In Between' / 'In Pieces' / 'The Little Things Give You Away'.
Label: Warner, Machine Shop.
Producer(s): Rick Rubin and Mike Shinoda.
Engineer(s): Andrew Scheps, Ethan Mates, and Dana Nielsen.
Recording Details: The Mansion, CA.
Songwriters: Linkin Park and Rick Rubin.
Length: 43:30.
UK Chart Position: Number one.
US Chart Position: Number one.
Special Editions: Special Tour Editions were issued in Asia, Europe and Japan in the year following the album's release. Wal-Mart and Best Buy released special packages of the album. iTunes included bonus tracks and there's a CD/DVD set.

Trivia

Made it to number one in over 20 countries and the top 10 in over 30 countries and also reached number one in five American charts. The US versions were released censored and uncensored (because of profanity in 'Hands Held High', 'Bleed It Out' and 'Given Up').

Reviews
Matt Stevenson
Powerplay

"Minutes To Midnight, *however, is plain disappointing... The most obvious departure from the* Hybrid Theory *and* Meteora *albums is that there is no longer the fluid cohesion of different musical styles that was genre defining. On* Minutes To Midnight *the styles are much more isolated, almost to the extent where there could be three bands contributing tracks to this album: an angry band, a rap band and a melancholic band.*"

Dan Silver
NME

"[Minutes To Midnight] *is the sound of a band trying and failing to forge a new identity – boy-band balladry, U2-style stadium rock and Metallica-esque melodic crunch are all attempted with predictably patchy results.*"

Jeff Vrabel
billboard.com

"*Rap-metal's sell-by date expired many, many years ago, and no one noticed more than Linkin Park, whose* Minutes To Midnight *finds the band throwing all manner of styles at the wall to distance it from a genre that currently enjoys a lower approval rating than* [Vice President Dick] *Cheney... Linkin Park's ambitions are nearly palpable, but songs likely conceived as homages end up sounding too close to their sources.*"

Notes

After the release of *Meteora* it was noted in the press that if the band were to progress and challenge themselves and their listeners, they should opt for a new direction in their sound and image. Over the years they had grown up and matured in their dress sense but their music was perhaps too contrived. *Minutes To Midnight* could not have been further from the over-produced nu-metal sounds of *Hybrid Theory* and *Metoera*. There's a lot less rapping, more classic rock and metal, less production/digital effects and a stronger vocal presence. However, while *Hybrid Theory* was an original sound that carried sombre and moody emotions akin to the likes of Depeche Mode, with *Meteora*

RECORDING STUDIOS

These days bands can record music practically anywhere, as long as they have the technology: a bedroom is often the chosen venue, particularly for electronic music. Of Linkin Park's three studio albums, *Hybrid Theory* and *Meteora* were recorded at NRG Studios, North Hollywood in California. The client list at NRG includes the Foo Fighters, Matchbox Twenty and Mike Shinoda's side-project Fort Minor, who recorded *The Rising Tied* there. There are 3 separate studios at NRG.

Minutes To Midnight was recorded at The Mansion in Laurel Canyon, owned by producer Rick Rubin, a building constructed in 1918. This studio is where Rubin records the majority of the artists he works with, a list which includes Red Hot Chili Peppers, Audioslave, The Mars Volta, Johnny Cash and numerous others. The Chili Peppers famously recorded *Blood Sugar Sex Magik* and *Stadium Arcadium* there.

In 2007 prior to the release of *Minutes To Midnight*, Brad Delson informed *Entertainment Weekly*:

"It's [The Mansion] *a really famous – or infamous – place.* [It has] *a timeless feel. You're almost not sure what decade it's in. I think that's reflected on the record, whether it was the Motown-inspired drums, or different pianos we experimented with, or vintage amps, or totally new electronic sounds."*

Visit *nrgrecording.com*

---

a less attractive twin brother, *Minutes To Midnight* is in some ways less creative because some of the melodies are too similar to other bands. 'Shadow Of The Day' has been compared to U2 in almost every published professional and fan review. Also, the album is notable for some guitar solos. Brad Delson had previously declined to show his skills on the fret board, but after some words of encouragement from the band, his guitar solos were added to: 'In Pieces', 'Shadow Of The Day', 'What I've Done' and 'The Little Things Give You Away'.

Minutes To Midnight aims to be more radio-friendly than the band's previous albums and while there's too much of an emphasis on balladry ('Valentine's Day' is unwanted) it is a thoroughly enjoyable rock-fuelled album. It's totally unlike anything they've done before; it's more creative, melodic and musical. The hugely talented Rick Rubin co-produced the album and had possibly helped the band from falling off the face of the earth in absolute embarrassment like their fellow nu-metallers Limp Bizkit. The piano opens 'What I've Done' and the odd influence here is John Carpenter's haunting score to his own film – the late seventies horror classic *Halloween*. There is still some rapping but not nearly as much as you'd expect from this band. 'No More Sorrow' is a screamer with

some punk-style grit and attitude. While there is little rapping there are still some hip-hop beats so they hadn't truly gotten away from their specially crafted formula. Some of the lyrics are more politically motivated; a track like 'Hands Held High' is totally unexpected on a Linkin Park album. However, it was an unwise choice to close a (mostly) exciting metal album with 'The Little Things Give You Away', a six-and-a-half-minute ballad.

PARENTAL ADVISORY

In the mid-eighties a powerful group of politically and socially inclined people came together over their concern for what they perceived as violence and profanity in music, particularly rock and heavy metal. The Parents' Music Resource Center (PMRC) was formed in 1985 by four women, led by Tipper Gore, wife of future Democratic Vice President Al Gore. The media dubbed them the "Washington Wives." One way to censor music and to warn parents about the lyrical content was to place a sticker on an album containing "explicit lyrics". Later in the decade and in the nineties, when rock and metal were

no longer as popular as they had been, hip-hop and rap came under attack from the PMRC. Indeed, the subject of censorship, with its "parental advisory" and "explicit lyrics" stickers, is still a "hot potato", with many artists refusing to change their music.

Linkin Park are not a particularly controversial band but their 2007 album *Minutes To Midnight* was given a "parental advisory" sticker because of the use of explicit language. However, there were censored versions of both the regular and the special editions: 'Bleed It Out',' 'Hands Held High' and 'Given Up' have profanity in the lyrics and were edited for the censored versions. In some far eastern and Asian countries the explicit lyrics were removed altogether. Naturally, 'Given Up' and 'Bleed It Out' were slightly edited for the radio. Songs that are cut in this way for the radio or for release as singles are often known as "clean versions."

The album feels as if Linkin Park know that nu-metal is well and truly dead so it's up to them to find fresh blood for their fanbase, whilst retaining the fans who have been there since the beginning. What they are doing is trying different sounds and attempting to re-invent themselves as a different kind of metal band. *Minutes To Midnight* is a total surprise; it shows that Linkin Park have matured considerably since their last album. The most important thing is that it's a forward-thinking album.

RE-MIXES & COLLABORATIONS

Whereas some bands work best on the road and loathe endless hours in a sweaty non-air conditioned studio, Linkin Park is a band that obviously loves being in the studio surrounded by expensive digital recording equipment and the latest technical devices. As such they like to remix and tinker with their original recordings as well as the work of other artists.

REANIMATION
Year Of Release: 2002.
Track Listing: 'Opening' / 'Pts. OF.Athrty' / 'Enth E Nd' / '[Cha-

li]' / 'Frgt/10' / 'P5hng Me A*wy' / 'Plc.4 Mie Hæd' / 'X-Ecutioner Style' / 'H! Vltg3' / '[Riff Raff]' / 'Wth>You' / 'Ntr\Mssion' / 'Ppr:Kut' / 'Rnw@y' / 'My<Dsmbr' / '[Stef]' / 'By_Myslf' / 'Kyur4 th Ich' / '1stp Klosr' / 'Krwlng'. *Label:* Warner.
Producer(s): Mike Shinoda.
Engineer(s): Jeff Chester.
Recording Details: Recorded at The Stockroom, Division One Studios, Total Recall Studios, DND Studios, Blue Room Studios, Adiar COR Studios, The Studio, Pressbox Studios, Rowena Projects, Olympic Studios, Pulse Recordings, Joe's Parents' House, The Humble Bros Studios, Elementree Studios and Bus #2.
Songwriters: Linkin Park and Mark Wakefield.
Length: 61:00.
UK Chart Position: Number three.
US Chart Position: Number two.

Special Editions: A DualDisc format was released with the audio CD on one side and the DVD audio on the other. A single DVD audio was also released to Linkin Park Underground members. As usual a Japanese edition was issued which included the Marilyn Manson remix of 'By Myself' retitled 'Buy Myself.'

Trivia
The album was made available to download on iTunes with bonus tracks (live versions of 'One Step Closer' and 'My December' and the aforementioned Marilyn Manson remix 'Buy Myself'.)

Reviews
Rob Sheffield
Rolling Stone
"Reanimation definitely goes overboard on the atmospherics: Without the high-resolution hooks and guitar-rock crunch of Hybrid Theory, *the tracks tend to blur together in unflattering patterns."*

Matt Stevenson
Powerplay
"Do you remember how Ali G enhanced his guests' music with samples and rapping? Would you buy a record like it? Hybrid Theory *wasn't broken, so this fix shouldn't have been attempted. 3/10."*

Caroline Sullivan
The Guardian
"Where would busy nu metallists be without the remix album...? They can even claim the finished item to be so different it comprises a whole new record... The word is 'stopgap'".

Notes
Essentially this was a filler album released in-between the band's first studio records *Hybrid Theory* and *Meteora*. It features remixes of Linkin Park mostly on their debut opus. Although it sold well, it split the fanbase; many wanted a brand new studio album with fresh songs not remixes, yet the band believe it *is* an original studio album simply because of the nature of the remixes (even the song titles have been radically altered). It also alienated the group's metal audience who craved for something heavier and more metal, whereas *Reanimation* is certainly focused on rap and hip-hop as it features many underground rap artists as well as Korn's Jonathan Davis, so the band are certainly not alone on this bold and controversial endeavour.

In no particular order, *Reanimation* includes guest appearances by: Jay Gordon, Kutmasta (featuring Motion Man), Alchemist (featuring Chali 2na), Stephen Richards, Amp Live (featuring Zio), Black Thought, Evidence (featuring Pharoahe Monch and DJ Babu), Chairman Hahn (featuring Aceyalone), Cheapshot and Jubacca (featuring Rasco and Planet Asia), Backyard Bangers (featuring Phoenix Orion), Mickey P. (featuring Kelli Ali), Josh Abraham, The Humble Brothers and Aaron Lewis. Basically the songs on *Hybrid Theory* (and 'My December' and 'High Voltage') have been dismantled and rebuilt, or "reinterpreted", as the band refer to in the sleeve notes. Consequently, there are even more studio tinkering and production effects than on the original piece of work. The guitars are fuzzy and the drum beats are too frequent. 'Wth>You' is not too far away from the original version of 'With You' but something like 'Pts.OF.Athrty' is too convoluted. Other tracks that are not easy to listen to are 'H! Vltg3' and '[Stef]'. It's a venture the band needed to get out of their system but it's not a startling

RIAA

The Recording Industry Association Of America. One of the many roles of the important RIAA is to award albums or singles with certificates according to their sales figures: Gold (500,000 units), Platinum (1,000,000 units), Multi-Platinum (2,000,000) or Diamond (10,000,000). With their first album *Hybrid Theory*, Linkin Park were already making a name for themselves in the industry.
In early 2002, the CEO of the RIAA, Hilary Rosen stated on *riaa.com*:

"By selling more than two million albums in one month, Linkin Park is setting a high standard for themselves in 2002. But I think it's safe to say this record has yet to reach its peak."

In regards to their three studio albums: in the United States *Hybrid Theory* was awarded Diamond status and in the UK it was awarded Platinum status four times; *Meteora* was given Platinum status four times in the US and twice in the UK and 2007's *Minutes To Midnight* was given Platinum status twice in the US and once in the UK. It has to be taken into account that when a new album is released an artist's back catalogue tends to sell more, so for a popular band like Linkin Park their album sales will continually be on the rise.
Visit *riaa.com*

BILLBOARD CHARTS

Newsletter | Mobile | Events | Biz | Classifieds

Billboard

SIRIUS XM | **Now Playin**
Sports, Com

SPECIAL FEATURES: Dads and Grads • Chart Game • Create a Billboard Cover

CHARTS | NEWS & REVIEWS | ARTISTS | SHOP | BIZ TOOLS | VIDEO

Artist Biography - Linkin Park

○ Artist Biography   ○ Discography   ○ Artist Chart History

Although rooted in alternative metal, Linkin Park became one of the most successful acts of the early 2000s by welcoming elements of hip-hop, modern rock, and atmospheric electronica into their music. The band's rise was indebted to the aggressive rap-rock movement made popular by the likes of Korn and Limp Bizkit, a movement that

There are numerous types of charts in the United States (some would say too many), but the most popular and highly-publicised is the *Billboard* 200 album chart which has been in operation since the mid-fifties, and the *Billboard* Hot 100 singles chart which was founded in 1958. It's named after the revered *Billboard* magazine, a leading publication of singles, albums and download sales as well as tour grosses and ticket sales, etc. There are *Billboard* charts for probably every type of genre of music, including rock, metal, R&B, hip-hop, country, Latin, gospel, jazz, reggae and even soundtracks. The *Billboard* 200 includes all types of popular music. It can play a big part in the career of any band in the United States since success in the *Billboard* charts can lead to greater public awareness of a band and its music.

Linkin Park have had increasingly successful runs in the *Billboard* 200: *Hybrid Theory* (number two), *Reanimation* (number two), *Meteora* (number one), *Live In Texas* (number 23), *Collision Course* (number one), *Minutes To Midnight* (number one) and *Road To Revolution* (number 41). Their highest charting singles in the *Billboard* Hot 100 are 'In The End' (number two), 'What I've Done' (number seven), 'Numb' (number 11) and 'Shadow Of The Day' (number 15).

In May 2007, *Billboard* reported on the huge chart success of *Minutes To Midnight*, which exceeded all expectations, selling 623,000 in its initial week of release. Chester Bennington spoke to *launch.com* about the album's success:

"I know that we're all extremely proud of this record, and we hoped that it would do well and I was thinking big and I was like, 'If we sell 250,000 copies of this thing in the first week, like, I'll be super happy,' but six hundred and twenty-something thousand in the first week is just unbelievable, especially nowadays, you know. That just doesn't happen anymore. So, you know, I can't express it enough, but we have the best fans in the world, hands down."

Visit *billboard.com*

or even memorable piece of work, which is why fans talk about it in hushed tones.

COLLISION COURSE
Year Of Release: 2004.
Chapter/Track Listing: (CD) 'Dirt Off Your Shoulder/Lying From You' / 'Big Pumpin'/Papercut' / 'Jigga What/Faint' / 'Numb/Encore' / 'Izzo/In The End' / 'Points Of Authority/99Problems/One Step Closer' *(DVD)* 'Intro' / 'In The Studio', /'Jay-Z Arrives' / 'Rehearsal' / 'Soundcheck' / 'Dirt Off Your Shoulder/Lying From You' / 'Big Pumpin'/Papercut' / 'Jigga What/Faint' / 'Numb/Encore' / 'Izzo/In The End' / 'Points Of Authority/99Problems/One Step Closer' / 'End Credits'.
Label: Warner, Machine Shop, Def Jam and Roc-A-Fella.
CD Producer(s): Mike Shinoda.
CD Engineer(s): Mike Shinoda, John Ewing Jr. and Mark Kiczula.
DVD Director(s): Kimo Proudfoot.
DVD Producer(s): Matt Caltabiano.
Recording Details: Recorded 18th July, 2004 at The Roxy Theatre in LA.
Songwriters: Linkin Park, Jay-Z, T. Mosley, Kanye West, K. Joshua, J. Burks, Rick Rubin, N. Landsberg, F. Pappalardi, J. Ventura, L. Weinstein, W. Squier, T. Marrow and A. Henderson.

Length: 21:18 *(CD)* 45:00 *(DVD)*.
UK Chart Position: Number 15.
US Chart Position: Number one.
Special Editions: There's no special edition per se, but the package does include a host of bonus features: a photo gallery, plus 'It's Goin' Down', 'Dirt off Your Shoulder/Lying From You', 'Big Pimpin'/Papercut', 'Jigga What/Faint', 'Numb/Encore', 'Izzo/In The End' and 'Points Of Authority/99 Problems/One Step Closer'. However, in the States there are censored and uncensored versions of the package with parental advisory stickers.

Trivia
The CD part of the package is an EP as it is only six tracks long; following Alice In Chains' *Jar Of Flies* in 1994, *Collision Course* was the second EP to hit number one in the US *Billboard* charts.

Reviews

Pat Long
NME

"At the time Jay claimed the gig to be a 'hybrid of the hot shit'. Sadly, however, the resulting EP and 45-minute DVD prove his words to be wildly untrue – apart from the 'shit' bit... Like trying to cross, say, a shoe with a satsuma or a lump of Edam with a house brick, Collision Course *is ultimately a pointless, unfathomable exercise."*

Vik Bansal
musicOMH.com

"For the most part, the results are genuinely interesting... the very concept of this collaboration will be enough for it to appeal to Jay-Z and Linkin Park fans alike, and perhaps it will inspire some even more innovative mash-ups in the future."

David Jeffries
All Music Guide

"If the CD were released on its own, the collection wouldn't be as exciting. Linkin Park's genuine excitement about the project on the 'behind the scenes' segment of the DVD is infectious... It's doubtful mash-ups will survive corporate handling this well again, and to paraphrase a post-show Linkin Parker, Collision Course *is awesomely fun."*

Notes

The basic premise of this album was to merge some songs of Jay-Z's – aka Shawn Carter – with some songs by Linkin Park as part of the MTV *Ultimate Mash-Ups*. The CD features the studio recordings while the DVD plays host to an entertaining 'behind the scenes' documentary as well as the actual concert which originally aired in November 2004. The studio recordings that Linkin Park chose to 'mash-up' are 'Lying From You', 'Papercut',' 'Faint', 'Number', 'In The End', 'Points Of Authority' and 'One Step Closer.' It was a controversial move for the band and the results are not exactly awe-inspiring. As with *Reanimation* there's much more rapping than metal and even Jay-Z fans were annoyed some of his songs from his revered 2003 CD *The Black Album* were tarnished. It's hard to think that this wasn't anything but a commercially motivated endeavour. The DVD is far more entertaining. Expertly directed by Kimo Proudfoot, there's an interesting glimpse of the band at work and their relationship with Jay-Z during the project. As for the concert, it isn't long but it is about as entertaining as a project like this is likely to be.

CD/DVD PACKAGES

There are far too many different versions (tour editions, special editions, etc.) of Linkin Park's albums, but what they seem to enjoy releasing are CD/DVD packages. Of course, the band's two live albums are CD/DVD releases, but the author has chosen to place those under the 'Live Albums' heading.

REANIMATION DVD-A
Year Of Release: 2002.
Chapter/Track Listing: 'Opening' / 'Pts.OF.Athrty' / 'Enth E Nd' / '[Chali]' / 'Frgt/10' / 'P5hng Me A*wy' / 'Plc.4 Mie Hæd' / 'X-Ecutioner Style' / 'H! Vltg3' / '[Riff Raff]' / 'Wth>You' / 'Ntr\ Mssion' / 'Ppr:Kut' / 'Rnw@y' / 'My<Dsmbr' / '[Stef]' / 'By_Myslf' / 'Kyur4 th Ich' / '1stp Klosr' / 'Krwlng'.
Label: Warner.

Trivia
Those fans who became members of Linkin Park Underground before 10th November, 2002 were given free copies of this DVD-A version of *Reanimation*.

Reviews
Sian Llewellyn
Classic Rock

"The menus are flashy and colourful, owing a lot to Japanese Manga comic design, although they aren't always easy to navigate; the remixes themselves work very well over the surround-sound spread, with, for example, MC Mike Shinoda's bleeps and samples hitting you from all angles of the room."

Notes
Reanimation was released in a number of formats, but the DVD-A was most interesting: it contains the complete album as well as music videos for 'Pts.OF.Athrty', 'Frgt/10' and 'Kyur4 th Ich'. Also included is a making of featurette on 'Pts.OF.Athrty'. The 5.1 surround sound gives the audio quality a sharpness which you may not get on an audio CD player (those fans who have a CD player that is compatible with a DVD-A would be able to play this version).

METEORA /MAKING OF METEORA

Year Of Release: 2003.
Chapter/Track Listing: (DVD) 'Intro' / 'Summer 2001' / 'Early 2002' / 'June 2002' / 'July 2002' / 'August 2002' / 'Early October 2002' / 'Late October 2002' / 'October 29, 2002' / 'Early November 2002' / 'Late November 2002' / 'December 6, 2002' / 'December 12, 2002' / '2003: Meteora'.
Label: Warner.

Trivia

This package was the blue version of the *Meteora* album cover.

Notes

Although the *Meteora* album is written about under the studio albums heading, this CD/DVD set deserves a mention of its own simply because it gives a glimpse into the band's hectic lifestyle. The package combines the album with a special edition DVD that is basi-

cally a documentary, albeit a short one, on the making of the album as well as life in the Linkin Park tour bus. Having said that, only true Linkin Park zealots would buy this set simply because the documentary is not long enough for the extra cost, but it is interesting to watch nonetheless. Some foreign territories (India and Asia) had a different DVD chapter listing: 'Behind Meteora', 'Somewhere I Belong', 'Faint', 'Numb', 'From The Inside', 'Breaking The Habit', 'Meteora CD Ad'

MINUTES TO MIDNIGHT /MAKING OF MINUTES TO MIDNIGHT

Year Of Release: 2007.
Chapter/Track Listing: (DVD) 'Making Of Minutes To Midnight' / 'What I've Done Music Video' / 'Making Of What I've Done'.
Label: Warner, Machine Shop.
DVD Producer(s): Devin Sarno, David May and Raena Winscott.

Trivia

This is one of six special edition versions of *Minutes To Midnight*.

Notes

As with the *Meteora/Making Of Meteora* CD/DVD, this deserves a little mention of its own simply because the album was so hugely successful and there are various editions of it. Produced by Films

Di Bovino and directed by Mark Fiore, the 'Making Of' featurette is an interesting glimpse into the band's inner sanctum although it is too short. Ditto the making of the music video for 'What I've Done', which was produced by Almost Midnight Productions and directed by Michael Perlmutter. Of course, fans will be familiar with the music video itself. There are also some odds and ends on the DVD-Rom such as wallpaper, screensavers and a PDF booklet etc.

LIVE ALBUMS (CD/DVD)

Despite being known as a studio band, Linkin Park has grown in stature over the years as a powerful live act, headlining stadiums all over the world. As such they have chosen to release CD/DVD packages as visual and audio mementos of their time on the road.

LIVE IN TEXAS
Year Of Release: 2003.
Chapter/Track Listing: (CD) 'Somewhere I Belong' / 'Lying From You' / 'Papercut' / 'Points Of Authority' / 'Runaway' / 'Faint' / 'From The Inside' / 'P5hng Me A*wy' / 'Numb' / 'Crawling' / 'In The End' / 'One Step Closer'

(DVD) 'Don't Stay' / 'Somewhere I Belong' / 'Lying From You' / 'Papercut' / 'Points Of Authority' / 'Runaway' / 'Faint' / 'From The Inside' / 'Figure.09' / 'With You' / 'By Myself' / 'P5hng Me A*wy' / 'Numb' / 'Crawling' / 'In The End' / 'A Place For My Head' / 'One Step Closer'.
Label: Warner, Machine Shop.
CD Producer(s): Matt Caltabiano, Josh Abraham, David May.
CD Engineer(s): Ryan Williams.
DVD Director (s): Kimo Proudfoot.
DVD Producer(s): Matt Caltabiano.
Songwriters: Linkin Park and Mark Wakefield.
Length: 41:40 *(CD)* 70:58 *(DVD)*.
Recorded: 2nd August, 2003 at the Reliant Stadium in Houston, Texas; 3rd August, 2003 at the Texas Stadium in Irving, Texas.

UK Chart Position: Number 47.
US Chart Position: Number 23.
Special Editions: This package came in a CD size case and a DVD size case; the DVD version has an alternative cover.

Trivia

The CD does not feature all the songs on the DVD; those can be located on *Linkin Park Underground Vol 3.0.*

Reviews
Johnny Loftus
All Music Guide

"...the casual listener might do well to steer toward the studio material... Live In Texas *will likely serve as a memento of the tour. But it's clear that top-shelf production and mixing plays a significant role in making Linkin Park's albums so powerful."*

Mark Hoaksey
Powerplay

"Strange one this: all the massive headlining shows that Linkin Park have played and they choose to record their live DVD at a festival at which they are only third on the bill behind Metallica and Limp Bizkit. Effective only as a live 'best of' collection from the band's first two studio albums, for an act of Linkin Park's stature this has to be seen as a badly wasted opportunity."

Rosanna Slater
Classic Rock

"This DVD/CD... is simply a no-frills, two-disc keepsake of the muscular Linkin Park live experience. Casual fans may curse the omission of extras (no interviews, no rarities, no previously unreleased material), and the predictable renditions of favourites from Meteroa *and the breakthrough debut* Hybrid Theory. *3/5."*

Notes

Filmed during the 2003 Summer Sanitarium Tour, the recording of the audio and DVD of *Live In Texas* is slightly complicated and as such the editing is not all that great. Simplistically, the band wore the same clothes for both the Dallas and Houston shows because the visual footage was edited together to make one seamless concert; however, if you look hard enough you will notice that Mike Shinoda is wearing two slightly different shirts and there are a few other little things that make the concert look like it was filmed at two (which it was) rather than at a single show. The audio recording from the Dallas show was used on the DVD. Artists often film more than one concert and edit the footage together to make it appear as though it was one single performance, but at least fans know *Live In Texas* was filmed at two shows.

The band open their performance with 'Don't' Stay' and follow it up with 'Somewhere I Belong.' The atmosphere isn't great throughout the DVD, which is often the case with gigs that were recorded during daylight. Bennington's voice is (mostly) on good form despite some strained moments that were due to an extensive touring schedule. Although it is difficult to hear the audience, which creates a lack of atmosphere, the looks on the faces tell a different story. Still, it's a good set-list and watching Joe Hahn scratch is what fans wanted to see just as much as hearing Shinoda's rapping or Bennington's voice. The crowd goes ballistic through 'Crawling' which is without a doubt a solid stadium metal song. The band sound well-rehearsed and despite the aforementioned qualms, *Live In Texas* was always going to please their legions of fans regardless.

The CD was mixed by Josh Abraham at Pulse Recordings in Los Angeles, California. At best the CD is just a bonus edition; there's barely any audience noise in between each song and there are only 12 tracks of the 17 performed, omitting 'Don't Stay', 'Figure.09', 'With You', 'By Myself' and 'A Place For My Head'. And for a live album the *Live In Texas* CD sounds too polished; the band sound almost identical as to how they do on an album. They're capable of a better live recording, especially with such a strong set of songs as those on *Hybrid Theory* and even *Meteora. Live In Texas* is more about the DVD, but despite that there are no interviews, bonus features or music videos.

It is not a great release by any means and critics pointed out that it was the band's fourth release in only three years so it was easy to attack Linkin Park for being interested in the corporate side of the music business.

ROAD TO REVOLUTION: LIVE AT MILTON KEYNES
Year Of Release: 2008.
Chapter/Track Listing: (CD) 'One Step Closer' / 'From The Inside' / 'No More Sorrow' / 'Given Up' / 'Lying From You' / 'Hands Held High' / 'Leave Out All The

Rest' / 'Numb' / 'The Little Things Give You Away' / 'Breaking The Habit' / 'Shadow Of The Day' / 'Crawling' / 'In The End' / 'Pushing Me Away' / 'What I've Done' / 'Numb/Encore' / 'Jigga What/Faint' / 'Bleed It Out' *(DVD)* 'One Step Closer' / 'From The Inside' / 'No More Sorrow' / 'Wake 2.0.' / 'Given Up' / 'Lying From You' / 'Hands Held High' / 'Leave Out All The Rest' / 'Numb' / 'The Little Things Give You Away' / 'Breaking The Habit' / 'Shadow Of The Day' / 'Crawling' / 'In The End' / 'Pushing Me Away' / 'What I've Done' / 'Numb/Encore' / 'Jigga What/Faint' / 'Bleed It Out'.
Label: Warner, Machine Shop.
CD Producer (s): Emer Patten.
CD Engineer(s): Mike Cox and Steve Nickson.
DVD Director(s): Blue Leach.
DVD Producer(s): David May.
Songwriters: Linkin Park, Jay-Z, Kanye West and Mark Wakefield.
Length: (CD) 77:28 (DVD) 85:06.
Recorded: 29th June, 2008 at the Milton Keynes National Bowl, England.
UK Chart Position: Number 58
US Chart Position: Number 41.

Trivia
The DVD contains secret footage: 'Somewhere I Belong', 'Papercut' and 'Points Of Authority'.

Reviews
Ryan Bird
Kerrang!
"Although the sheer magic of the occasion is something you had to witness first hand in order to fully understand its brilliance, Road To Revolution *is the next best thing to reliving a night which has rightfully earned legendary status."*

Stephen Thomas Erlewine
All Music Guide
"It's big but not ballsy, an appropriate sound for an immaculate performance from Linkin Park – one that may not exactly replicate the details of their studio versions but certainly doesn't find them colouring outside of the lines. It's something that will surely please fans, the ones that have the other two Linkin Park live sets, but it's not a bracing testament to the band's on-stage prowess."

Rick Florino
Artistdirect.com
"The interplay between Shinoda and Bennington channels the classic dual harmonies of Layne Staley and Jerry Cantrell. However, both vocalists also possess a hip-hop swagga, canvassing the stage like wolves on the hunt... Road To Revolution *as a live record packs*

the punch of a Linkin Park show, without the stench and sweat."

Notes

Just what fans wanted: the band's biggest headlining concert in the UK filmed for an audio/DVD release. It's far superior to *Live In Texas*. This package is also a special memento for fans because the performance was the first time the band had staged the now massive Projekt Revolution touring package in the UK: on the day a host of bands performed (Innerpartysystem, The Bravery, Enter Shikari, N*E*R*D, Pendulum and Jay-Z) prior to Linkin Park.

The DVD opens with 'One Step Closer' and the camera work, editing and direction are all excellent. It was filmed during sunset and into the evening so the stage lighting and atmospherics look highly professional and visually alluring. The stage is huge and despite a long day the audience is alive and energetic. The concert was staged just after the mammoth Glastonbury Festival, which is the biggest in the UK and held annually. Bennington tells the crowd after playing 'From The Inside':

"Holy Shit. This is fucking amazing. This is one of the most beautiful things I've ever seen in my life."

And then after the track 'Wake', he bawls:

"How the fuck you doin' out there? Today's officially the biggest Projeckt fucking Revolution to date and the most beautiful fucking day of my life..."

Highlights of the evening include the stunning climax 'Bleed It Out' which just proves how good a drummer Rob Bourdon is, and the hit single 'What I've Done' is finely performed. 'Points Of Authority' includes songs from Fort Minor's back catalogue: 'Petrified' and 'There They Go'. Jay-Z makes an enthusiastic appearance for 'Numb/Encore' and 'Jigga What/ Faint'. The set-list had been wisely picked, concentrating on the hits. The 5.1 surround sound gives the DVD an excellent sound quality. There is also some hidden content: 'Somewhere I Belong', 'Papercut' and 'Points Of Authority.' 22 songs were played on the night and are featured on the DVD although only 19 tracks are listed.

As with *Live In Texas* the CD is really just a bonus, simply because it does not contain all the songs played during the gig. Only 18 tracks are listed and it is odd they chose to list only 18 songs on the back of the package's cover sleeve when *Road To Revolution* is obviously more about the DVD than the CD. 'Wake 2.0', 'Somewhere I Belong', 'Papercut' and 'Points Of Authority' are omitted from the CD but feature on the DVD (including the hidden content) and 'Bleed It Out' was edited for the CD. Again the audio qual-

ity of the CD sounds too polished but it seems as if that's Linkin Park's style. The audience can be heard better than they are on *Live In Texas*. It is altogether a better release than *Live In Texas* and more worthy of the band. What it does show is how far the band has come in such a short space of time from the pubs and clubs of America in 2000 to the biggest stadiums of Europe in 2008, less than eight years later. It would take some bands that time to get a record deal. They are also a stupendous live act, putting plenty of energy into their performances as well as the stage designs. They are very good at what they do and this CD/DVD shows that to full effect.

CONCEPT ALBUMS

The term 'concept album' is self-explanatory: it's an album that has one idea or theme running right through it, making all the songs thematically linked. Concept albums have enjoyed huge popularity since the late sixties and also critical derision. Often created by progressive rock bands, some of the most famous concept albums of all time were composed by the likes of Yes (*Tales From Topographic Oceans*), Pink Floyd (*Dark Side Of The Moon*), Jethro Tull (*Thick As A Brick*) and Genesis (*The Lamb Lies Down On Broadway*) – all released in the seventies. However,

it would be inaccurate to say only progressive rock bands make concept albums. Other types of rock bands have released them too and enjoyed great success: The Who (*Tommy*), Queensrÿche (*Operation: Mindcrime*), W.A.S.P. (*The Crimson Idol*) and Green Day (*American Idiot*). Most recently, the American progressive metal band Coheed & Cambria released four concept albums and the British heavy metal band Judas Priest released their first of the type, *Nostradamus* in 2008. In late 2008, Linkin Park announced plans for one such opus of their own.

DEMOS

It can be very difficult to compile a list of demos recorded by successful bands, but with Linkin Park they have chosen to re-record and re-name some of their demo material. This has made it easier to locate past work and they are not secretive about their recordings prior to **Hybrid Theory.**

XERO
Year Of Release: 1997.
Track Listing: (Side A) 'Rhinestone' / 'Reading My Eyes' *(Side B)* 'Fuse' / 'Stick N' Move'.
Label: Independent.
Producer(s): Mike Shinoda.
Songwriters: Mike Shinoda, Brad Delson, Joe Hahn and Mark Wakefield.
Length: 12:41. *Line-up:* Mike Shinoda, Brad Delson, Joe Hahn, Dave Farrell and Mark Wakefield.

Trivia
According to the *Collins English Dictionary & Thesaurus* the word 'Xero' means 'indicating dryness.'

Notes
Recorded in 1996, this is the tape that started it all. Before changing their name from Hybrid Theory to Linkin Park, the band was called Xero which they evidently named their initial demo after (as most bands do). This is the only tape that Xero made before singer Mark Wakefield left the fold to become manager of the band Taproot and commit to other musical endeavours. The first track 'Rhinestone' (3:38) evolved into 'Forgotten,' the tenth track on *Hybrid Theory*. An amended version of 'Reading My Eyes' (2:56) was played live at various concerts in 2006 and 2008 (it can be heard on the fan club release *Linkin Park Underground Vol 6.0*). 'Fuse' is the second longest track on the demo at three minutes and 16 seconds. It is often the case that bands use discarded songs to form the basis of new ones: the guitar riff on 'Stick N' Move' (2:44) is the core riff in the song 'Runaway', the sixth track on *Hybrid Theory*. It has been said that Xero also

recorded two songs which did not feature on this demo: 'Esaul' (an earlier versions of what would become 'A Place For My Head', the ninth track on *Hybrid Theory*) and the obscure 'Pictureboard' which was played live at least once prior to the release of *Hybrid Theory*, so around 1999-2000.

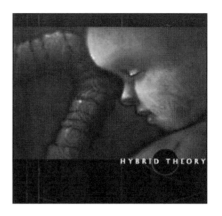

EPs

As mentioned in the 'Demos' section Linkin Park have made their fans aware of some of the older recordings. But they've also released a batch of EPs over the years, especially for members of their fan club. Some of the initial releases have proved to be rather valuable among fans.

HYBRID THEORY
Year Of Release: 1999.
Track Listing: 'Carousel' / 'Technique' / 'Step Up' / 'And One' / 'High Voltage' / 'Part Of Me'.
Label: Zomba.
Producer(s): Mike Shinoda.
Songwriters: Mike Shinoda, Chester Bennington, Joe Hahn and Brad Delson.
Length: 22:30.
Line-up: Mike Shinoda, Chester Bennington, Joe Hahn, Rob Bourdon, Brad Delson and Kyle Christener.

Trivia
There is a hidden instrumental (9:58) at the end of the EP (tagged on to 'Part Of Me') that, although unnamed by the band, fans have taken it upon themselves to call 'Ambient' and 'Secret.'

Notes
After changing their name from Xero to Hybrid Theory as well as recruiting a new singer (Chester Bennington) and bassist (Kyle Christener), the band that would become Linkin Park showed incredible persistence by creating a second demo. Only a thousand copies were produced specifically for the purposes of promotion and to attract the attention of a record label. As with *Xero* this is a very rare recording; it was actually remixed and remastered in 2001 specifically for the band's fan club Linkin Park Underground. The

art work (a baby in the womb) was designed by Shinoda and Hahn. Some of the songs are included on B-sides on later releases: 'And One' (4:33) and 'Part Of Me' (12:43) are featured on *Songs From The Underground*. 'Step Up' (3:55) is included as a B-side on the single 'In The End' and 'Somewhere I Belong.' A re-recording of 'High Voltage' (3:30) is included as a B-side to the band's first single from *Hybrid Theory*, 'One Step Closer.' In their original incarnations 'Carousel' (3:00), 'And One' and 'Part Of Me' have been played live, whereas the rest of the songs on this EP have yet to be played on stage. The shortest song on the EP is 'Technique' which lasts only 40 seconds.

IN THE END: LIVE & RARE
Year Of Release: 2002.
Track Listing: 'In The End' / 'Papercut' / 'Points Of Authority' / 'A Place For My Head' / 'Step Up' / 'My December' / 'High Voltage'.
Label: Warner.
Producer(s): Don Gilmore, Andy Rodgers and Mike Shinoda.
Songwriters: Linkin Park and Mark Wakefield.
Length: 25:25.
Line-up: Mike Shinoda, Chester Bennington, Joe Hahn, Rob Bourdon, Brad Delson and Dave Farrell.

Trivia
This is an exclusive Japanese release although all tracks (except 'Step Up') were included on the special edition version of *Hybrid Theory.*

Notes
The Japanese market is huge for Western rock and metal bands, which is why so many of them release exclusive packages (or add bonus tracks) over there. To those who don't live in Japan *In The End: Live & Rare* is obviously available to buy on import and has become a collectors item over the years. It's basically an odds-and-sods EP with the tracks culled from CD singles. 'In The End' (3:36) is the album version; 'Papercut' (3:12), 'Points Of Authority' (3:29) and 'A Place For My Head' (3:10) were recorded at the London Docklands Arena and were included as B-sides to the two-part 'In

The End' CD singles. 'Step Up' (3:55) is a demo from 1999 which is a treat for Linkin Park archivists, while 'My December' (4:20) and 'High Voltage' (3:45) were B-sides on the 'One Step Closer' single. The EP photography was taken by Clay McBride and as ever with Linkin Park it's quite distinctive. These types of releases tend to be for serious fans only, yet even the more casual one will enjoy the live tracks.

LIVE FROM SOHO
Year Of Release: 2008.
Track Listing: 'Wake' / 'Given Up' / 'Shadow Of The Day' / 'My December' / 'In Pieces' / 'Bleed It Out'.
Label: iTunes
Producer(s): Mike Shinoda.
Songwriters: Linkin Park and Mike Shinoda ('My December').
Length: 21:39.

Line-up: Mike Shinoda, Chester Bennington, Joe Hahn, Rob Bourdon, Brad Delson and Dave Farrell.

Trivia
It was recorded live at a gig at the Apple Store in SoHo (NYC) on 20th February, 2008 and released just two weeks later on 4th March.

Notes
As downloading takes over the music industry and CDs are becoming less popular, many bands are releasing exclusive Downloads. This EP (the band's third) was recorded specifically for the popular iTunes *Live From SoHo* EPs which you can download from the Apple iTunes website. As a live recording it's good enough but it's especially interesting to hear the acoustic version of 'My December' (Shinoda on keyboard with singer Bennington) which shows that there is more shade to Linkin Park; they're not simply black and white. 'Wake' (1:39), 'Given Up' (3:28), 'Shadow Of The Day' (4:16), 'In Pieces' (3:59) and 'Bleed It Out' (3:26) feature on *Minutes To Midnight* while 'My December' (3:51) is an older track written by Mike Shinoda just four weeks after the release of *Hybrid Theory*.

SONGS FROM THE UNDERGROUND

Year Of Release: 2008.

Track Listing: 'Announcement Service Public' / 'Qwerty' / 'And One' / 'Sold My Soul To Yo Mama' / 'Dedicated' / 'Hunger Strike' / 'My December' / 'Part Of Me' / 'Crawling' *(Bonus Track).*

Label: Warner.

Producer(s): Mike Shinoda.

Songwriters: Mike Shinoda, Chester Bennington, Joe Hahn, Rob Bourdon, Brad Delson and Dave Farrell and Chris Cornell.

Length: 36:45 and 41:34 *(inc. Bonus Track).*

Line-up: Mike Shinoda, Chester Bennington, Joe Hahn, Rob Bourdon, Brad Delson and Dave Farrell.

Trivia

The live versions of 'Hunger Strike' and 'My December' are exclusive to this EP.

Notes

This compilation EP is basically a collection of songs that had proven to be the most popular from the fan club only releases, *Linkin Park Underground.* They are all original tracks recorded exclusively for the band's fan club; the Temple Of The Dog song 'Hunger Strike' (4:15) was recorded live at the 2008 Projekt Revolution and features

iTUNES

Owned and maintained by the American software company Apple Inc., iTunes is an Internet site that allows users, for a fee, to download music and video files. It has became hugely successful over the past five years and downloads in general have outsold the CD single. Many believe that downloads will become even more popular than the CD album in the coming years. Like most bands, Linkin Park make their music available to download on iTunes and other similar sites and, as an incentive for fans, Linkin Park also release otherwise unavailable tracks exclusively as downloads or record songs specifically for release on iTunes. Linkin Park even performed a six-song set in front of 200 radio contest winners at an Apple iTunes store in SoHo, NYC on 22nd February 2008. The set-list ran: 'Wake', 'Given Up', 'Shadow Of The Day', 'My December', 'In Pieces' and 'Bleed It Out'.

Visit *apple.com/itunes*

Chris Cornell, and the piano version of 'My December' (4:18) was also recorded live in 2008. The studio tracks were culled from *LPU 1.0, 2.0, 4.0,* and *6.0* whereas the other LPU releases (*3.0, 5.0,* and *7.0*) featured only live recordings. There was a catch to the release of this EP: fans could only buy it from *Best Buy*, the America retailer. Fans who were already members of LPU could download (for free) a live version of 'Crawling' (featuring Chris Cornell) which was recorded in 2008 on the Projekt Revolution tour. 'Announcement Public Service' (2:26) and 'Qwerty' (3:23) were taken from *LPU 0.6*; 'And One' (4:31) was taken from the *Hybrid Theory EP/LPU 1.0*; 'Sold My Soul To Yo Mama' was taken from *LPU 4.0*; 'Dedicated' (3:13) is a demo that was recorded in 1999 and taken from *LPU 2.0* and the hidden instrumental 'Part Of Me' (12:43) was initially included on *Hybrid Theory EP/LPU 1.0*. All tracks were recorded between the years 1999 and 2008 and as such it serves as a memento of the band's first decade.

DVDs

Linkin Park seem to prefer to release CD/DVD packages rather than DVD sized products

so what follows is a surprisingly short list of standard DVDs.

FRAT PARTY AT THE PANKAKE FESTIVAL
Year Of Release: 2001 (re-released in CD packaging in 2003).
Track/Chapter Listing: 'Intro' / 'Papercut' / 'Beginnings' / 'Points Of Authority' / 'The Live Show' / 'Crawling Video Shoot' / 'Crawling' / 'Touring' / 'Cure For The Itch' / 'The Band' / 'One Step Closer' / 'The Future' / 'In The End' / 'The End'.
Label: Warner Bros / Warner Music Vision.
Details: Produced by Bill Berg-Hillinger, Joe Hahn, David May and Angela Smith.
Special Features: Various live performances and making of featurettes, including 'Points Of Authority' (Live at the Dragon Festival) / 'Crawling' (Live at the Dragon Festival) / Making of 'In The End' / Audio version of 'My December' / Audio version of 'High Voltage' / Audio version of 'Crawling' by Bryson Jones and The Sweethearts of The Rodeo All-Star Band / '1Stp Klosr' (Humble Brothers remix) / Mike and Joe's Art & Chester's Tattoos / 'One Step Farther' (Basically, the 'One Step Closer' music video

with the audio played backwards hence the title).

DVD Features: Main Language, English / Dolby Digital 2.0 Stereo / Audio Tracks / Additional Backstage Footage / Length, 90 minutes.

Trivia

This was the band's first DVD (it was also released on VHS). The photos on the inner sleeve of the DVD were used on the 2002 Japanese release *In The End: Live & Rare*.

Reviews
Josh Harper
Classic Rock

"The effort that has gone into this product is certainly the factor that has promoted it above the area of mediocrity which most band videos and DVDs inhabit... it makes for an enjoyable and informative package."

Notes

This oddly named DVD is something of a "bits and bobs" compilation from the band's *Hybrid Theory* tour (their first national tour). If truth be told it would have made a better second/bonus disc (as a partner to a complete concert) than a proper full scale DVD release. The main feature

disc includes live footage filmed in various locations, which if you look at now – several years later – shows how far the band have come (and how mature they look) these days. Nevertheless, there are all sorts of entertaining special features to please fans. What is especially interesting (and also infuriating for the less patient viewer) are the five hidden Easter eggs scattered throughout the DVD; if you unlock them using your remote control you gain access to further bonus material: music videos, live performances, audio tracks and some interesting behind-the-scenes type footage such as the featurette on Mike Shinoda, Joe Hahn's stunning art and Chester Bennington's obsession

with tattoos. Some of the remixes are just filler material but the live footage filmed at the Dragon Festival is good stuff. There's also some footage of the band in London (England).

For a debut DVD it could be regarded as a bit predictable, but it's a good insight into the band's inner world. Despite being slightly disorganised and lacking in focus, it was obviously a build-up towards something bigger and better, and as such is really for the committed fan only.

BREAKING THE HABIT
Year Of Release: 2004.
Track/Chapter Listing: 'Breaking The Habit' (Video Version) / Making of 'Breaking The Hab-

it' / 'Breaking The Habit (5.28.04 3:37 P.M.)'.
DVD Features: Main Language, English / Length, 27:13.
Label: Warner Music Vision / Warner Reprise Video.
Details: Produced by Matt Caltabiano and Jasper Tomlinson; directed by Joe Hahn and Kazuto Nakazawa and Kimo Proudfoot.

Trivia
A two-disc promo version was released; the first disc is the audio track and the second disc is a DVD of the official video.

Notes
'Breaking The Habit' was created at NRG Studios and Soundtrack Studios. Both the Hahn/Nakazawa video version and the Kimo Proudfoot version are included on this DVD. (See Music Videos for details on the video's premise). Intriguingly, the DVD comes with a Manga book created by the anime/Manga publisher Tokyopop. The book is basically about the video itself and offers biographies of the personnel involved, storyboards and visual prints relating to the video(s).

SINGLES (SELECTIVE LIST)

The following section is a list of the band's singles released in both the US and the UK on the CD format. It would be pointless to repeat some information on the songs because the majority of it is discussed in the albums section, for example, a run through the verse/chorus of each song, the instruments played and the style of production etc. Also, some songs are discussed in detail in '10 Most Memorable Linkin Park Songs' later in Part Three. Basically, this is a quick and easy guide to the band's back catalogue of CD singles. (NB: The length of each track refers to what is actually on the CD single; and the US chart positions refer to the Billboard Hot 100.)

band released. Further elaboration is offered in the '10 Most Memorable Linkin Park Songs' later in this section.

CRAWLING
Year Of Release: 2001.
Label: Warner.
Length: 2:21.
UK Chart Position: Number 16.
US Chart Position: Number 74.

Notes
Essentially about drug addiction (Chester Bennington has admitted he was addicted to drugs prior to the Linkin Park years) 'Crawling' is a very angry song that ac-

ONE STEP CLOSER
Year Of Release: 2001.
Label: Warner.
Length: 2:39.
UK Chart Position: Number 24.
US Chart Position: Number 75.

Notes
One of Linkin Park's most popular songs and famous for the line *"Shut up when I'm talking to you!"* It appears on the *Hybrid Theory* album and was the first single the

tually includes very little rapping from Mike Shinoda, probably because it's such a personal song for Bennington. It is taken from *Hybrid Theory*. Detailed discussion is offered in the '10 Most Memorable Linkin Park Songs' further on in Part Three.

IN THE END
Year Of Release: 2001.
Label: Warner.
Length: 3:38.
UK Chart Position: Number eight.
US Chart Position: Number two.

Notes
The band's first big hit in the American and British singles charts, 'In The End' remains one of their biggest-selling singles to date. The song is probably one of the band's most famous choruses. It was conceived at a studio in New Orleans in 2000 and features on *Hybrid Theory*. Further information is given in the '10 Most

Memorable Linkin Park Songs' later in Part Three.

SOMEWHERE I BELONG
Year Of Release: 2003.
Label: Warner.
Length: 3:34.
UK Chart Position: Number 10.
US Chart Position: Number 32.

Notes
The first single taken from the band's second studio album *Meteora* is a typically loud and aggressive nu-metal tune, although it hints at a straightforward metal sound, as if the band are distancing themselves from the (mostly) derided nu-metal scene.

FAINT
Year Of Release: 2003.
Label: Warner.
Length: 2:42.
UK Chart Position: Number 15.
US Chart Position: Number 48.

Notes

Still regarded as one of the band's most popular tracks, 'Faint' was released as two singles 'Faint 1' (with blue cover) and 'Faint 2' (with brown/green cover) which is more a marketing ploy than anything else. It is taken from the album *Meteora*.

NUMB
Year Of Release: 2003.
Label: Warner.
Length: 3:07.
UK Chart Position: Number 14.
US Chart Position: Number five.

Notes

The third single released from the massively successful but slightly underwhelming *Meteora*, 'Numb' is an excellent song and was a good choice as a single. It was recorded in New Orleans in 2003 and is the closing track on *Meteora*.

BREAKING THE HABIT
Year Of Release: 2004. ***Label:*** Warner. ***Length:*** 3:16. ***UK Chart Position:*** Number 39. ***US Chart Position:*** Number 20.

Notes

As with 'Crawling' this single is about drug addiction but written by Mike Shinoda (about a drug-addicted friend of his) rather than Chester Bennington. It was the final track taken from *Meteora*. *"I had this theme in my head that I wanted to write about,"* Shinoda explained to *musicOMH.com*, *"and I kept trying it, and it would always be too dorky or too cheesy.*

And somehow, when I sat down with this particular music, what I had been trying to write about for five years came out in two hours – just fell out on the page."

NUMB/ENCORE
Year Of Release: 2004.
Label: Warner / Roc-A-Fella.
Length: 3:25.
UK Chart Position: Number 14.
US Chart Position: Number 20.

Notes
A very famous collaboration that divided the band's fan base: the rap fans and the metal fans. Obviously some metal aficionados were not too keen on hearing Linkin Park collaborate with Jay-Z on the album *Collision Course*. Nevertheless, it was a massive hit and stayed on the US airwaves for around six months. The song is a combination of Linkin Park's 'Numb' and Jay-Z's 'Encore.'

WHAT I'VE DONE
Year Of Release: 2007.
Label: Warner.
Length: 3:25.
UK Chart Position: Number six.
US Chart Position: Number seven.

Notes
The lead single for the band's third studio album *Minutes To Midnight*. It's a terrific metal song that begins with an eerie piano melody. The band have clearly developed their sound from their nu-metal roots by not including any rapping. And with the help of producer Rick Rubin the band created one of their best singles.

BLEED IT OUT
Year Of Release: 2007.
Label: Warner.
Length: 2:44.
UK Chart Position: Number 29.
US Chart Position: Number 52.

Notes

The second single taken from *Minutes To Midnight* received better reviews but lower sales than 'What I've Done'. Less then three minutes in total, it's a short song but it makes an instant impact on the listener. There's some rapping and the song also contains the word "fucking" which provoked some broadcasters to censor it. As with previous Linkin Park lyrics, the premise concerns paranoia, frustration and despair.

doesn't contain any rapping and is clearly inspired by U2's 'With Or Without You.' It's a strong ballad with an obvious melody and has some effective moments. It is taken from *Minutes To Midnight*.

LEAVE OUT ALL THE REST

Year Of Release: 2008.
Label: Warner.
Length: 3:19.
UK Chart Position: Number 90.
US Chart Position: Number 94.

Notes

This single is the lowest charting one the band has had in the UK, aside from the Digital Release 'Given Up', which surprisingly did

SHADOW OF THE DAY

Year Of Release: 2008.
Label: Warner.
Length: 4:16.
UK Chart Position: Number 46.
US Chart Position: Number 15.

Notes

Another commercially minded single, certainly one of the band's more radio friendly releases as it

not chart at all. It's a big metal ballad perfect for a single release and it had a huge special effects laden video to accompany it. It was the final single taken from the mega-selling *Minutes To Midnight*.

OTHER SINGLES RELEASES (SELECTIVE LIST)

Some of the band's singles have only been released in the UK as Digital Downloads; this is now commonplace and has been since 1ˢᵗ September 2004 when the official UK Download Chart was kick-started in the UK. In early 2005, CD singles were outsold by download releases for the first time. This has meant that some artists have only released download singles rather than the more familiar CD; some have released singles on both formats. The same has happened in the States; since February 2005, Digital Download singles have been incorporated in the official **Billboard** **Hot 100** *singles chart simply because downloads are so popular. What follows is a selective list of singles that were either made available as* *downloads only or on the radio but not in CD format.*

PAPERCUT
Year Of Release: 2001.
Label: Warner. *Length:* 3:05. *UK Chart Position:* Number 14. *US Chart Position: Not released in the States.*

Notes
This song could well be another personal composition about Chester Bennington's past: it's essentially about a lonely man who is besieged with bouts of paranoia and feelings of isolation. 'Papercut' was recorded way back in July 1999 at a studio in New Orleans. Like all the singles released off *Hybrid Theory* it remains a favourite amongst committed fans. The single features only live recordings of the song rather than an unreleased B-side.

Pts.OF.Athrty
Year Of Release: 2002.
Label: Warner. *Length:* 3:38.
UK Chart Position: Number nine.
*US Chart Position: Not released
in the States.*

Notes
Written by Linkin Park (with
Derek Murphy, Lorenzo Decha-
lus and Maxwell Dixon), 'Pts. Of.
Athrty' was the first single taken
from *Reanimation*. It was remixed
by Orgy's Jay Gordon and is a mix
of 'High Voltage,' 'By Myself' and
'Points Of Authority.' The single
features two B-sides: 'H! Vltg3'
and 'Buy Myself'. The former was
remixed by Evidence and Pharoahe Monch but the Marilyn Manson
remixed version of 'By Myself'
(dubbed 'Buy Myself') which appears on the CD single is different
to that on *Reanimation*.

FROM THE INSIDE
Year Of Release: 2004.
Label: Warner.
Length: 2:55.
UK Chart Position: Download only.
US Chart Position: Did not chart.

Notes
An excellent metal track (with a
lengthy scream by Bennington) that
was surprisingly not a chart hit at
all. It didn't make the top 10 in any
country it was released in. It's tak-
en from the album *Meteora*. It just
managed to make the top 40 in Australia, Germany, France, Italy and
Switzerland.

LYING FROM YOU
Year Of Release: 2004.
Label: Warner.
Length: 2:55.
*UK Chart Position: Not released
in the UK.*
US Chart Position: Number 58.

Notes

This song (from *Meteora*) is one song which was mashed up on the Jay-Z collaboration *Collision Course*. It's a pretty good song with big production but some fuzzy guitars prevent it from being one of the band's better tracks. It was not released at all in the UK and performed only modestly in the famed American *Billboard* Hot 100 yet it was a hit in the separate *Billboard* rock charts.

DIRT OFF YOUR SHOULDER/LYING FROM YOU

Year Of Release: 2005.
Label: Warner / Roc-a-Fella.

Length: 4:04.
UK Chart Position: Download only.
US Chart Position: Download only.

Notes

Taken from the album *Collision Course* (with Jay-Z), this single did not actual chart; it was a download release only. It was initially released in 2005 and later reissued in 2006. It contains explicit lyrics.

GIVEN UP

Year Of Release: 2008.
Label: Warner.
Length: 3:09.
UK Chart Position: Did not chart *(download only).*
US Chart Position: Number 99.

Notes

The fourth single taken from *Minutes To Midnight* was the worst performing Linkin Park single in the UK – it did not chart at all. It's a ballsy song that features Chester Bennington screaming for an unbelievable 17 seconds.

MUSIC VIDEOS (SELECTIVE LIST)

Since the launch of MTV on 1ˢᵗ August, 1981 most commercially released singles are accompanied by promotional music vid-

eos. The following section is basically a list of all the music videos Linkin Park made between their 2000 debut album Hybrid Theory *right up to 2007's* Minutes To Midnight. *There's no doubt they'll continue to make more exciting (and expensive) videos for future releases. You can download the following videos from the band's official website linkinpark.com: 'Leave Out All The Rest', 'What I've Done', 'Points Of Authority' (Remix), 'Papercut', 'One Step Closer', 'Shadow Of The Day', 'Given Up', 'In The End', 'From The Inside', 'Faint', 'Breaking The Habit' and 'Bleed It Out'.*

ONE STEP CLOSER
Year Of Release: 2000.
Album: *Hybrid Theory.*
Director(s): Gregory Dark (concept by Joe Hahn).

Notes
A typically stylish video that is not dissimilar in some ways to Prodigy's famous 'Firestarter' promo video. The band certainly looks a lot younger; Chester Bennington is almost unrecognisable with bleached blonde hair and Mike Shinoda's dyed red. There's another noticeable thing about the video: the bassist is Scott Koziol who was briefly David Farrell's replacement. The video ba-sically shows a group of teenage kids hanging out in an alley way, who follow some guy into a tunnel which leads them to the place where the band are playing the song. The teens are spooked out by the band, and the weirdo whom they follow chases them out of the tunnel. There are some visual tricks going on and the use of neon colours gives it a cyberpunk edge. The video was actually shot in an abandoned subway tunnel in Los Angeles.

"It's an extremely scary place to hang out," Mike Shinoda told shoutweb.com, *"and shoot a video. The air was very thick and filled with minerals and dust and dirt. It's very hard to breathe down there. But we endured. We had a lot of fun."*

It would be the first in a stream of well-directed and visually alluring promo videos.

CRAWLING
Year Of Release: 2001.
Album: *Hybrid Theory.*
Director(s): Brothers Strause.

Notes

Perhaps more plausible than their first video, 'Crawling' actually has a story premise: the actress Katelyn Rosaasen (who appeared in The Offspring's 'Want You Bad' as well as some other music videos) plays a women whose relationship is in turmoil because she is being abused by her spouse. The video shows Rosaasen trying to deal with the mental and psychical abuse. The CGI crystals surround her as she struggles to cope with her life but by the end of the film the crystals explode, which is obviously a metaphor for her triumph over the relationship. Meanwhile, the band is playing the song in a crystal room said to be a Fortress Of Solitude (i.e. Superman.) It's a high-tech, well-directed video which obviously had a lot of money spent on it and one that certainly appeals to the MTV generation.

PAPERCUT
Year Of Release: 2001.
Album: *Hybrid Theory.*

Director(s): Nathan "Karma" Cox and Joe Hahn.

Notes

Another big-budget video with some cool special effects that has become the hallmark of the band. This one is set in a haunted house where there are lots of spooky things happening in the vicinity, even though Rob Bourdon seems to be the only one to see what's going on around them. One interesting piece of trivia for fans is that the picture in the room where the band are playing was painted by Mike Shinoda the day before the shoot, and was initially used as the cover artwork for their Xero demo way back when. Another point worth mentioning is that both Brad Delson and David Farrell play – gasp – acoustic guitars in the video even though there are actually no acoustic instruments in the song. Drummer Rob Bourdon is not playing drums in the video either! Such small details could make the video seem ill-conceived. Yet some of the im-

agery (obviously produced using some impressive special effects) sees Shinoda's fingers stretching and Bourdon's eyes melt. Very weird! But it all helps to make the lyrics (of paranoia and despair) more potent; you just have to spend time watching the video to understand its premise. One argument often made against music videos of this type is that they take away the songs meaning and are merely about the effects, but that is clearly not so on this occasion.

IN THE END
Year Of Release: 2001.
Album: Hybrid Theory.
Director(s): Nathan Cox, Joe Hahn and Mike Shinoda.

Notes
This award winning video is certainly one of the most ambitious music videos by any band of Linkin Park's generation. While the group performed their part at a sound studio in LA, the background was filmed in a desert somewhere in southern California, and the fantasy setting/imagery was created purely by CGI and special effects.

Admittedly, it can be feasibly argued that at this point the band is getting carried away with high-tech videos: too much money and

too many special effects didn't help the group fight accusations of being just another corporate rock outfit. There's one especially entertaining bit towards the end when it starts raining as Shinoda raps and the clouds turn oppressively dark, but then the sun shines and the wasteland turns green.

POINTS OF AUTHORITY
Year Of Release: 2001.
Album: *Hybrid Theory.*
Director(s): Nathan Cox, Joe Hahn and Mike Shinoda.

Notes
This video is basically a montage of live clips that were filmed during the band's 2001 world tour. If anything it shows just how much energy they have on stage. There

was no single release for this song; it was made to promote their debut DVD *Frat Party At The Pancake Festival.*

Pts.OF.Athrty
Year Of Release: 2002.
Album: Reanimation.
Director(s): Joe Hahn.

Notes
Reportedly inspired by the CGI film *Final Fantasy: The Spirits Within*, 'Points Of Authority' is a complete CGI film, in other words it's completely animated. In a nutshell (and that's all which is required on this one), the human race no longer exists and all that remains are robots (with the heads of the six Linkin Park members) and an alien race that don't really get on with each other. Obviously they do battle for governorship of the planet. The leader of the alien race is killed at the end of the video. It's fun but way, way over the top. Only a metal band could get away with something as concep-

tual as this; Linkin Park are artistic people (certainly Shinoda and Hahn are) with a keen visual eye, so they're not going to settle for something lame. It has to be big, edgy and expensive.

Frgt/10
Year Of Release: 2002.
Album: Reanimation.
Director(s): Joe Hahn.

Notes
Another CGI film and like 'In The End' there is an ecological message. The opening and closing scenes are the only parts of the film which are not CGI. Essentially the video shows a person (dressed in a green jump suit complete with gas mask) who walks around a grim city spray painting the words 'LP' on walls and buildings. Those words must have some magical quality because wherever 'LP' is painted, vegetation and greenery starts to grow in the oppressive cityscape. The governmental officials track the person down until the end of the video when it is revealed the person is actually a woman named Chali; in fact, it is Chali who first appears on screen at the start of the film. We don't know it is her who paints the city until she is being chased and jumps from one rooftop to an-

other and consequently her paint tank falls off, which distracts the officials so she has time to get back to her bedroom where she takes her mask off.

Enth E Nd
Year Of Release: 2002.
Album: *Reanimation.*
Director(s): Joe Hahn.

Notes
What makes this Linkin Park video stand out from the rest is not the use of CGI or special effects because there aren't any (at least not as elaborate as in previous videos) but because it only features Mike Shinoda, the rapper Motion Man and Kutmasta Kurt. The video takes place in the back of a car.

Kyur4 Th Ich
Year Of Release: 2002.
Album: *Reanimation.*
Director(s): Joe Hahn.

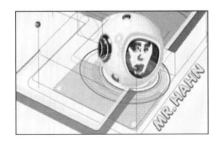

Notes
The song is nothing special and neither is the music video. It is basically a montage of footage of breakdancers in various venues, indoor and out; it looks like the footage was filmed at breakdancing festivals or gatherings. The final shot is of Joe Hahn staring at the camera.

SOMEWHERE I BELONG
Year Of Release: 2003.
Album: *Meteora.*
Director(s): Joe Hahn.

Notes
Considering what the band had conceived in earlier videos, this one is less interesting, although it did pick up the gong for 'Best Rock Video' at the 2003 MTV Video Music Awards. With a fire in the background, the band performs the song with the usual amount of gusto and the camera sporadically cuts to Bennington and Shinoda singing in front of a waterfall. Bennington and Shin-

oda are not just singing in peaceful surrounding, there are weird creatures hanging around them.

FAINT
Year Of Release: 2003.
Album: Meteora.
Director(s): Mark Romanek.

Notes
Members of Linkin Park Underground, the band's official fan club, make an appearance in this film as the band performs in a graffiti-infested, dilapidated building. However, one nifty little filmic trick is that the band are filmed from behind so you only see them as silhouettes until the end when there's a cool shot of the band from the front. It's a good video, basic and visually it's quite easy to watch – certainly more than some previous.

NUMB
Year Of Release: 2003.
Album: Meteora.
Director(s): Joe Hahn.

Notes
This excellent video follows a social outcast girl portrayed by Briana Evigan. She is extremely unpopular at school and is mocked for her artistic vices (drawing and sketching) and her mother lambastes her for being weak and misguided, basically not what she wanted her daughter to be like. In one shot you can see the word

NUMB on her fingers which she inflicted on herself. The church scenes, where the band is singing, was filmed in LA and the outdoor scenes were filmed in Prague.

FROM THE INSIDE
Year Of Release: 2004.
Album: Meteora.
Director(s): Joe Hahn.
Notes
This video was filmed in Prague during their 2003 European tour.
A familiar event for some bands, 'From The Inside' sees Bennington and Shinoda struggling to cope during a city riot. The troops are

called out to arrest the culprits and calm everyone down. The video focuses on Bennington and Shinoda singing/rapping in the streets, although they are not standing together. In fact, Bennington's son, Jamie Bennington, is at the centre of the riot after he is seperated from his carer. By the end of the video, the riot is stopped after Jamie screams and consequently, buildings start to collapse and the people in the street fall to the ground. It has to be seen to be believed. The final 30 seconds or so

have the band playing the song together in the street.

BREAKING THE HABIT
Year Of Release: 2004.
Album: Meteora.
Director(s): Joe Hahn and Kazuto Nakazawa.

Notes
Blatantly influenced by the anime/Japanese cartoon animation in the film *Kill Bill: Volume 1* (which was directed by Nakazawa), 'Breaking The Habit' was created by the animation company Studio 4°C. The video revolves around a dead man found on top of a car roof. The police get involved and the video shows the reaction of other characters presumably, people who knew him. There are several characters in the video, all of whom have negative habits and are shown trying to break those habits hence their obvious relation to the song title. The smoke that flows around the characters is Chester Bennington's soul and towards the end the smoke goes into the dead body which is obviously Bennington. The video finishes with the *entire* band playing the song on top of the roof of the car.

Interestingly a second video (directed by Kimo Proudfoot) called 'Breaking The Habit (5.28.04 3:37 PM)' was filmed; far less elaborate, it merely shows the band playing the song in a recording studio.

NUMB/ENCORE
Year Of Release: 2004.
Album: Collision Course.
Director(s): Kimo Proudfoot and Joe Hahn.

Notes

This is a simple video that sees Jay-Z and the band performing the song at the famed Roxy Theatre in LA. Behind-the-scenes footage is in black and white and is spliced into the live performance.

WHAT I'VE DONE
Year Of Release: 2007.
Album: Minutes To Midnight.
Director(s): Joe Hahn.

Notes

This politically conscious video covers a wide range of topics that affect our planet, from disease and poverty to bigotry, ignorance and racism. The band performs the song as footage of world crises are edited together. The video also features a whole bunch of great historical figures such as John F. Kenney, Mother Teresa and Abraham Lincoln as well as tyrants like Hitler, Stalin and Saddam Hussein. If anything, this video shows how politically and socially inclined the band are.

BLEED IT OUT
Year Of Release: 2007.
Album: Minutes To Midnight.
Director(s): Joe Hahn.

Notes

A toned down video, 'Bleed It Out' sees the band perform the song in a bar whilst a bar fight is going on. It was actually filmed in one long continuous shot which further demonstrates the band's (or rather Joe Hahn's) flirtations with various cinematic techniques.

SHADOW OF THE DAY
Year Of Release: 2008.
Album: Minutes To Midnight.
Director(s): Joe Hahn.

Notes

A dystopian inspired video, 'Shadow Of The Day' is set between 11:55pm and 11:59pm when presumably at 12:00am Doomsday occurs.
Hahn spoke to *punktv.ca*:

"When making this video, it was important to shoot it at night. I wanted to show that this city was awake while the rest of the world is sleeping. I don't really have a philosophy when it comes to lighting; it's a matter of what feels right. For me, it's a mat-

ter of going to the location and brainstorming with my photographer to dramatically embellish the environment as it pertains to the narrative."

The video follows Chester Bennington around the city during what is absolute civil unrest. We watch Bennington as he wakes up, gets ready and walks around the city: buildings are set on fire and the police and SWAT teams are obviously involved. The rest of the band does not feature in the video and there is not a song performance but you can hear sound effects in the background despite the song being played. One point worth mentioning is that there are three differently edited videos available on the Internet but the basic premise remains the same regardless of different scenes and edits.

GIVEN UP
Year Of Release: 2008.
Album: Minutes To Midnight.
Director(s): Mark Fiore.

Notes
'Given Up' is basically a montage of live clips (filmed at the Manchester Evenings News Arena and London's O2 Arena in January 2007) with various special

effects spliced into the footage. These kinds of videos are usually quite lame and made only because the artists in question are busy on tour so Linkin Park did well to "spice" it up with the special effects. It's an interesting way of blending the footage together rather than quick edits which is so common in these types of videos.

LEAVE OUT ALL THE REST
Year Of Release: 2008.
Album: Minutes To Midnight.
Director(s): Joe Hahn.

Notes
Possibly the best video they have made so far – and also another one influenced by recent American films – 'Leave Out All The Rest' is an obvious nod towards the Danny Boyle directed sci-fi film *Sunshine*. The video follows the daily lives of the band members as they live in deep reaches of outer space. The band doesn't actually perform in this video although Bennington sings his parts.

10 MOST MEMORABLE LINKIN PARK SONGS

This is certainly not a definitive selection of Linkin Park's '10 Most Memorable Songs' but taking into account sales and chart success in the UK, the United States and elsewhere, the following songs have become hugely famous and are either consistent parts of their live set-list or frequently played on music stations on the TV and radio. Some of the details below have previously been listed, but as this is a separate section that isolates 10 of their most popular tracks, there is added emphasis on the recording details.

(NB: The B-sides listed below only include original recordings – no live tracks or remixes. Track lengths are approximate and album versions only.)

ONE STEP CLOSER

Recording Information: Written by Linkin Park; produced by Don Gilmore; length, 2:36; taken from *Hybrid Theory*; released in 2000. B-sides: 'My December' and 'High Voltage'.

Trivia
The song was initially called 'Plaster.' It was composed while the band was working on the track 'Runaway.' It also features on *Rock Band 2,* the interactive video game.

Notes
Certainly one of the most popular Linkin Park songs, 'One Step Closer' was not actually a chart hit. It peaked at a lowly number 75 on the American *Billboard* Hot 100 and only reached number 24 in the UK top 40, where it spent four weeks in the charts. However, it had some success in Australia where it reached number four in the national charts. It has since become a firm live favourite and has been played at every Linkin Park gig to date, usually as the climax. The song was remixed for the album *Reanimation*: it was renamed '1Stp Klosr' and features Jonathan Davis of Korn and also The Humble Brothers.

'One Step Closer' opens with a memorable electric riff but only a few seconds in it quickly becomes clear the song is not going to be your average metal anthem. There are lots of production effects and during the chorus you can hear Mike Shinoda's screams over Chester Bennington's vocals. The lyrics are quite catchy and the chorus remains one of their most popular compositions. There's a fair bit of scratching which is another way the band distinguished themselves from acts of their ilk in the early years. Sure, it's an angry song but the anger is passionate, apparent both in Bennington's vocals and Shinoda's rapping. It remains one of their most famous tracks.

CRAWLING

Recording Information: Written by Linkin Park; produced by Don Gilmore; length, 3:29; taken from *Hybrid Theory*; released in 2000.

Trivia

It won the band their first Grammy in 2002 for 'Best Hard Rock Performance.' First Linkin Park video to feature David Farrell. A remixed version of the song named 'Krwlng' is included on *Reanimation* and features Aaron Lewis. Also, it was covered by the German band Angelzoom.

Notes

Hitting number 74, 'Crawling' only made it one position higher on the American *Billboard* Hot 100 than 'One Step Closer.' Meanwhile, in the UK it peaked at a reasonably healthy number 16 where it spent eight weeks in the charts. It performed especially strongly in Ireland and Austria, reaching the top 10 in both countries.

'Crawling' opens with some fuzzy production sounds, but then in creeps a steady bass line, before heading straight to the lyrics –

the chorus in fact. It's an odd song that quickly changes tempo from slow dulcet vocals to the really bitter hard edged choruses. It's another firm fan favourite and one that is still regularly played live. There isn't much of Shinoda's rapping; the melody makes the song one of the edgiest tracks they have composed. The track is basically about an addiction to Crystal Meth, which makes the addict feel like there are insects crawling up his skin. Bennington allegedly had an addiction to the drug, hence the song's introspective nature.

IN THE END

Recording Information: Written by Linkin Park; produced by Don Gilmore; length, 3:36; taken from *Hybrid Theory*; released in 2001. B-sides: 'Step Up'.

Trivia

It was covered by XP8, the Italian band and the Christian rock band ApologetiX recorded a parody version.

XP8

Notes

'In The End' was one of Linkin Park's first big hits and it remains a famous song, played by the band on tour and consistently liked by fans. It peaked at number two on the American *Billboard* Hot 100 while in the UK it reached number eight where it spent nine weeks in the charts. It was a top five hit in Switzerland, Austria, Mexico and Denmark.

This is certainly one of the most intriguing Linkin Park songs. There's a whole bunch of things going on here: the song opens with a piano melody (which runs through the whole piece) before the vocals and production effects kick in. There's a lot of rapping in this song, courtesy of Mr. Shinoda, more than there are actual vocals in fact. This is an authentic nu-metal track – in capital letters. Bennington makes himself heard as a rock star to be reckoned with and Rob Bourdon beats the hell out of his drum kit throughout the whole track. If you pay close attention to everything that is happening in the song it becomes clear why Linkin Park have endured past the nu-metal era, leaving most of their peers way behind.

SOMEWHERE I BELONG

Recording Information: Written by Linkin Park; produced by Don

Gilmore; length, 3:33; taken from *Meteora*; released in 2003.

Trivia

The Jamaican sprinter Usain Bolt used the song for his profile video at the 2008 Beijing Olympics.

Notes

The first single taken from the band's second studio opus, 'Somewhere I Belong' only reached a disappointing number 32 on the *Billboard* Hot 100, while in the UK it peaked at number 10 and spent eight weeks in the charts. It was a top 10 hit in New Zealand, Ireland and Canada.

'Somewhere I Belong' is an untypically sombre Linkin Park song and despite what some of their critics have noted, shows this band has conviction and depth. It's certainly more 'metal' than nu-metal' and there is a feeling of the band wanting to move away from being pigeon-holed in the highly-derided yet once popular genre. Again, the chorus is quite catchy and there's a raspy edge to Bennington's vocals that give hints toward a change in vocal style and direction.

FAINT

Recording Information: Written by Linkin Park; produced by Don

Gilmore; length, 2:42; taken from *Meteora*; released in 2003.

Trivia

The CD single was released in two parts – CD one features 'Lying From You' (Live from the LUP 2003 tour) and the video for 'Somewhere I Belong'. CD two includes 'One Step Closer' (Live from the LUP 2003 tour) and a live video of 'Faint.'

Notes

'Faint' peaked at number 48 on the American *Billboard* Hot 100 but it had a higher degree of success in the UK where it spent eight weeks in the charts, reaching number 15. It performed only modestly in other territories missing the top 10 in big markets like Japan.

'Faint' is an odd track: the first few seconds prove this is going to be no ordinary song. Shinoda starts his rapping before Bennington comes in and begins screaming the chorus. There's a 'classical' melody that comes up sporadically in the tune (which actually starts the song) with a John Berry feel to it. And it's over-produced – but that's their style!

BREAKING THE HABIT

Recording Information: Written by Linkin Park; produced by Don

Gilmore; length, 3:16; taken from *Meteora*; released in 2004.

Trivia

Does not include lead vocals from Mike Shinoda.

Notes

The final single release from *Meteora*, 'Breaking The Habit' peaked at number 20 on the *Billboard* Hot 100 in the States. And in the UK it just about made the top 40, reaching a poor 39 and spending just two weeks in the charts.

'Breaking The Habit' is an interesting experiment; it's obviously influenced by electronica and there's an itching for the song to get heavy and more aggressive but the band keep a tight leash on the melody and it stays at mid-paced level. The story goes that the lyrics are about a friend of Mike Shinoda who was addicted to drugs, thus 'Breaking The Habit'. It's not necessarily memorable for its quality but rather its style and distinction from previous Linkin Park songs. It's just something different.

NUMB/ENCORE

Recording Information: Written by Linkin Park, Jay-Z and Kanye West; produced by Mike Shinoda; length, 3:25; taken from *Collision Course*; released in 2004.

Trivia

At the 2006 Grammy Awards whilst performing this song, Paul McCartney joined the band to sing 'Yesterday' – the Beatles song.

Notes

The most successful single from the mash-up album *Collision Course*, 'Numb/Encore' is a combination of the *Meteora* track 'Numb' and the Jay-Z song 'Encore' (from *The Black Album*.) It peaked at number 20 in the *Billboard* Hot 100 in the States and number 14 in the UK where it spent a respectable 23 weeks in the charts.

OK, so this isn't really metal and some fans (of either genre) may prefer the original recordings of 'Numb' and 'Encore', but this track was a hit and is still popular with zealots. It's only around two and a quarter minutes into the song that Linkin Park's 'Numb' becomes recognisable as Jay-Z starts the controversial collision proceedings with 'Encore.' It sounds more like a Jay-Z song than anything else; it's unbalanced because with it lasting only three minutes and 25 seconds, it's only the last minute that Linkin Park take front stage so to speak, and even then Jay-Z can still be heard in the background. The CD single features an instrumental version of the song. 'Numb/Encore' is popular because it's a collaboration rather than a fine piece of work.

WHAT I'VE DONE

Recording Information: Written by Linkin Park; produced by Rick Rubin and Mike Shinoda; length, 3:25; taken from *Minutes To Midnight*; released in 2007
.

Trivia

Features on *Guitar Hero World Tour*, the interactive video game.

Notes

This globally successful single was released on iTunes as a download as well as a CD single; a radio edit was also released. It peaked at a very healthy number seven on the *Billboard* Hot 100; it hit number six in the UK and was a number one smash hit in Germany and Austria. Linkin Park like to keep their songs at a crisp three or so minutes and this one is no exception. It starts off with a creep piano melody before the guitars and drums kick into action. In fact, many critics pointed out the resemblance of the piano intro to John Carpenter's piano score for his horror classic *Halloween*. There's no rapping at all; it's pure mainstream contemporary metal but surprisingly subdued, not like a ballad, more like a consistently paced hard rock song with an infectious chorus. Like the rest of the album this song is a massive departure from what we previously knew of Linkin Park. It's a further step away from the whole nu-metal thing.

SHADOW OF THE DAY
Recording Information: Written by Linkin Park; produced by Rick Rubin and Mike Shinoda; length, 4:50; taken from *Minutes To Midnight*; released in 2007.

INTERACTIVE VIDEO GAMES

In recent years there has been a spate of interactive video games that concentrate specifically on rock music. The *Guitar Hero* series was first released in 2005 on the Playstation Two. There have been numerous sequels, including *Guitar Hero: Metallica*. The premise is simple: the player uses a toy guitar to riff along with the selected songs. *Guitar Hero III: Legends Of Rock* on the Playstation Three and Xbox360 has a feature that allows users to download songs (for a fee) from the software stores; among the songs available is Linkin Park's 'No More Sorrow', while *Guitar Hero: On Tour* includes 'One Step Closer'.

Another interactive rock game is the phenomenally successful *Rock Band*, which was launched on the Playstation Three and Xbox360 in 2007. It basically allows four players to perform in a virtual band: singer, drummer, bassist and guitarist. *Rock Band 2* was launched in mid-2008 after the first one made around $600 million. It's a billion-dollar success. Linkin Park allowed the makers to use 'One Step Closer' on *Rock Band 2*, while other artists include Thin Lizzy, Megadeth, Alice In Chains and Soundgarden.

Trivia

Linkin Park is one of four bands (Foo Fighters, R.E.M. and U2) to have had four tracks in the top 20 US Modern Rock Chart, 'Shadow Of The Day' made that happen.

Notes

This song peaked at number 15 on the American *Billboard* Hot 100 but in the UK it only managed to make it to number 46. However, it reached the top 10 in Latvia, Israel and Singapore. It also made it into the top 20 in Portugal, Sweden, Switzerland, Germany, France, New Zealand, Canada and Czech Republic.

'Shadow Of The Day' starts life as some production effects that are reminiscent of eighties U2, in particular 'With Or Without You'; Bennington's vocals are full yet restrained and you wouldn't guess it was the same singer heard on a song like 'In The End.' The last 20 seconds or so of the song are instrumental, giving it a moody vibe. It's an intriguing song and during production they apparently played around with various effects and loops till settling on this official version. The sleeve notes in the CD state that they played various instruments (piano, acoustic guitar, marimba, xylophone and electric banjo) and they chose the reversed/edited keyboard. An-

other interesting thing about this track is that it does not feature Mike Shinoda singing/rapping. It's a further development from previous songs and after several repeats is actually quite moving.

LEAVE OUT ALL THE REST

Recording Information: Written by Linkin Park; produced by Rick Rubin and Mike Shinoda; length, 3:29; taken from *Minutes To Midnight*; released in 2008.

Trivia

Originally named 'Fear' and 'When My Time Comes'.

Notes

This song only reached number 94 on the *Billboard* Hot 100 and in the UK it only managed number 90, but with the album having been in stores for months and the singles market said to be in a dying state, it's not a surprise than major artists struggle to shift units in the singles market. It made the top 20 in Austria, Finland and Germany. Opening with some effects (strings and electronic keys), 'Leave Out All The Rest' is an introspective track and although it references one character it can be about everyone: the general premise is the choices we make in life and how they affect us. It's a ballad and a pretty good one too; Bennington gives a sturdy vocal performance and the electronic piano that creeps through the song is familiar to Linkin Park fans.

10 KICK-ASS LIVE RECORDINGS

As with the '10 Most Memorable Linkin Park Songs', this little section is not a definitive account of the band's live recordings but a worthwhile selection of some of their finest live tracks. They are a powerful live band that can perform as magnetically on stage as they do on CD – and why not celebrate that with this little list.

PAPERCUT
Details: Can be heard on *Live In Texas*; recorded live at the Reliant Stadium in Texas on 2nd August and Texas Stadium in Irving on 3rd August, 2003; length, 3:06.

Notes
A stunning version of the song that is almost identical to the album version which is a difficult task considering the amount of production effects going on. Shinoda's rapping is a little too fast

but the band maintains tight control over the melody.

RUNAWAY
Details: Can be heard on *Live In Texas*; recorded live at the Reliant Stadium in Texas on 2nd August and Texas Stadium in Irving on 3rd August, 2003; length, 3:08.

Notes
One, two, three, and the band immediately encourage the audience to join in on the manic action and help create quite a thrilling live version of 'Runaway.' Bennington over-eggs the screaming a little but when he slows down and actually sings his voice is in good shape. Credit due to the rest of the band for keeping superb pace.

FROM THE INSIDE
Details: Can be heard on *Live In Texas*; recorded live at the Reliant Stadium in Texas on 2nd August and Texas Stadium in Irving on 3rd August, 2003; length, 3:01.

Notes
Mike Shinoda is probably the centre voice through this song, his rapping is concise and clear which makes it memorable. Bennington does a lot of screaming but there's an edge to his voice on this song which keeps him in focus.

NO MORE SORROW

Details: Can be heard on *Road To Revolution: Live At Milton Keynes*; recorded live at Milton Keynes National Bowl in England on 29th June, 2008; length, 5:06.

Notes

The crowd led the way from some instrumental bits to introduce the song: Brad Delson's crisp and loud lead guitar riff paves the way for the rest of the band to begin their path to destruction, and then there's around two minutes of relentless headbanging. Bennington starts singing around two-and-a-half minutes into the track and his voice is in good shape. You can sporadically hear the audience singing along but it's quite faint.

THE LITTLE THINGS GIVE YOU AWAY

Details: Can be heard on *Road To Revolution: Live At Milton Keynes*; recorded live at Milton Keynes National Bowl in England on 29th June, 2008; length, 7:20.

Notes

A piano melody begins this seven-minute opus and despite the cheers and cries of the crowd, the piano is not drowned out. After about a minute, some recording effects come into play and the song slowly builds up pace. It's a slow song but Bennington sings it with conviction; despite being known for their metal-rap crossovers, they are pretty good at ballads and this is a good example. This is a fine testament to their live skills.

HANDS HELD HIGH

Details: Can be heard on *Road To Revolution: Live At Milton Keynes*; recorded live at Milton Keynes National Bowl in England on 29th June, 2008; length, 1:27.

Notes

This is Mike Shinoda rapping. That's all. But he's pretty good at it.

National Bowl, Milton Keynes

POINTS OF AUTHORITY

Details: Can be heard on the 2001 'Papercut' single; recorded live on BBC Radio One; length, 3:25.

Notes

An enjoyable version of the song that is not quite as frantic as something they'd perform in an arena or on stage.

A PLACE FOR MY HEAD

Details: Can be heard on the 2001 single 'In The End' (CD single two); recorded live at the London Docklands Arena; length, 3:12.

Notes

Before Linkin Park progressed to outdoor venues like Milton Keynes Bowl they used to play medium sized arenas like the London Docklands. The crowd are pretty manic showing that they have a strong UK fanbase.

LYING FROM YOU

Details: Can be heard on the 2003 single 'Faint' (CD single one); recorded live during the 2003 Linkin Park Underground Tour; length, 3:03.

Notes

The band is really on fire throughout this three minute track recorded in the States. When they're playing to home-grown fans on a head-lining tour of their own they're practically unbeatable.

FAINT

Details: Can be heard on the 2007 single 'What I've Done' (CD single one); recorded live in Japan; length, 2:45.

Notes

The Japanese fans love Western metal bands and listening to this version of 'Faint' you can tell such enthusiasm for the music invigorates Linkin Park. They play with precision and passion.

If you want to go further into the archives the following live tracks are certainly worth checking out:

'Papercut'

Recorded live at BBC Radio One. *(Available on the 2001 CD single 'Crawling').*

'Papercut'

Recorded live at London's Docklands Arena. *(Available on the 2001 CD single 'Papercut').*

'In The End'

Recorded live at BBC Radio One. *(Available on the 2001 CD single 'In The End', CD single one).*

'Points Of Authority'
Recorded live at London's Docklands Arena. *(Available on the 2001 CD single 'In The End', CD single one).*

'Step Up'
Recorded live during the 2002 Projekt Revolution Tour. *(Available on the 2003 CD single 'Somewhere I Belong').*

'My December'
Recorded live during the 2002 Projekt Revolution Tour. *(Available on the 2003 CD single 'Somewhere I Belong').*

'One Step Closer'
Recorded live during the 2003 Linkin Park Underground Tour. *(Available on the 2003 CD single 'Faint', CD single two).*

'Crawling'
Recorded live at the 2003 Reading Festival in the UK. *(Available on the 2004 CD single 'Breaking The Habit').*

'From The Inside'
Recorded live in Japan. *(Available on the 2007 CD single 'What I've Done', CD single two).*

'Bleed It Out'
Recorded live at Holmdel, New Jersey on 29th August during the 2007 Projekt Revolution Tour. *(Available on the 2007 CD single 'Shadow Of The Day').*

BOOTLEGS –
THE UNOFFICIAL LINKIN
PARK RECORDINGS

Anybody can make a bootleg: all you have to do is take a recording device into a gig, record the gig, make multiple copies and sell them to whoever wants to buy one. Some bootlegs are so good the artists themselves have gotten involved and released them professionally; or at the

other end of the spectrum, they've brought in their legal team to cease production, which only has varying degrees of success. Bootlegs can also be made from demo recordings or archival material. It's an infamously profitable underworld of the

music business – not to mention highly illegal.
However, to combat the illegal recording of and trading in bootlegs some bands, including Linkin Park and Pearl Jam, have made it possible for fans to purchase gig recordings via an MP3 link on their website seven

days after each gig. The correct name is "Digital Souvenir Package" but it has also been referred to as "instant bootlegging". Linkin Park first made this happen on their 2008 North American tour. They preferred fans to buy high quality recordings via official sources than dreadful recordings made via mobile phones.
Speaking during a conference call with journalists, and reported on the news site blabbermouth. com, Mike Shinoda stated:

"The best part about it, to me, is that our live mixer, our official mixer who mixes our show every night, you know, finishes his night with us, then goes back to his hotel or bus or backstage and mixes the show for you... It's intended to be played, you know, in your headphones and in your car, and it's done by our official guy."

Chester Bennington said:

"For those who get this thing, you know, our sets change, we play songs maybe one night that we don't play the next, and so if you want to get those songs, you know, we encourage our fans to go on and trade them and kind of get to know each other and communicate and share and exchange things with each other, *and this is one of those things that we would really like our fans to kind of do that with..."*

There are too many Linkin Park bootlegs to name here. But here's a small(ish) list, spanning most of their career to date:

LIVE IN ORLANDO *(2000)*
Track Listing: 'Papercut' / 'Forgotten' / 'Points Of Authority' / 'With You' / 'Runaway' / 'And One' / 'In The End' / 'A Place For My Head' / 'One Step Closer'

LIVE IN HOLLYWOOD, CALIFORNIA *(2000)*
Track Listing: 'A Place For My Head' / 'Forgotten' / 'Papercut' / 'By Myself' / 'Points Of Authority' / 'In The End' / 'With You' / 'Runaway' / 'One Step Closer'

KROQ ALMOST ACOUSTIC CHRISTMAS *(2000)*
Track Listing: 'My December' / 'A Place For My Head' / 'Papercut' / 'Points Of Authority' / 'In The End' / 'With You' / 'Runaway' / 'One Step Closer'

LIVE AT THE ROSELAND BALLROOM, NEW YORK *(2000)*
Track Listing: 'A Place For My Head' / 'Forgotten' / 'Papercut' / 'By Myself' / 'In The End' / 'With You' / 'One Step Closer'

LONDON – END SESSIONS *(2001)*
Track Listing: 'Intro'/ 'A Place For My Head' / 'Forgotten' / 'Papercut' / 'By Myself' / 'Points Of Authority' / 'And One' / 'In The End' / 'With You' / 'Runaway' / 'Talking' / 'One Step Closer'

SEATTLE – END SESSIONS *(2001)*
Track Listing: 'Intro' / 'Crawling' / 'Papercut' / 'Points Of Authority' / 'In The End' / 'One Step Closer'

LIVE AT THE ROSELAND BALLROOM, NEW YORK *(2001)*
Track Listing: 'With You' / 'Runaway' / 'Papercut' / 'By Myself' / 'Points Of Authority' / 'High Voltage' *(Remix)* / 'Crawling' / 'Pushing Me Away' / 'And One' / 'In The End' / 'A Place For My Head' / 'Forgotten' / 'One Step Closer'

LIVE AT THE DRAGON FESTIVAL, CALIFORNIA *(2001)*
Track Listing: 'Intro' / 'With You' / 'Runaway' / 'Papercut' / 'By Myself' / 'Points Of Authority' / 'High Voltage' / 'Crawling' / 'Pushing Me Away' / 'And One' / 'In The End' / 'A Place For My Head' / 'Forgotten' / 'One Step Closer'

LIVE IN LAS VEGAS *(2001)*
Track Listing: 'With You' / 'Runaway' / 'Papercut' / 'By Myself' / 'Points Of Authority' / 'High Voltage' / 'Crawling' / 'Pushing Me Away' / 'And One' / 'In The End' / 'A Place For My Head' / 'Forgotten' / 'One Step Closer'

LIVE AT ROCK AM RING, GERMANY *(2001)*
Track Listing: 'Intro' / 'With You' / 'Runaway' / 'Papercut' / 'By Myself' / 'Points Of Authority' / 'High Voltage' / 'Crawling' / 'Pushing Me Away' / 'And One' / 'In The End' / 'A Place For My Head' / 'Forgotten' *(Guns N' Roses parody)* / 'One Step Closer'

LIVE AT OZZFEST, CHICAGO *(2001)*
Track Listing: 'A Place For My Head' / 'Forgotten' / 'Papercut' / 'Points Of Authority' / 'By Myself' / 'In The End' / 'Crawling' / 'With You' / 'Runaway' / 'One Step Closer'

LIVE AT THE MANCHESTER APOLLO, ENGLAND *(2001)*
Track Listing: 'Intro' / 'With You' / 'Runaway' / 'Papercut' / 'By Myself' / 'Points Of Authority' / 'Crawling' / 'In The End' / 'Λ Place For My Head' / 'Forgotten' / 'One Step Closer'

LIVE IN NEW YORK – PROJEKT REVOLUTION TOUR (2002)
Track Listing: 'With You' / 'Runaway' / 'Papercut' / 'Points Of Authority' / 'Step Up' / 'Pushing Me Away' / 'In The End' / 'A Place For My Head' / 'Forgotten' / 'It's Goin' Down' / 'Crawling' / 'My December' / 'By Myself' / 'My Own Summer' *(Deftones cover)* / 'One Step Closer'

WALMART SOUNDCHECK (2007)
Track Listing: 'Breaking The Habit' / 'In The End' / 'No More Sorrow' / 'What I've Done' / 'Pushing Me Away' *(Piano)* / Interview

SPLITTING THE DNA (2007)
Track Listing: 'Technique' / 'High Voltage' / 'Step Up' / 'Carousel' / 'And One' / 'Part Of Me' / 'Esaul' *(Demo)* / 'Superxero' *(Demo)* / 'Points Of Authority' *(Demo)* / 'With You' *(Demo)* / 'Papercut' *(Live)* / 'Forgotten' *(Live)* / 'Points Of Authority' *(Live)* / 'With You' *(Live)* / 'Runaway' *(Demo)* / 'And One' *(Live)* / 'In The End' *(Live)* / 'A Place For My Head' *(Live)*

LINKIN PARK: BEST OF *(2008)*
Track Listing: 'Pushing Me Away' / 'Faint' *(Live In Texas)*

/ 'Somewhere I Belong' / 'One Step Closer' / 'Crawling' *(Hyper Remix)* / 'Easier To Run' / 'More Sky' / 'Vertical Limit' / 'B12' / 'Starting To Fly' / 'Spin' / 'By Myself' / 'Papercut' / 'From The Inside' / 'It's Going Down' / 'In The End' / 'With You' *(Reanimation)* / 'Crawling' / 'A Place For My Head' / 'Anything, Anything' / 'Lying From You' / 'My December' / 'Numb' / 'With You' / 'Drag' / 'Don't Say'/ ' Numb' *(Live In Texas)*

METEORA LIVE *(2008)*
Track Listing: 'Foreword' / 'Don't Say' / 'Somewhere I Belong' / 'Lying From You' / 'Hit The Floor' / 'Easier To Run' / 'Faint' / 'Faint.09' / 'Breaking The Habit' / 'From The Inside' / 'Nobody's Listening' / 'Session' / 'Numb'

LIVE IN ROCK LISBOA *(2008)*
Track Listing: 'What I've Done' / 'Faint' / 'No More Sorrow' / 'Wake 2.0' / 'Given Up' / 'Lying From You' / 'Don't Say' / 'In Pieces' / 'Somewhere I Belong' / 'Points Of Authority' / 'Leave Out All The Rest' / 'Numb' / 'Shadow Of The Day' / 'Valentines Day' / 'Crawling' / 'In The End' / 'Bleed It Out' / 'Pushing Me Away' / 'Breaking The Habit' / 'A Place For My Head' / 'One Step Closer'

PAYING HOMAGE - LINKIN PARK TRIBUTE BANDS

For those wannabe rock stars who missed the boat on fame and fortune, one good way of earning a decent living (if you're good at it) is on the tribute band circuit. The most famous such acts tend to be ones paying tribute to bands no longer in existence (The Beatles, Queen, and the like) or to those bands who are very theatrical and offer a visually exciting show (KISS for example). Believe it or not, however, there are some Linkin Park tribute bands in the world.

PIKNIK PARK *(Hungary)*
Since 2005, Hungary's Piknik Park has covered a reported 25 songs by Linkin Park. They are the only known existing Linkin Park tribute band in Europe. They also write original songs under the moniker AtomorA. Inevitably the

recent success of *Minutes To Midnight* aided the band: 2007 saw them perform at a number of European festivals. In 2009 Piknik Park is: singer Szabi 'Kju' Oláh, bassist Tamas Madácsy, guitarist Balázs Mónos and drummer Zoli Csányi.

The band's website says,

"The world famous Linkin Park mixes the elements of rock, hip-hop and electronic music. Their only European tribute band is the Hungarian Piknik Park.
Three young and talented musicians formed the group in 2005: Gabesz Várkonyi on bass, Balázs Mónos on guitar and Ákos 'Axy' Danyi on drums and asked Zoli Csányi, drummer of several well known Hungarian bands, if he wanted to join in as a singer. Csilla Fehér, Zoli's wife, also pressed him and got involved too as the manager of the band. Zoli soon took the kind offer and the guys were ready to roll.
Since 2005 they covered over 25 songs thus they have enough music for concerts nearing 140 minutes. Piknik Park also has self-written songs, playing them under the name of AtomorA.
2007 and 2008 were successful years for the band. Piknik Park toured all summer, played at Hungarian venues and at sever-

al international festivals. Unfortunately in the beginning of 2008 Gabesz had to quit the band due to a hand injury. Tamas Madácsy (Electric Ocean) joined on bass, and Szabi 'Kju' Oláh (Freshfabrik) as singer and MC."

Their official website is *piknik-park.hu.*

Here's a list of links to other tribute/covers bands performing Linkin Park songs:

Witness a Japanese Linkin Park tribute band with a female lead singer –
vids.myspace.com/index.cfm?fuseaction=vids.individual&VideoID=26797338

Rather oddly, here's a 'virtual' Linkin Park covers band –
uk.youtube.com/watch?v=dhas5W9nE_8

This seven minute video of a Linkin Park tribute band is reasonably entertaining – *uk.youtube.com/watch?v=56Zf-JTQBP8*

This covers band perform a decent version of 'No More Sorrow' – *uk.youtube.com/watch?v=E88y0 C45ryw&feature=related*

This popular video has had thousands of visits. See the kids' Linkin Park covers band with a girl singer – *uk.youtube.com/ watch?v=qBqlsNMZl- A&feature=related*

TRIBUTE ALBUMS (SELECTIVE LIST)

Let's face it, most of what's listed below is pretty odd stuff – a bluegrass tribute album? Tribute albums are mostly hit or miss affairs and there's nothing especially outstanding listed here. Most of these albums are available from online retail sites.

This covers band from Brazil have a go at singing 'What I've Done' – *uk.youtube.com/watch?v=D6JDo AhOs9k&feature=related*

An American High School band covers the ever popular 'What I've Done' – *uk.youtube.com/ watch?v=1IouRS8k- oo&feature=related*

A TRIBUTE TO LINKIN PARK
Year Of Release: 2002
Label: Anagram
Track Listing: 'Crawling' *(Fredco's Demon)* / 'With You' *(Sinister)* / 'High Voltage' *(Razed In Black)* / 'Runaway' *(Dkay.Com Version)* / 'My December' *(Dead Girls Corp)* / 'Papercut' *(Razor)*

/ 'Place For My Head' *(Joolz)* /
'One Step Closer' *(Leather Fire)* /
'In The End' *(Forward To Death)*
/ 'Forgotten' *(Razed In Black)* /
'Pushing Me Away' *(Dictated)* /
'By Myself' *(Fixer)* / 'Points Of
Authority' *(DJ Chiller Vs Big Ed)*

**IN THE CHAMBER
WITH... LINKIN PARK –
THE STRING QUARTET
TRIBUTE**
Year Of Release: 2003
Label: Vitamin
Track Listing: 'One Step Clos-
er' / 'Crawling' / 'In The End' /
'Pushing Me Away' / 'Runaway' /
'Points Of Authority' / 'Cure For
The Itch' / 'Can't Stop What I'm
Hearing Within' / 'Somewhere
I Belong' / 'By Myself'

**GUITAR TRIBUTE
TO LINKIN PARK**
Year Of Release: 2004
Label: Tribute Sounds
Track Listing: 'Crawling' / 'Hit
The Floor' / 'Papercut' / 'With
Me' / 'Easier To Run' / 'Pushing
Me Away' / 'Don't Stay' / 'Some-
where I Belong' / 'Numb' / 'In
The End'

**DUB TRIBUTE
TO LINKIN PARK**
Year Of Release: 2005

Label: Vitamin
Track Listing: 'Somewhere I Belong' / 'One Step Closer' / 'Crawling' / 'Points Of Authority' / 'Hit The Floor' / 'In The End' / 'Papercut' / 'Numb' / 'Place For My Head' / 'Dubble Parked'

ULTIMATE TRIBUTE TO LINKIN PARK

Year Of Release: 2005
Label: Redline
Track Listing: 'Hit The Floor' *(Dark One)* / 'Crawling' *(Fredco's Demon Vision)* / 'Papercut' *(Gothacoustic Ensemble)* / 'With You' *(Dark One)* / 'Somewhere I Belong' *(Gothacoustic Ensemble)* / 'Numb' *(Gothacoustic Ensemble)* / 'Easier To Run' *(Dark One)* / 'In The End' *(Forward To Death Version)* / 'Forgotten' *(Razed In Black Version)* / 'My December' *(Gothacoustic Ensemble)* / 'One Step Closer' *(Gothacoustic Ensemble)* / 'High Voltage' *(Razed In Black Version)* / 'Pushing Me Away' *(Dark One)* / 'Place For My Head' *(Gothacoustic Ensemble)* / 'By Myself' *(Fixer Version)* / 'Don't Stay' *(Dark One)* / 'Runaway' *(Gothacoustic Ensemble)* / 'Points Of Authority' *(DJ Chiller Vs Big Ed)*

BLUEGRASS TRIBUTE TO LINKIN PARK

Year Of Release: 2005
Label: CMH
Track Listing: 'Breaking The Habit' / 'Points Of Authority' / 'Somewhere I Belong' / 'One Step Closer' / 'Easier To Run' / 'Runaway' / 'Don't Stay' / 'Pushing Me Away' / 'Numb' / 'Crawling' / 'In The End'

A GOTHIC ACOUSTIC TRIBUTE TO LINKIN PARK

Year Of Release: 2005
Label: Anagram
Track Listing: 'Somewhere I Belong' / 'Forgotten' / 'High Voltage' / 'My December' / 'One Step Closer' / 'Papercut' / 'Numb' / 'Place For My Head' / 'Pushing Me Away' / 'Runaway' / 'With You' / 'Idiot Music' *(Zeromancer)* / 'Unclean' *(Pitbull Daycare)* / 'Why' *(Razed In Black)*

THE STRING QUARTET TRIBUTE TO LINKIN PARK'S METEORA

Year Of Release: 2006
Label: Vitamin
Track Listing: 'Foreword' / 'Don't Say' / 'Somewhere I Belong' / 'Lying From You' / 'Hit The Floor' / 'Easier To Run' / 'Faint' / 'Figure 09' / 'Breaking The Habit' / 'From The Inside' / 'Nobody's Listening' / 'Session' / 'Numb'

LINKIN PARK UNDERGROUND - FAN CLUB ONLY RELEASES

Since their fan club, Linkin Park Underground, was created in 2001, the band have released an EP every year via their own label Machine Shop Recordings and they are only available to fans.

HYBRID THEORY

Year Of Release: 2001
Track Listing: 'Carousel' / 'Technique' / 'Step Up' / 'And One' / 'High Voltage' / 'Part Of Me'

Trivia

This is a remixed and remastered version of the band's 1999 EP (when they were known as Hybrid Theory). The first 500 copies were signed by each member of the band. The artwork on both offers is slightly different.

LINKIN PARK UNDERGROUND VOL 2.0

Year Of Release: 2002
Track Listing: 'A.06' / 'With You' *(Live)* / 'Pts.OF.Athrty' *(Crystal Method Remix)* / 'Dedicated' *(Demo 1999)* / 'High Voltage' *(Live)* / 'My December'

Trivia
The track 'Dedicated' is a demo that was left-over from the *Hybrid Theory (EP)* sessions. The live tracks were recorded at London Docklands Arena on 16th September, 2001.

LINKIN PARK UNDERGROUND VOL 3.0
Year Of Release: 2003
Track Listing: 'Don't Stay' / 'Figure.09' / 'With You' / 'By Myself' / 'A Place For My Head'

Trivia
This release includes enhanced footage and the video for 'From The Inside.'

LINKIN PARK UNDERGROUND VOL 4.0
Year Of Release: 2004
Track Listing: 'Sold My Soul To Yo Mama' / 'Breaking The Habit' *(Live)* / 'Standing In The Middle' *(Motion Man featuring Mike Shinoda)* / 'Step Up' – 'Nobody's Listening' – 'It's Goin' Down' *(Live)* / 'Wish' *(Live)* / 'One Step Closer' *(Live; featuring Jonathan Davis)*

Trivia
'Wish' is a Nine Inch Nails cover. 'Wish' and 'One Step Closer' were recorded during the Projekt Revolution tour in 2004 and 'Breaking The Habit' was record-

ed at their appearance at the Rock Am Ring festival.

LINKIN PARK UNDERGROUND VOL 5.0
Year Of Release: 2005
Track Listing: 'Somewhere I Belong' / 'Breaking The Habit' / 'Public Service Announcement' *(Intro)* / 'Dirt Off Your Shoulder' – 'Lying From You' / 'Big Pimpin'' – 'Papercut' / 'Jigga What' – 'Faint'

Trivia
All tracks are live and were performed with Jay-Z. They were recorded during the Live 8 Philadelphia benefit event on 2nd July, 2005. The only tracks missing from their complete performance are 'In The End' and 'Numb'/ 'Encore' (which are available on the *Live 8* DVD) and 'Crawling.'

LINKIN PARK UNDERGROUND VOL. 6.0
Year Of Release: 2006
Track Listing: 'Announcement Service Public' / 'QWERTY' / 'QWERTY' *(Live)* / 'Pushing Me Away' [Piano version] *(Live)* / 'Breaking The Habit' *(Live)* / 'Reading My Eyes' *(Live)*

Trivia
The cover for the fan club release was green but copies with a red

cover were also sold during the 2007 Projekt Revolution tour. The live tracks were recorded during the Summer Sonic Festival at the Chiba Marine Stadium in Tokyo, Japan in August 2006.

LINKIN PARK UNDERGROUND VOL. 7.0
Year Of Release: 2007
Track Listing: 'No More Sorrow' [Toronto, ON] / 'What I've Done' [Hartford, CT] / 'One Step Closer' [Syracuse, NY] / 'Given Up' [West Palm Beach, FL] / 'Numb' [The Woodlands, TX] / 'Crawling' [Holmdel, NJ] / 'The Little Things Give You Away' [Atlantia, GA] / 'In The End' [Toronto, ON] / 'Bleed It Out' [Raleigh, NC] / 'Faint' [Holmdel, NJ]

Trivia
All tracks were recorded during the 2007 Projekt Revolution tour. A tour edition of this LPU release was sold at their shows in 2008.

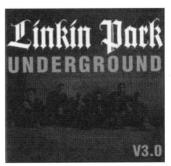

MMM... COOKIES – SWEET HAMSTER LIKE JEWELS FROM AMERICA!
Year Of Release: 2008
Track Listing: 'You Ain't Gotsta Gotsta' / 'Bubbles' / 'No Laundry' / 'Da Bloos' / 'PB n' Jellyfish' / '26 Lettaz In Da Alphabet'

Trivia

Mike Shinoda penned a message to fans on the LPU website regarding this release. He wrote:

"In previous years, we've released LPU CDs that contain B-sides, live tracks, and lesser-known songs from the band. This year, we have decided to do something totally unprecedented and unexpected. The LPU8 CD contains six totally new, original studio songs that Chester and I recorded in our free time in the past couple of years. But these aren't normal Linkin Park songs. Working on a song for an album is sometimes a lot of work, and occasionally we need some time to unwind. When Chester and I unwind, sometimes we make another kind of lighter, fun song. We call these songs 'cookies.' I think this came from the idea that you get your dessert (your cookies) after you eat all the rest of your meal. The songs on the LPU8 CD are random, silly, and they fall into a variety of styles, from a James-Brown-Meets-Bobby-Mc-Ferrin track called 'You Ain't Gotsta Gotsta' to a mock electro-club-banger called '26 Lettaz In Da Alphabet.'"

GUEST APPEARENCES/ FEATURED VOCALS (SELECTIVE LIST)

(NB: What follows is a simple discography. Detailed examinations of guest appearances and featured vocals of members of Linkin Park are in PART 2 under SOLO PROJECTS. The following merely provides a handy chronology of the individual members' output away from the Linkin Park camp.)

BUILT FROM SCRATCH – THE X-ECUTIONERS *(Album)*
Year Of Release: 2001
Label: Loud Records
Track Listing: 'Intro' / 'XL' / 'Xecutioners Scratch' / 'A Journey Into Sound' / 'Hip Hop Awards' *(Skit)* / '3 Boroughs' / 'Let It Bang' / 'Xecutioners Theme Song' / 'Feel The Bass' / 'You Can't Scratch' *(Skit)* / 'It's Goin' Down'* / 'Premier's Execution' / 'Yall Know The Game' / 'Genius Of Love' / 'B-boy Punk Rock 2001' / 'Who Wants To Be A Mutha Fuckin Millionaire' *(Skit)* / 'Play That Beat' / 'Dramacyde' / 'Xecution Of A Bum Rush' / 'Play That Beat Lo Fi'

Notes
*'It's Going' Down' features Linkin Park on guitars and vocals

WE MADE IT – BUSTA RHYMES *(Single)*
Year Of Release: 2008
Label: Flipmode/Interscope/Aftermath
Track Listing: 'We Made It' *(Album Version)* / 'We Made It' *(A Capella Edit)* / 'We Made It' *(Instrumental)* / 'We Made It' *(Video)*

Notes
Features Linkin Park with co-production by Mike Shinoda and Brad Delson with Cool & Dre

CHESTER BENNINGTON

The following details the artists Bennington has collaborated with outside of Linkin Park...

Features on 'Wonderful' by Stone Temple Pilots and 'Push It' by Static-X on the *Family Values Tour 2001* compilation *(2001)*

Features on 'Karma Killer' by Cyclefly on the album *Crave (2002)*

Features on 'System' (written by Jonathan Davis of Korn) on the *Queen Of The Damned* soundtrack *(2002)*

Features on 'State Of The Art' by DJ Lethal of Limp Bizkit *(2004)*

Features on 'Rock N' Roll (Could Never Hip-Hop Like This) Part 2' by Handsome Boy Modelling School on the album *White People (2004)*

Features on 'Walking Dead' by DJ Z-Trip on the album *Shifting Gears (2005)*

Features on a remake of the song 'Home Sweet Home' with Mötley Crüe *(2005)*

Features on 'Slow Ya Roll' by Young Buck on the album *Buck The World (2007)*

Features on a cover of the Nine Inch Nails song 'Head Like A Hole' by Korn *(TBA)*

MIKE SHINODA

The following details the artists Shinoda has collaborated with (as producer) outside of Linkin Park...

'Marco Polo' by Styles Of Beyond; features on the album *2000 Fold* (1998)

'It's Goin' Down' by The X-Ecutioners; features on the album *Built From Scratch* (2002)

'Enjoy The Silence 04' by Depeche Mode (remixed and produced by Shinoda) (2004)

'The Instrumental' by Lupe Fiasco; features on the album *Lupe Fiasco's Food & Liquor (2006)*

'You Cannot Fuck With This' by Styles Of Beyond (featuring Celph Titled); features on the album *Razor Tag* mixtape *(2007)*

'Hard' [MS Remix] by Styles Of Beyond; features on the album *Razor Tag* mixtape *(2007)*

'Second To None' by Styles Of Beyond; features on the album *Reseda Beach (2008)*

'Death To Analog' [Mike Shinoda Remix] by Julien-K *(2009)*

FORT MINOR

STUDIO ALBUMS

THE RISING TIED
Year Of Release: 2005.
Track Listing: 'Introduction' / 'Remember The Name' / 'Right Now' / 'Petrified' / 'Feel Like Home' / 'Where'd You Go' / 'In Stereo' / 'Back Home' / 'Cigarettes' / 'Believe Me'/ 'Get Me

Gone' / 'High Road' / 'Kenji' / 'Red To Black' / 'The Battle' / 'Slip Out The Back'.
Label: Machine Shop/Warner.
Producer(s): Mike Shinoda, Shawn Carter (Jay-Z).
Engineer(s): Mark Kiczula.
Recording Details: NRG Studios in LA. **Songwriter(s):** Mike Shinoda, Joe Hahn, Lonnie Rashid Lynn, R. Maginn, T. Bashir, T. Trotter.
Length: 61:54.

Special Editions: There is a Tour Edition with 'Be Somebody', 'There They Go' and 'The Hard Way' and a Special Edition version with a remix of 'Petrified'.

Reviews
Henry Adaso
about.com
"The Rising Tied doesn't necessarily break any new grounds, but it's loaded with melodies that tug

HIP-HOP & RAP

Hip-hop and rap are controversial styles of music that have become increasingly popular with youths (especially urban/working class) in the past two decades. It was started in the seventies in New York by African-Americans, but since the eighties it has rapidly diversified and now there are many white rappers, the most famous being the iconic Eminem. Some have even claimed that the flamboyant English rock band Queen started the genre with the groovy bass-laden hit single 'Another One Bites The Dust' in 1980, which was remixed by the hip-hop star Wyclef Jean in 1998. Whether that is true or not is certainly debatable, but they did have an impact in bringing the genre to a mass audience. Some rock bands have even collaborated with hip-hop stars (in a genre dubbed rap-rock) and had huge success, the most famous being Aerosmith and Run DMC with 'Walk This Way' (1986) and Anthrax and Public Enemy with 'Bring The Noise' (1991). Like rock and metal music, hip-hop and rap have been criticised by some cultural commentators for negatively impacting on the youth of today because of the lyrical content and the image of the artists. >>

and bang at the same time. Overall, Fort Minor comes across as fluent in the edgy rhetoric of hip-hop."

David Jeffries
allmusic.com
"On The Rising Tied, *Fort Minor* can strike the baller pose a little too hard and sometimes the club-minded tracks shout loud while saying nothing. Softening the blow of these standard rock-dude-doing-rap clichés is the production, with constructions that are like House Of Pain meets the Crystal Method and a whole synthetic orchestra in tow."

OTHER

WE MAJOR (OFFICIAL MIXTAPES)
Year Of Release: 2005.
Track Listing: 'Green Lantern Intro' / '100 Degrees' / 'Dolla' / 'Bloc Party' / 'S.C.O.M.' / 'Remember The Name' *(Funkadelic Remix)* / 'Bleach' *(Jimi Remix)* / 'Spraypaint & Ink Pens' / 'Petrified' *(Doors*

HIP-HOP & RAP

<< What does this have to do with Linkin Park? Linkin Park has successfully merged rap vocals and beats with metal to make a unique style of music. Mike Shinoda is the band's rap vocalist and MC (microphone jockey) and his side-project, Fort Minor, is a hip-hop orientated band. Linkin Park has collaborated with a number of hip-hop/rap artists, most notably on *Reanimation* (which features several hip-hop artists) and *Collision Course* with Jay-Z. The band also collaborated with Busta Rhymes on the 2007 single 'We Made It'. Outside of the Linkin Park camp, Chester Bennington has worked with Young Buck and DJ Lethal, DJ Z-Trip and Handsome Boy Modelling School. Mike Shinoda has worked with Lupe Fiasco, Styles of Beyond and The X-Ecutioners. As the band's turntablist (he scratches the discs), Joe Hahn has also worked with The X-Ecutioners.

Back in 2005 Mike Shinoda shared his views on rap music with *antimusic.com*:

"Hip-hop right now is mostly based on keyboard music. One of my goals of the Fort Minor album was to keep the big sound of a hip-hop album, but make it using live instruments and hand-played keyboard parts. It's an organic hip-hop album. When you hear a tambourine, bass, or guitar, it's played by hand."

Remix) / 'Get It' / 'Be Somebody' / 'Respect 4 Grandma' / 'There They Go' *(Green Lantern Remix)* / 'All Night' / 'Nobody's Listening' *(Green Lantern Remix)* / 'Cover And Duck' / 'Remember The Name' *(Album Version)* / 'Petrified' *(Album Version)* / 'Outro'.
Label: Machine Shop.
(NB: This was available to download for free prior to its official release on CD.)

WE MAJOR EP *(vinyl)*
Year Of Release: 2005.
Track Listing: Side A: 'Spraypaint & Ink Pens' *(Clean)* / 'Spraypaint & Ink Pens' *(Dirty)* / 'Nobody's Listening' *(Green Lantern Remix) (Dirty)* / 'Nobody's Listening' *(Green Lantern Remix) (Clean) Side B:* 'S.C.O.M.' *(Dirty)* / 'S.C.O.M.' *(Clean)* / 'There They Go' *(Green Lantern Remix) (Dirty)* / 'There They Go' *(Green Lantern Remix) (Clean)*.
Label: Machine Shop.

SINGLES

PETRIFIED
Year Of Release: 2005.
Label: Machine Shop/Warner.
Album: The Rising Tied

BELIEVE ME
Year Of Release: 2005.
Label: Machine Shop/Warner.
Album: The Rising Tied

REMEMBER THE NAME
Year Of Release: 2005.
Label: Machine Shop/Warner.
Album: The Rising Tied

WHERE'D YOU GO
Year Of Release: 2006.
Label: Machine Shop/Warner.
Album: The Rising Tied

S.C.O.M./DOLLA
Year Of Release: 2006.
Label: Machine Shop/Warner.
Album: We Major

GET IT/SPRAYPAINT & INK PENS
Year Of Release: 2006.
Label: Machine Shop/Warner.
Album: We Major

MUSIC VIDEOS

PETRIFIED
Year Of Release: 2005.
Album: The Rising Tied.
Director: Robert Hales

REMEMBER THE NAME
Year Of Release: 2005.
Album: The Rising Tied.
Director: Kimo Proudfoot

BELIEVE ME
Year Of Release: 2005.
Album: The Rising Tied.
Director: Laurent Briet

WHERE'D YOU GO
Year Of Release: 2006.

Album: The Rising Tied.
Director: Philip Andelman

COMPILATIONS FEATURING LINKIN PARK (SELECTIVE LIST)

Linkin Park has featured on quite a number of compilations over the years so the author has compiled a selective list only...

MTV'S RETURN OF THE ROCK VOLUME 2
Year Of Release: 2000
Label: Roadrunner
Track Listing: 'Show Me What You Got' [Live] *(Limp Bizkit)* / 'Legacy' *(Papa Roach)* / 'Synthetic' *(Spineshank)* / 'God Of The Mind' *(Disturbed)* / 'Just Got Wicked' *(Cold)* / 'Change' *(In The House Of Flies)* [Acoustic] *(Deftones)* / 'Leader Of Men' *(Nickelback)* / 'One Step Closer' *(Linkin Park)* / 'Waiting To Die' *((hed) p.e.)* / 'Freestyle' [Knock 'Em Out The Box Mix] *(P.O.D.)* / 'Down' *(Fuel)* / 'Mechanical Animals' [Live] *(Marilyn Manson)* / 'Back To The Primitive' *(Soulfly)* / 'Goin' Down' *(Godsmack)* / 'Godless' *(U.P.O.)* / 'Spectrum' *(Orgy)*

THE FAMILY VALUES TOUR 2001
Year Of Release: 2002
Label: Elektra
Track Listing: 'Vasoline' *(Stone Temple Pilots)* / 'Runaway' *(Linkin Park)* / 'Fade' *(Staind)* / 'Wonderful' *(Stone Temple Pilots)* / 'Push It' *(Static-X, featuring Chester Bennington)* / 'It's Been A While' *(Staind)* / 'Wicked Garden' *(Stone Temple Pilots)* / 'Cold' *(Static-X)* / 'Black' *(Aaron Lewis of Staind)* / 'Creep' *(Stone Temple Pilots)* / 'Tom Sawyer' *(Deadsy One Step)* / 'Closer' *(Linkin Park, featuring Aaron Lewis)*

OZZFEST 2001: SECOND MILLENNIUM
Year Of Release: 2002
Label: Epic
Track Listing: 'The Wizard' *(Black Sabbath)* / 'The Love Song' *(Marilyn Manson)* / 'New Abortion' *(Slipknot)* / 'Blood Brothers *(Papa Roach)* / 'With You' *(Linkin Park)* / 'Super Terrorizer' *(Black Label Society)* / 'Fear' *(Disturbed)* / 'Death Blooms' *(Mudvayne)* / 'South Texas Deathride' *(The Union Underground)* / 'Fillthee' *(Otep)* / 'What A Day' *(Nonpoint)* / 'Last Breath' *(Hatebreed)* / 'Deep Colors Bleed' *(Systematic)* / 'Kiss Of Death' *(Pure Rubbish)* / 'Reach And Touch' *(American Head Charge)*

KERRANG! THE ALBUM 2008
Year Of Release: 2008
Label: WMTV
Notes: A two-disc set featuring 42 songs, including Linkin Park's 'Given Up.'

SOUNDTRACKS FEATURING LINKIN PARK (SELECTIVE LIST)

LITTLE NICKY
Year Of Release: 1999
Label: Eastworld
Track Listing: 'School Of Hard Knocks' *(P.O.D.)* / 'Pardon Me' *(Incubus)* / 'Change (In The House Of Flies)' *(Deftones)* / '(Rock) Superstar' *(Cypress Hill)* / 'Natural High' *(Insolence)* / 'Points Of Authority' *(Linkin Park)* / 'Stupify' [Remix] *(Disturbed)* / 'Nothing' *(Ünloco)* / 'When Worlds Collide' *(Powerman 5000)* / 'Cave' *(Muse)* / 'Take My Picture' *(Filter)* / 'Be Quiet And Drive (Far Away)' *(Deftones)*

DRACULA 2000
Year Of Release: 2000
Label: Sony BMG
Track Listing: ''Ultra Mega' *(Powerman 5000)* / 'Welcome Burden' *(Disturbed)* / 'Bloodline' *(Tom Araya)* / 'Metro' *(System Of A Down)* / 'Head Explode' *(Monster Magnet)* / 'Break You Down' *(Godhead & Marilyn Manson)* / 'One Step Closer' *(Linkin Park)* / 'Avoid The Light' *(Pantera)* / 'Ostego Undead' *(Static-X)* / 'Swan Dive' *((hed) p.e.)* / 'Day By Day' *(Taproot)* / 'Malice' *(Endo)* / 'Blind World' *(Flybanger)* / 'Sober' *(Half Cocked)* / 'Your Disease' *(Saliva)*

VALENTINE
Year Of Release: 2001
Label: Warner
Track Listing: 'Superbeast' *(Rob Zombie)* / 'God Of The Mind' *(Disturbed)* / 'Love Dump' *(Static-X)* / 'Pushing Me Away' *(Linkin Park)* / 'RX Queen' *(Deftones)* / 'Opticon' *(Jay Gordon)* / 'Valentine's Day' *(Twiggy Ramirez)* / 'Filthy Mind' *(Amanda Ghost)* / 'Fall Again' *(Roman Marisak)* / 'Smartbomb' *(Brian Transeau)* / 'Son Song' *(Max Cavalera)* / 'Take A Picture' *(Richard Patrick)* / 'Breed' *(Jason Slater)* / '1 A.M.' *(Darrin Jay Ashba)*

MATRIX RELOADED
(Various Artists)
Year Of Release: 2003
Label: WEA
Track Listing: Disc 1: 'Session' *(Linkin Park)* / 'This Is The New Shit' *(Marilyn Manson)* / 'Reload' *(Rob Zombie)* / 'Furious Angels' *(Rob Dougan)* / 'Lucky You' *(Deftones)* / 'The Passportal' *(Team Sleep)* / 'Sleeping Awake' *(P.O.D.)* / 'Bruises' *(Unloco)* / 'Calm Like A Bomb' *(Rage Against The Machine)* / 'Dread Rock' *(Oakenfold)* / 'Zion' *(Fluke)* / 'When The World Ends' *(Dave Matthews)*
Disc 2: 'Main Title' *(Don Davis)* / 'Trinity Dream' *(Don Davis)* / 'Tea House' *(Juno Reactor)* / 'Chateau' *(Rob Dougan)* / 'Mona Lisa Overdrive' *(Juno Reactor)* / 'Burly Braw' *(Don Davis Vs. Juno*

Reactor) / 'Reloaded Suite' *(Don Davis)*

TWILIGHT *(Various Artists)*
Year Of Release: 2008
Label: Atlantic
Track Listing: 'Supermassive Black Hole' *(Muse)* / 'Decode' *(Paramore)* / 'Full Moon' *(The Black Ghosts)* / 'Leave Out All The Rest' *(Linkin Park)* / 'Spotlight' [Twilight Mix] *(MuteMath)* / 'Go All The Way (Into The Twilight)' *(Perry Farrell)* / 'Tremble For My Beloved' *(Collective Soul)* / 'I Caught Myself' *(Paramore)* / 'Eyes On Fire' *(Blue Foundation)* / 'Never Think' *(Rob Pattinson)* / 'Flightless Bird, American Mouth' *(Iron & Wine)* / 'Bella's Lullaby' *(Carter Burwell)*

Linkin Park also allowed their songs to be used in the following films and TV shows:

FILMS

The One
Released in: 2001
Song(s): 'Papercut'

S.W.A.T.
Released in: 2003
Song(s): 'Figure 0.9'

Riding Giants (Documentary)
Released in: 2004

Song(s): 'Don't Say' and 'Cure The Itch'

Rock Bottom (Documentary)
Released in: 2004
Song(s): 'Somewhere I Belong'

The Work Of Director Mark Romanek (Compilation DVD)
Released in: 2005
Song(s): 'Faint'

Miami Vice
Released in: 2006
Song(s): 'Numb/Encore'

TV SHOWS

Roswell
Episode: 'Meet The Dupes'
Aired in: 2000.
Song(s): 'With You'

ER
Episode: 'On The Beach'
Aired in: 2002
Song(s): 'One Step Closer'

The Sopranos
Episode: 'In Camelot'
Aired in: 2004
Song(s): 'In Session'

CSI: Crime Scene Investigators
Episode: 'Leave Out All The Rest'
Aired in: 2008
Song(s): 'Leave Out All The Rest'

CHAPTER 12

THE LIVE CAREER OF LINKIN PARK

THE GIGS & TOURS

The following section is a list of gigs and tours Linkin Park have played since the release of their first album in 2000. Not every single concert (including festivals and charity gigs) is listed; such an endeavour would fill half this book, no doubt, but most, if not all of the major tours/gigs, are mentioned below.

HEADLINING TOURS

Aside from all the festivals the band play on a regular basis and as well as their hugely successful Projekt Revolution tour, Linkin Park have played sporadic headlining tours since the release of Hybrid Theory *in 2001. The author has listed them in chronological order, with several batches of tour dates.*

2000

Linkin Park didn't actually begin headlining tours until the release of *Hybrid Theory* in 2001, but it is interesting to look at the preceding tour dates just to see how the band's audiences grew over the years.

US TOUR DATES

24th July, Orlando, FL (The Sapphire); 15th August, Phoenix, AZ (Mason Jar, 98KUPD Show); 20th September, New York City, NY (Roseland Ballroom, KROCK Low Dough Show); 1st October, Atlanta, GA (Hi-Fi Buys Amphitheatre, 99X's 'Big Day Out'); 3rd October, Des Moines, IA (Super Toad Entertainment Centre, Kottonmouth Kings Riding High tour); 11th October, Springfield, MO, Juke Joint (Kottonmouth Kings Riding High tour); 31st October, Hollywood, CA, The Palace (Kottonmouth Kings Riding High tour); 10th November, New York City, NY (Roseland Ballroom, P.O.D's The King Of Game tour); 11th November, Westminster, CA (Best Buy Parking Lot, KROQ Jocks Signing Calendars); 28th November, Toronto, ON (Legendary Horseshoe Tavern); 30th November, Providence, RI (Lupo's Heartbreak Hotel, WBRU Radio Show) and 17th December, Universal City, CA (Universal Amphitheatre, KROQ Almost Acoustic X-Mas.)

2001-2002

Linkin Park's debut headlining tour, dubbed (*Street Soldier's Tour*), took place in the States in 2001 in support of *Hybrid Theory*. The tour began on 26th January in Seattle and went through at least 20 US cities. In a press statement published on the Internet and made available on *linkinpark.com*, Mike Shinoda said:

"...we're really looking forward to the headline tour because it will give us a chance to play some new material we haven't played yet."

US TOUR DATES
26th January, Seattle (Showbox); 27th January, Portland, Oregon (Roseland); 29th January, Sacramento, California (Crest Theatre); 30th January, San Francisco (Fillmore); 1st February, San Diego (Cane's); 2nd February, Las Vegas (House Of Blues); 3rd February, San Bernardino, California (Dragon Festival); 5th February, Salt Lake City, Utah (Salt Air Pavilion); 6th February, Denver (Gothic Theatre); 8th February, Minneapolis (Quest); 9th February, Lawrence, Kansas. (Liberty Hall); 10th February, St. Louis (Pop's); 11th February, Chicago (House Of Blues); 13th February, Columbus, Ohio (Newport Music Hall); 14th February, Detroit (Clutch's Cargo); 15th February, Pittsburgh (Club Laga); 21st February, New York (Irving Plaza); 22nd February, Washington, D.C. (9:30 Club); 23rd February, Philadelphia (Electric Factory) and 24th February, Providence, R.I. (Lupo's.)

SET-LIST
(House Of Blues, Las Vegas, 2nd February, 2001)
'With You' / 'Runaway' / 'Papercut' / 'By Myself' / 'Points Of Authority' / 'High Voltage' / 'Crawling' / 'Pushing Me Away' / 'And One' / 'In The End' / 'A Place For My Head' / 'Forgotten' / 'One Step Closer'

After a support slot on the Deftones European tour (in March) as well as some festival shows and special performances, they played a series of headlining dates in and outside of America as part of a road jaunt called *US To Europe*, which lasted several weeks and included some non-US and European dates.

US & EAST ASIA TOUR DATES
16th April, Los Angeles, CA (Hollywood Palladium); 17th April, Mesa, AZ Mesa (Amphitheatre);

Hollywood Palladium

20th April, Boston, MA (Roxy); 22nd April, Spring, TX (CWM Pavilion); 27th April, Miami, FL (Bayfront Park Amphitheatre); 28th April, Zephyr Hills, FL (Festival Park); 2nd May, Newtown, Australia (Enmore Theatre); 4th May, West Melbourne, Australia (Festival Hall); 5th May, Brisbane, Australia (Festival Hall); 8th May, Auckland, New Zealand (Town Hall); 14th May, Tokyo, Japan (Zepp); 15th May, Osaka, Japan (IMP Hall); 16th May, Nagoya, Japan (Diamond Ballroom); 30th May, Copenhagen, Denmark (Pumphuset) and 4th June, Brixton, London (Brixton Academy.)

SET-LIST
(Enmore Theatre, Newtown, Australia, 2nd May, 2001)
'With You' / 'Runaway' / 'Pushing Me Away' / 'Crawling' / 'By Myself' / 'High Voltage' / 'Papercut' / 'And One' / 'Forgotten' / 'In The End' / 'Points Of Authority' / 'A Place For My Head' / 'One Step Closer'

After some festival performances, the band played on the Ozzfest tour in the summer before a major headlining tour of Europe (dates as follows):

EUROPEAN/UK TOUR DATES
11th September, Hamburg, Germany (Grosse Freiheit); 12th September, Berlin, Germany (Columbia Halle); 15th September, Manchester, UK (Apollo Theatre); 16th September, London, UK (Docklands Arena); 18th September, Paris, France (L'Elysee Montmarte); 20th September, Vienna, Austria (Libro Music Hall); 21st September, Munich, Germany (Zenith) and 23rd September, Koln, Germany (Palladium).

SET-LIST
(L'Elysee Montmarte, Paris, France, 18th September, 2001)
'With You' / 'Runaway' / 'Papercut' / 'Points Of Authority' / 'Step Up' / 'Pushing Me Away' / 'And One' / 'In

Family Values tour

The End' / 'A Place For My Head' / 'Forgotten' / 'Crawling' / 'My December' / 'By Myself' / 'Sweet Child O' Mine' / 'One Step Closer'

They played on the *Family Values* tour from October through to November and then finished off the year with a headlining tour of the States (*Countdown To Revolution*) featuring, (hed)pe, DJ Ztrip and The X-Ecutioners.

US TOUR DATES

27th November, Kansas City, MO (Hale Arena); 28th November, St. Louis, MO (Family Arena); 29th November, Grand Rapids, MI (DeltaPlex); 30th November, Cedar Rapids, IA (US Cel-
lular); 1st December, Lincoln, NE (Pershing Auditorium); 3rd December, West Valley City, UT (E-Centre); 5th December, Spoakane, WA (Spokane Convention Centre); 6th December, Seattle, WA (Paramount Theatre); 7th December, San Francisco, CA and 8th – 9th December Los Angeles, CA (Universal Amphitheatre.)

(NB: The last four dates on the tour were special performances for various State radio stations, so not strictly part of the tour.)

In 2001 they toured 325 out of the 365 days of the year. And then they committed themselves to the first ever Projekt Revolution tour in the States, before a headlining jaunt around Europe, beginning in March 2002 with shows in the usual hotspots: UK, Germany, France, Holland and Austria. Mike Shinoda told *onstagemag.com*:

"We all have a lot of pent-up aggression from the past few months, and we're planning to let it out. This upcoming tour includes some of the biggest venues we have played. We practically sold out London [Docklands] arena without announcing an opener, which is a first for us."

2003-2004

To promote their second studio opus *Meteora*, Linkin Park played a European tour (beginning late February) with low-key dates in the UK and France, amongst others. The UK performances were held in London, Nottingham and Manchester.

Writing in *The Guardian*, Adam Sweeting said of the Brixton Academy show on 5th March:

"The band deliver their bludgeoning metal barrage with digitally enhanced expertise, Brad Delson's guitar roaring out of the mix like a multi-vehicle pile-up over booming drums and bass notes that make the floor wobble."

A 10 date headlining tour was then planned for America which allowed fan club members free admission and some fans were given a chance to attend meet and greets (basically a chance to meet the band backstage before a show). Fans in Europe had also been given this opportunity, hence the name of the tour: *LP Underground Tour*.

At the time, it was estimated that there was at least 25,000 members of the Linkin Park Underground. The tour started on 11th March and finished on 25th March in Los Angeles.

In a press statement made available on *linkinpark.com* as well as on various other websites Rob Bourdon said:

"Since before we were even signed, we took an active roll in communicating with our fans... And the purpose of the LP Underground is to maintain that relationship with them as we grow as a band. Our fans are the reason we can continue to play our music."

EUROPEAN/US TOUR DATES
23rd February, Milan, Italy (Alcatraz); 27th February, Hamburg, Germany (The Docks); 2nd March, Paris, France (L'elysee Montmarte); 3rd March, Nottingham, England (Rock City); 5th March, London, England (Brixton Academy); 7th March, Manchester, England (Apollo The-

Brixton Academy

Reading Festival

atre); 11th March, Worcester, MA (Palladium); 12th March, New York City, NY (Roseland Ballroom); 14th March, Chicago, IL (Riviera Theatre); 15th March, Minniapolis, MN (Quest Club); 17th March, Detroit, MI (State Theatre); 18th March, St. Louis, MO (The Pageant); 20th March, Dallas, TX (Bronco Bowl); 23rd March, San Francisco, CA (Warfield Theatre); 24th March, Los Angeles, CA (Wiltern Theatre) and 25th March, Los Angeles, CA (Wiltern Theatre.)

In April, they headlined another Projekt Revolution tour before joining Metallica on the Summer Sanitarium tour of North America.

Later on in the year, Chester Bennington was taken to hospital with severe back pains and spasms, which forced the band to cancel some of their headlining European dates. A press statement on the band's behalf was published on the Internet and stated:

"All touring and video shoot plans in Europe have been put on hold this month as we make sure Chester fully recovers... We wish him the best, and will keep everyone posted as to his condition."

Linkin Park carried on playing shows to the end of 2003, which included a tour of Australia and Asia.

AUSTRALIAN/ASIAN TOUR DATES

11th October, Sydney, Australia (Moore Park); 12th October, Melbourne, Australia (Melbourne Park); 15th October, Kuala Lumpur, Malasia (Stadium Merdeka); 18th October, Brisbane, Australia (RNA Showgrounds); 21st October, Yokohama, Japan

(Yokohama Arena); 22nd October, Osaka, Japan (Osaka Castle Hall); 24th October, Tokyo, Japan (Nippon Budokan); 25th October, Tokyo, Japan (Nippon Budokan); 27th October, Tokyo, Japan (Nippon Budokan) and 29th October, Seoul, Korea (Olympic Gymnastic Gymnasium.)

They returned to the UK in November for what was their biggest UK tour up to that point. No doubt the success of their headlining performances at the Leeds and Reading festivals gave them a much larger fanbase, hence the size of the venues compared to previous UK shows.

UK TOUR DATES
20th November, Glasgow (SECC); 21st November, Manchester (M.E.N. Arena); 22nd November, London (Wembley Arena); 24th November, Birmingham (NIA) and 25th November, Cardiff (Cardiff Arena.)

They played a handful of radio sponsored Christmas festivals between 7th December and 13th December.

However, in 2004 Linkin Park commenced a complete full scale headlining tour (in support of *Meteora*) of North America dubbed *Meteora World Tour*. The US jaunt commenced on 16th January in Washington DC. They were on the road for a full three months and were supported by P.O.D., Hoobastank and Story Of The Year.

They played shows in the following cities: Washington, DC; Worcester, MA; New York, NY; Philadelphia, PA; Cleveland, OH; Montreal, QC; Toronto, ON; Columbus, OH; Detroit, MI; Chicago, IL; Madison, WI; St. Paul, MN; Colorado Springs, CO; Los Angeles, CA; Salt Lake City, UT; Vancouver, BC; Portland, OR; Tacoma, WA; San Jose, CA; San Diego, CA; Sacramento, CA; Las Vegas, NV; Oklahoma City; Dallas, YX; San Antonio, TX; Houston, TX; Little Rock, AR; Greensboro, NC; Atlan-

Wembley Arena

Sonny Sandoval

Speaking to *billboard.com*, Mike Shinoda said:

"We're playing an all-new set and we've added some songs that people haven't heard us play live before and some songs we haven't played live in a long time... So, even though I know a lot of our fans are going to check out Live In Texas, *the set that we will be playing in January and February is longer, has more songs and it has a lot of stuff that people haven't heard."*

ta, GA; Jacksonville, FL; Tampa/ St. Petersburg, FL; and Ft. Lauderdale, FL. Extra dates were added due to high demand.

Speaking about the tour, Dave Farrell told *livedaily.com*:

"Actually, P.O.D. was a band that we toured with quite a long time ago – in early 2000 – before our first record, Hybrid Theory, *even came out... Hoobastank, a couple of the guys in our group actually went to school up in the valley of LA... Story Of The Year is a band that we heard their record, and really liked what they were doing, researched them a little bit and figured they would be a great addition to the tour. It's a great record."*

P.O.D. mainman Sonny Sandoval told *Rolling Stone*:

"We always connected with those guys more on the human side of things rather than music... We know they're good people, and they know we're good people. It's important to tour with bands that you get along with."

They finished the US leg of the world tour with a 90 minute set at the Great Western Forum in LA on 15th March, which was actually postponed from a previous date. Songs played included 'From The Inside,' 'Numb,' 'Somewhere I Belong,' 'Lying From You,' 'Faint,' 'Crawling,' 'In The End' and 'One Step Closer.'

After playing to audiences in North America they travelled to Europe and other parts of the world. The *Meteora World Tour* finished in Brazil on 11th September, 2004; in total they played 150 gigs across five continents. In between those haphazard dates they also managed to play another Projekt Revolution tour, between July and August.

2007-2008

Up to and after the release of *Minutes To Midnight* in 2007, Linkin Park played a bunch of headlining dates and festivals around the world as well as the Projekt Revolution tour. The headlining solo

tour included a sold out show at the small Astoria venue in central London and they were special guests at a Pearl Jam gig on 13th June in Chorzow, Poland at the Stadion Slaski.

The headlining dates were:

28th April, Berlin, Germany (Kesselhaus); 3rd May, London, UK (Astoria);
24th May, Copenhagen, Denmark (Forum); 27th May, Hamburg, Germany (Colorline Arena); 30th May, Paris, France (Bercy); 5th June, St. Petersburg, Russia (New Arena); 11th June, Zurich, Switzerland (Hallenstadion); 12th June, Prague, Czech Republic (Sazka Arena)

Some of the shows were supported by the Swedish band Blindside. These were in Denmark, Sweden and Germany. On their website *myspace.com/blindside* they said:

"We heard that Linkin Park were doing a European tour and thought it'd be a nice time to catch up with them. They were kind enough to offer us three dates in Northern Europe."

In November, the band embarked on a successful headlining tour of Asia.

Hannover, Germany

ASIAN TOUR DATES

11th November, Bangkok, Thailand (Aktive Square); 13th November, Singapore, Singapore (Singapore Indoor Stadium); 16th November, Taipei, Taiwan (Taipei County Stadium); 18th November, Shanghai, China (Hong Kou Stadium); 20th November, Hong Kong, Hong Kong (Asia-World Arena); 23rd November, Saitama-Shi, Japan (Saitama Super Arena Chou-ku); 24th November, Saitama-Shi, Japan (Saitama Super Arena Chou-ku); 26th November, Nagoya, Japan (Nippon Gaisha Hall/Rainbow Hall) and 27th November, Osaka, Japan (Prefectural Gymnasium Naniwa.)

Fast forward to early 2008 and the band hit the road in Europe and the UK.

EUROPEAN TOUR DATES

16th January, Hannover, Germany (TUI Arena); 17th January, Amnéville, France (Galaxie); 18th January, Basel, Switzerland (St. Jakobshalle); 20th January, Frankfurt, Germany (Festhalle); 21st January, Köln, Germany (Kölnarena) and 22nd January, Paris, France (Bercy.)

On 24th January they played a packed show at the Nottingham Arena, the first night of their UK tour. Supported by Julien-K, the UK tour was totally sold out:

UK TOUR DATES

24th January - Nottingham Arena; 25th January - Sheffield Arena; 27th January - Manchester MEN Arena ; 28th- 29th January - London O2 Arena

The UK tour sold out within hours, so quickly that a second date was added at London's massive 22,000 capacity O2 Arena. Brad Delson told *nme.com*:

"The recent news of our show at the O2 selling out almost immediately is kind of emotional for us because we've been able to play big shows around the world...
I really do love London in particular, when the weather's nice – we're spoilt because I live in Los Angeles. I love the culture, and we had a lot of support very early on from the UK..."

Reviewing the show at the MEN, one journalist wrote in Manchester's *City Life*:

"There's a close connection between Linkin Park and their fans, with plenty of in-between song banter from Chester and his rapping co-pilot Mike Shinoda. This is definitely one of their greatest strengths."

In November 2007, the band announced ticket sales for the first two US shows of their 2008 North American tour: Joe Louis Arena in Detroit, MI on 16th February and Verizon Wireless Arena in Manchester, NH on 18th February. Indeed on 12th February, 2008, the North American leg of the tour began at the Qwest Center in Omaha Nebraska and finished in early March. The road jaunt rolled through 14 cities and was supported by progressive metal band Coheed and Cambria and the Michigan band Chiodos.

Prior to the tour, Coheed and Cambria guitarist Travis Stever told the American online newspaper *The Gateway* (*unogateway.com*):

"It's going to be exciting. We're really interested to see how things will work. They've [Linkin Park] been around just as long as we have and what I've heard of their new stuff, I like. They have also experienced changing things up like we have. It will be interesting to be on this bill with three different bands."

US TOUR DATES

12th February, Omaha, NE (Qwest Centre); 13th February, St. Paul, MN (Xcel Energy Centre); 15th February, Columbus, OH (Na-

tionwide Arena); 16ᵗʰ February, Detroit (Joe Louis Arena); 18ᵗʰ February, Manchester, NH (Verizon Wireless Arena); 19ᵗʰ February, Baltimore (1st Mariner Arena); 21ˢᵗ February, New York (Madison Square Garden); 22ⁿᵈ February, Montreal (Bell Centre); 23ʳᵈ February, London, Ontario (LaBatt Centre); 25ᵗʰ February, Lexington, KY (Rupp Arena); 26ᵗʰ February, Nashville (Sommet Centre); 29ᵗʰ February, Oklahoma City (Ford Centre); 1ˢᵗ March, Albuquerque, NM (Tingley Coliseum); 2ⁿᵈ March, El Paso, TX (Don Haskins Centre) and 8ᵗʰ March, West Valley, UT (E Centre.)

However, the band had to cancel two shows (Tingley Coliseum in Albuquerque, NM on 1ˢᵗ March and Don Haskins Center in El Paso, TX on 3ʳᵈ March) after Chester Bennington was diagnosed with tracheobronchitis.

They also managed to squeeze in a couple of other dates in Europe as well as the festivals and Projekt Revolution tour of the States and Europe:

17ᵗʰ June, Brno, Czech Republic (Velodrom); 22ⁿᵈ June, Dublin, Ireland (RDS Arena)

SELECTIVE LIST OF SUPPORT BANDS

The following list shows the eclectic range of bands Linkin Park have taken on the road with them outside of the festival circuit. It's basically a mix of rap and rock/metal bands, thus appealing to many Linkin Park fans. The author has listed them in alphabetical order.

Ashes Divide *(2008)*

Atreyu *(2008)*

Biffy Clyro *(2008)*

Chiodos *(2008)*

Chris Cornell *(2007)*

Coheed and Cambria *(2008)*

(hed)pe *(2001)*

DJ Ztrip *(2001)*

HIM *(2007)*

Hoobastank *(2004)*

Julien-K *(2008)*

P.O.D. *(2004)*

Xecutioners *(2001)*

Story Of The Year *(2004)*

Taproot *(2001)*

Too Phat *(2003)*

FESTIVALS
(SELECTIVE LIST)

Like most major (and not so major) bands, Linkin Park have played most of the big global festivals. Here is a list of many of those festivals. They have also played touring festivals in the States and Europe, and of course, have headlined their ownversionl, Projekt Revolution. The author has listed them in alphabetical order.

ALIVE FESTIVAL

Linkin Park performed at the 2007 Alive Festival in Libson, Portugal, which was held on 8th, 9th and 10th June. Other acts included Beastie Boys, The Smashing Pumpkins, The White Strips and over 20 others. Linkin Park performed on the 8th.

BAMBOOZLE FESTIVAL

Bamboozle is an annual alternative rock festival that takes place on the parking lot of the Giants Stadium in East Rutherford, New Jersey. It began in 2003. Linkin Park headlined the 2007 Bamboozle festival with My Chemical Romance. It was held on 5th and 6th May (Linkin Park played on the second day) and other acts on the bill included Taking Back Sunday and Hawthorne Heights.

DOWNLOAD FESTIVAL

Download is seen as a successor to the hugely successful Monsters Of Rock which was held (almost annually) at Donnington Park, England between 1980 and 1996. Download was first held in 2003 and has taken place every year since. Donnington Park is a huge outdoor space in Leicestershire.

Linkin Park headlined the Main Stage on the first of two days (4th and 5th June, 2004). The other bands on the bill were: Sum 41, The Stooges, The Hives, The Distillers, Cradle Of Filth, Monsters Magnet, Opeth and Dillinger Escape Plan. The second day was headlined by Metallica and also featured Korn, Slipknot, Slayer, Machine Head, Damage Plan, Soulfly, Ill Nino, Turbonegro and Breed 77.

In 2004, for the first time Download was also held at another venue as well as Donnington and was arranged for the Glasgow Green, Scotland on 2nd and 3rd June: Metallica headlined the first day and Linkin Park the second day's bill. Bands that played in Glasgow included Slipknot, Lost Prophets, Korn, Iggy Pop, The Distillers and Machine Head.

On Saturday, 9th June 2007, Linkin Park headlined the second day of the three day Download festival, which also featured

Download Festival

Marilyn Manson, Slayer, Machine Head, Bowling For Soup, 30 Seconds To Mars, Aiden, Shadows Fall, HELLYEAH and Turisas. My Chemical Romance headlined the first day with Iron Maiden on the top spot for the final night.

DRAGON FESTIVAL

Linkin Park headlined California's Dragon Festival at the New Orange Shows Event Center on 3rd February, 2001. The hip-hop and metal focused festival featured GZA, Kottonmouth Kings, Taproot, Blackalicious, Shuvel and Ugly Duckling among others.

EDGEFEST

Originally created in 1987 to celebrate 10 years of 102.1 FM the Edge Toronto, Edgefest ran for the next 20 years, and in 2006 celebrated its 20th anniversary – albeit prematurely. In 2007, organisers forced the event to take a break but it returned in 2008 with Linkin Park and Stone Temple Pilots as headliners at Downsview Park on 12th July. Sam Roberts Band, The Bravery, Ashes Divide and Attack in Black also took part in the event.

FAMILY VALUES TOUR

This American touring festival is one that appeals to nu-metal fans only. It was the brainchild of the band Korn with the idea being to promote rock and rap/hip-hop bands. Because of hard competition from other touring festivals, whether metal-orientated ones like Ozzfest or similarly themed ones like Anger Management tour, Family Values has only been a sporadic event since its creation in 1998. The first line-up featured Korn, Limp Bizkit, Ice Cube, Incubus, Orgy and Rammstein.

Linkin Park joined in 2001 as headliners next to Stone Temple Pilots and main act Staind. The other performers were Puddle Of Mudd, Static-X, Deadsy and Spike 1000. Reviewing a show held at the San Jose Compaq Center in California, one journalist said on the American online entertainment magazine *livedaily.com*:

"With singer Chester Bennington and rapper Mike Shinoda mixing it up on sledgehammer songs like 'Crawling' and 'Papercut,' Linkin Park showed once again that it is the best young rap-metal band in the industry, and is one of the only acts in this genre that appears worth watching in the long term."

TOUR DATES

26th October, Hartford, CT (Hartford Civic Centre); 27th October, Worchester, MA (The Centrum); 28th October, Buffalo, NY (HSBC

Arena); 30th October, Charlotte, NC (Charlotte Coliseum); 31st October, Atlanta, GA (Philips Arena); 2nd November, Fort Lauderdale, FL (National Car Rental Centre); 3rd November, Tampa, FL (Ice Palace); 4th November, Biloxi, MS (Miss. Coast Coliseum); 6th November, Dallas, TX (Reunion Arena); 8th November, Denver, CO (Pepsi Centre); 10th November, Anaheim, CA (Arrowhead Pond); 11th November, Phoenix, AZ (America West Arena); 13th November, San Jose, CA (Compaq Centre); 14th November, Sacramento, CA (Arco Arena); 16th November, Portland, OR (Rose Garden Arena) and 17th November, Tacoma, WA (Tacoma Dome.)

SET-LIST

(HSBC Arena, Buffalo, New York, 28th October, 2001)
'With You' / 'Runaway' / 'Papercut' / 'By Myself' / 'Points Of Authority' / 'Step Up' / 'Pushing Me Away' / 'In The End' / 'A Place For My Head' / 'Crawling' / 'One Step Closer'

FESTIMAD

Held over two days in Madrid, Spain the Festimad is an alternative rock festival that has been staged yearly since 2004. Linkin Park headlined the second day

(7th June) in 2008. Around 40,000 people attend each year.

FESTIVAL d'été de QUEBEC

An outdoor festival in Quebec, Canada which took place in 2008 from 3rd July to 13th July. Linkin Park headlined the event on the final night. An outdoor event, it took place on the Bell Stage at Plains Of Abraham.

HEINEKEN JAMMIN' FESTIVAL

This festival is held in Venice, Italy and was first organised in 1998. In 2007 it was to be held at Mestre, Parco San Giuliano on 15th June, but when a tornado hit the outdoor venue it was wisely cancelled which meant there were no performances by Linkin Park, Pearl Jam, The Killers and My Chemical Romance. Linkin Park returned in 2008 as a headlining act alongside Sex Pistols and The Police.

NOVA ROCK FESTIVAL

Held in Nickelsdorf, Austria the Nova Rock Festival first began in 2005 and is Austria's most famous and successful annual festival. The 2007 edition was held over three days from 15th to 17th June and featured Linkin Park. The headlining acts were Smashing Pumpkins, Marilyn Manson,

Billy Talent, Pearl Jam, The Killers and Slayer.

OZZFEST

As the name suggests, Ozzfest is named after heavy metal legend Ozzy Osbourne, the original lead singer of Black Sabbath. After Ozzy was turned down by the organisers of the festival Lollapalooza (it was alleged they thought he was past it and not popular with kids anymore), Ozzy and his wife and manager Sharon created the metal touring juggernaut Ozzfest, which was first held in the States on 25th and 26th October 1996. The first stage featured headliner Ozzy with Slayer, Danzig, Biohazard, Sepultura, Fear Factory and Narcotic Gypsy. The second stage had headliner Neurosis with Earth Crisis, King Norris, Powerman 5000, Coal Chamber and Cellophane.

Since then it has become a hugely successful annual touring festival playing all around North America and occasionally the UK and Europe as well as other parts of the world. It was integral in resurrecting Ozzy's career and helping metal become more popular again during what was essentially a poor decade for the genre.

Linkin Park joined Ozzfest in 2001 for the American touring jaunt. The line-up for the main stage was the original Black Sabbath, Marilyn Manson, Slipknot, Papa Roach, Linkin Park, Disturbed, Crazy Town and Black Label Society. The second stage featured differing line-ups but the following bands played at some point: Mudvayne, The Union Underground, Taproot, Systematic, Godhead, Nonpoint, Drowning Pool, Spineshank, Hatebreed, Otep, No One, Pressure 4-5, American Head Charge, Pure Rubbish, Beautiful Creatures, Project Wyze and Slaves On Dope.

TOUR DATES

8th June, Tinley Park, IL (New World Music Theatre); 9th June, East Troy, WI (Alpine Valley Music Theatre); 12th – 13th June, Noblesville, IN (Verizon Wireless Music Centre); 16th June, Somerset, WI (Float Rite Park Amphitheatre); 18th June, Maryland Heights, MO (Riverport Amphitheatre); 19th June, Bonner Springs, KS (Sandstone Amphitheatre); 22nd June, Denver, CO (Mile High Stadium); 25th June, George, WA (The Gorge); 27th June, Marysville, CA (Sacramento Valley Amphitheatre); 29th June, Mountainview, CA (Shoreline Amphitheatre); 30th June, San Bernadino, CA (Blockbuster Pavilion); 3rd July, Selma, TX (Verizon Wireless Amphitheatre); 5th July, Dallas, TX (Smirnoff

Music Centre); 7ᵗʰ July, Atlanta, GA (HiFi Buys Amphitheatre); 9ᵗʰ July, Camden, NJ (Tweeter Centre); 13ᵗʰ July, West Palm Beach, FL (Mars Music Amphitheater); 14ᵗʰ July, Tampa, FL (Zephyr Hills); 17ᵗʰ July, Charlotte, NC (Verizon Wireless Amphitheatre); 20ᵗʰ July, Bristow, VA (Nissan Pavilion at Stoneridge); 21ˢᵗ July, Camden, NJ (Tweeter Centre); 24ᵗʰ July, Toronto, Ontario (The Docks); 26ᵗʰ July, Cuyahoga Falls, OH (Blossom Music Centre); 28ᵗʰ July, Burgettstown, PA (Post-Gazette Pavilion); 30ᵗʰ – 31ˢᵗ July, Clarkston, MI (DTE Energy Music Theatre); 3ʳᵈ August, Columbus, OH (Polaris Amphitheatre); 5ᵗʰ August,

Hartford, CT (Meadows Music Theatre); 7ᵗʰ – 8ᵗʰ August, Mansfield, MA (Tweeter Centre) and 11ᵗʰ – 12ᵗʰ August, Holmdel, NJ (PNC Bank Arts Centre.)

SET-LIST
(Nissan Pavillion, Bristow, Virginia, 20ᵗʰ July, 2001)
'With You' / 'Runaway' / 'Papercut' / 'By Myself' / 'Points Of Authority' / 'Crawling' / 'In The End' / 'A Place For My Head' / 'One Step Closer'

PINKPOP FESTIVAL
This festival takes place on a yearly basis in Landgraaf, Netherlands and it has been running since 1970. Since 2007, it has been a three day festival with an average of 60,000 fans attending. Linkin Park played the 2007 festival.

PROJEKT REVOLUTION
Ozzy and Korn weren't the only artists to jump in on the independent touring festival wagon: Linkin Park created the Projekt Revolution tour in 2002 with the aim of bringing different types of bands together to celebrate music (rather than a specific genre of music).

Projekt Revolution started as a small affair in 2002 (29th January to 24th February) with just one stage and a handful of bands (Linkin Park, Cypress Hill, Ade-

Ozzfest, Devore

ma and DJ Z-Trip.) A *second* one stage tour followed in 2003 with Linkin Park, Mudvayne, Xzibit and Blindside, and that particular jaunt ran for 16 shows from 9th April to 26th April. Chester Bennington suffered from a throat infection which meant the band had to rearrange some shows and move them from April to July.

Due to the success of the first two tours, a third was scheduled for 2004 with two stages: the first saw performances from Linkin Park, Korn, Snopp Dogg, The Used and Less Than Jake. The second stage (dubbed the Revolution Stage) was meant for younger up-and-coming bands and saw the following acts perform: Ghostface Killah, Funeral For A Friend, Downset, M.O.P., Mike V. and The Rats, Instruction, No Warning and Autopilot Off. They played 32 dates between 23rd July and 5th September.

In a press statement published on the Internet, Mike Shinoda said:

"It's an amazing feeling to experience an artist's music live, standing right there in the same room as the person who wrote the songs... and I think that these three headline-quality acts will show the Projekt Revolution crowd what a powerful feeling that can be."

There was a break for three years but Projekt Revolution resumed in 2007. Because of the sheer amount of carbon emissions used on all the tour buses from each band involved, Linkin Park decided to become more environmentally conscious and use bio-diesel and they chose to donate $1 from every ticket to the charity American Forests. The main headlining stage featured Linkin Park, My Chemical Romance, Taking Back Sunday, HIM, Placebo and Julien-K, while Mindless Self Indulgence, Saosin, The Bled, Styles of Beyond and Madina Lake played the Revolution Stage.

In a press statement Chester Bennington said:

"Linkin Park is thrilled to be joined by this amazing group of artists and I know the audience will share in our excitement..."

The 2007 road jaunt ran from 25th July to 3rd September, playing 29 shows and for the first time they took the festival to Canada.

And so in 2008, the tour travelled outside of America for the first time: they hit Germany on 21st June for three dates and played the Milton Keynes Bowl in England on 29th June. There was a different bill for each show; aside from the main act, Linkin Park, the following artists made at least one appearance: HIM, N*E*R*D, The Used, The Blackout, The Bravery, Innerpartsystem, Jay-Z, Pendulum and Enter Shikari.

They moved on to the States to begin touring on 16th July and finished on 24th August. The following acts played the main stage: Linkin Park, Chris Cornell, The Bravery, Ashes Aside, Steel Drum Corps and for only 11 shows Busta Rhymes (he apparently had a spat with Mike Shinoda and consequently left the tour). The Revolution Stage featured: Atreyu, 10 Years, Hawthorne Heights, Armour For Sleep and State Your Cause. 24 shows were played on the 2008 tour.

Prior to the 2008 shows Chester Bennington is quoted on *hypemagazine.com* as saying:

"We started Projekt Revolution six years ago and have been lucky to have toured with some great bands... This year, however, might just be the best line-up yet. We're looking forward to taking this show on the road and bringing great music to the masses."

TOUR DATES
Projekt Revolution I - 2002
29th January, Colorado Springs, CO (World Arena); 30th January, Wichita, KS (Kansas Coliseum); 1st February, Chicago, IL (UIC Pavilion); 2nd February, Madison, WI (Alliant Energy Centre Memorial Coliseum); 4th February, Detroit, MI (Cobo Arena); 5th February, Dayton, OH (Nutter Centre); 7th February, Wilkes-Barre, PA (First Union Centre); 8th February, Uniondale, NY (Nassau Coliseum); 9th February, State College, PA (Bryce Jordan Centre); 11th February, Lowell, MA (Tsongas Arena)

12th February, Fairfax, VA (Patriot Centre); 13th February, Philadelphia, PA (First Union Centre); 16th February, Memphis, TN (Mid-South Coliseum); 17th February, Dallas, TX (Fort Worth Convention Centre); 18th February, Oklahoma City, OK (Fairgrounds Arena); 20th February, Phoenix, AZ (American West Arena); 22nd February, Long Beach, CA (Long Beach Arena); 23rd February, San Diego, CA (Cox Arena) and 24th February, Las Vegas, NV (Thomas & Mack Centre).

Projekt Revolution II – 2003
9th April, State College, PA (Bryce Jordan Centre); 11th April, Evansville, IN (Robert's Stadium); 12th April, Memphis, TN (Mid-South Coliseum); 13th April, New Orleans, LA (Keifer UNO Lakefront Arena); 15th April, El Paso,

TX (Don Haskins Centre); 16th April, Albuquerque, NM (Tingley Coliseum); 18th April, Phoenix, AZ (American West Arena); 19th April, Tucson, AZ (Tucson Convention Centre); 21st April, West Valley City, UT (E Centre); 22nd April, Boise, ID (Idaho Centre); 23rd April, Spokane, WA (Spokane Arena); 25th April, Billings, MT (Metra Park Arena); 26th April, Rapid City, SD (Rushmore Plaza Civic Centre); 22nd July, Rochester, NY (Blue Cross Arena) (Originally intended for 8th April); 29th July, Council Bluffs, IA (Mid-America Centre) (Originally intended for 28th April) and 30th July, Valley Centre, KS (Kansas Coliseum) (Originally intended for 29th April).

Projekt Revolution III - 2004

23rd July, Cincinnati, OH (Riverbend Music Centre); 24th July, Columbus, OH (Germain Amphitheatre); 26th July, Clarkston, MI (DTE Energy Music Theatre); 27th July, Darien Center, NY (Darien Lake Performing Arts Centre); 29th July, Mansfield, MA (Tweeter Centre For The Performing Arts); 30th July, Holmdel, NJ (PNC Bank Arts Centre); 31st July, Hartford, CT (Meadows Music Centre); 2nd August, Wantagh, NY (Jones Beach Amphitheatre); 3rd August, Camden, NJ (Tweeter Centre At The Waterfront); 5th August, Cuyahoga Falls, OH (Blossom Music Centre);

6th August, Noblesville, IN (Verizon Wireless Music Centre); 7th August, Tinley Park, IL (Tweeter Centre); 9th August, Burgettstown, PA (Post Gazette Pavilion); 10th August, Bristow, VA (Nissan Pavilion Stone Ridge); 11th August, Virginia Beach, VA (Verizon Wireless Amphitheatre); 13th August, Atlanta, GA (HiFi Buys Amphitheatre); 14th August, Charlotte, NC (Verizon Wireless Amphitheatre); 17th August, West Palm Beach, FL (Sound Advice Amphitheatre); 18th August, Tampa, FL (Tampa Bay Amphitheatre); 20th August, Dallas, TX (Smirnoff Centre); 21st August, Selma, TX (Verizon Wireless Amphitheatre); 22nd August, Spring, TX (Cynthia Woods Mitchell Pavilion); 24th August, Bonner Springs, KS (Verizon Wireless Amphitheatre); 25th August, Maryland Heights, MO (UMB Bank Pavilion); 27th August, East Troy, WI (Alpine Valley Music Theatre); 28th August, Somerset, WI (Float-rite Park); 30th August, Englewood, CO (Coors Amphitheatre); 31st August, Albuquerque, NM (Journal Pavilion); 1st September, Phoenix, AZ (Cricket Pavilion); 3rd September, Chula Vista, CA (Coors Amphitheatre); 4th September, Devore,

CA (Hyundai Pavilion at Glen Helen) and 5ᵗʰ September, Mountain View, CA (Shoreline Amphitheatre).

Projekt Revolution IV - 2007

25ᵗʰ July, Auburn, WA (White River Amphitheatre); 27ᵗʰ July, Marysville, CA (Sleep Train Amphitheatre); 28ᵗʰ July, San Bernardino, CA (Hyundai Pavilion); 29ᵗʰ July, Mountain View, CA (Shoreline Amphitheatre); 31ˢᵗ July, Chula Vista, CA (Coors Amphitheatre); 1ˢᵗ August, Phoenix, AZ (Cricket Pavilion); 3ʳᵈ August, Selma, TX (Verizon Wireless Amphitheatre); 4ᵗʰ August, Dallas, TX (Smirnoff Music Centre); 5ᵗʰ August, Woodlands, TX (Cynthia Woods Mitchell Pavilion); 7ᵗʰ August, Atlanta, GA (HiFi Buys Amphitheatre); 8ᵗʰ August, Charlotte, NC (Verizon Wireless Amphitheatre); 10ᵗʰ August, West Palm Beach, FL (Sound Advice Amphitheatre); 11ᵗʰ August, Tampa, FL (Ford Amphitheatre); 13ᵗʰ August, Raleigh, NC (Walnut Creek Amphitheatre); 14ᵗʰ August, Virginia Beach, VA (Verizon Wireless Virginia Beach Amphitheatre); 15ᵗʰ August, Wantagh, NY (Nikon at Jones Beach Theatre); 17ᵗʰ August, Cuyahoga Falls, OH (Blossom Music Centre); 18ᵗʰ August, Darien Centre, NY (Darien Lake Performing Arts Centre); 19ᵗʰ August, Bristow, VA (Nis-

san Pavilion); 21ˢᵗ August, Toronto, Ontario (Molson Amphitheatre); 22ⁿᵈ August, Clarkston, MI (DTE Energy Music Theatre); 24ᵗʰ August, Mansfield, MA (Tweeter Centre For The Performing Arts); 25ᵗʰ August, Camden, NJ (Tweeter Centre at the Waterfront); 26ᵗʰ August, Hartford, CT (New England Dodge Music Centre); 28ᵗʰ August, Syracuse, NY (NY State Fair); 29ᵗʰ August, Holmdel, NJ (PNC Bank Arts Centre); 31ˢᵗ August, Noblesville, IN (Verizon Wireless Music Centre); 1ˢᵗ September, Tinley Park, IL (First Midwest Bank Amphitheatre) and 3ʳᵈ September, Englewood, CO (Coors Amphitheatre).

Projekt Revolution V - 2009

21ˢᵗ June, Munich, Germany (Reitstadion Riem); 27ᵗʰ June, Berlin, Germany (Waldbühne); 28ᵗʰ June, Düsseldorf, Germany (LTU Arena); 29ᵗʰ June, Milton Keynes, England (The Bowl); 16ᵗʰ July, Mansfield, MA (Comcast Centre For Performing Arts); 18ᵗʰ July,

Tinley Park

Burgettstown, PA (Post-Gazette Pavilion); 19th July, Camden, NJ (Susquehana Bank Centre); 20th July, Hartford, CT (New England Dodge Music Centre); 22nd July, Wantagh, NY (Nikon, Jones Beach Theatre); 23rd July, Holmdel, NJ (PNC Bank Arts Centre); 25th July, Raleigh, NC (Time Warner Cable Music Pavilion, Walnut Creek); 26th July, Virginia Beach, VA (Verizon Wireless Virginia Beach Amphitheatre); 27th July, Bristow, VA (Nissan Pavilion); 30th July, Charlotte, NC (Charlotte Verizon Wireless Amphitheatre); 1st August, West Palm Beach, FL (Cruzan Amphitheatre); 2nd August, Tampa, FL (Ford Amphitheatre); 3rd August, Atlanta, GA (Lakewood Amphitheatre); 7th August, Phoenix, AZ (Cricket Wireless Pavilion); 9th August, Mountain View, CA (Shoreline Amphitheatre); 10th August, Irvine, CA (Verizon Wireless Amphitheatre); 12th August, Greenwood Village, CO (Fiddler's Green Amphitheatre); 15th August, Cincinatti, OH (Riverbend Music Centre); 16th August, East Troy, WI (Alpine Valley Music Theatre); 17th August, Noblesville, IN (Verizon Wireless Music Centre Indianapolis); 19th August, Cuyahoga Falls, OH (Blossom Music Centre); 21st August, St. Louis, MO (Verizon Wireless Amphitheatre, St. Louis); 23rd August, Dallas, TX (Superpages.com Centre) and 24th August, Woodlands, TX (Cynthia Woods Mitchell Pavilion).

ROCK AM/IM RING

Rock Am Ring (Rock At The Ring) is held at Nürburgring racetrack in West Germany and Rock Im Park (Rock In The Park) is held in Frankenstadion in Nürnberg, South East Germany. Both festivals are scheduled to play at the same time.

Linkin Park played the 2001 event held on 1st to 3rd June. They were supposed to play (as headliners) at the 2003 event but they had to drop out after Chester Bennington was hospitalised and Placebo replaced them. In 2004 (4th to 6th June) Linkin Park made a full appearance and they returned as headliners for the 2007 (1st to 3rd June) event along side artists such as Smashing Pumpkins and Slayer, amongst others.

ROCK IN RIO

Traditionally held in Rio, Brazil, Rock In Rio was first staged in 1985 and famously headlined by Queen. The second event took place in 1991 and then in 2001. In 2004, Rock In Rio was moved (confusingly) to Lisbon in Portugal; there was a second one held in 2006 and a third in 2008. The lat-

Rock In Rio, Lisbon

ter event ran from 30th to 31st May, 1st June and 5th to 6th June. Linkin Park headlined the final night which also featured The Offspring, Muse, Kaiser Chiefs and Orishas. The event was held at the Parque da Bela Vista.

SUMMER SANITARIUM

Headlined by Metallica, who at the time were promoting *St. Anger*, the Summer Sanitarium 2003 tour featured Limp Bizkit, Linkin Park, Deftones and Mudvayne. Not strictly a festival – more like a mini-festival – Metallica's previous Summer Sanitarium tour was in 2001 and featured Korn, Kid Rock, System Of A Down and Powerman 500. The tour commenced in Detroit at the Pontiac Silverdome on 4th July and visited New York, Philadelphia, Washington D.C, Baltimore, Chicago, Atlanta, LA, San Francisco and in Canada, Montreal and Toronto. As a warm up to the tour Linkin Park played a show on 27th June at Las Vegas' Hard Rock Hotel

TOUR DATES

4th July, Pontiac, MI (Pontiac Silverdome); 5th July, Toronto, Ontario (Toronto Skydome); 6th July, Foxboro, MA (Gillette Stadium); 8th July, East Rutherford, NJ (Giants Stadium); 11th July, Atlanta, GA (Turner Field); 12th July, Philadelphia, PA (Veterans Stadium); 13th July, Orlando, FL (Citrus Bowl); 18th July, Landover, MD (FedExField); 19th July, Columbus, OH (Ohio Stadium); 20th July, Montreal, Quebec (Parc Jean-Drapeau); 25th July, St. Louis, MO (Edward Jones Dome); 26th July, Cicero, IL (Hawthorne Racetrack); 27th July, Minneapolis, MN (Metrodome); 1st August, Denver, CO (Invesco Field At Mile High); 2nd August, Houston, TX (Reliant Stadium); 3rd August, Irving, TX (Texas Stadium); 7th August, Seattle, WA (Seahawk Stadium) and 9th August, Los Angeles, CA (Los Angeles Memorial Coliseum).

SUMMER SONIC

Summer Sonic is a yearly two day festival held in Chiba and Osaka, Japan. The first festival was organised in 2004; Linkin Park played the 2006 festival alongside Metallica (who hosted the show),

Muse, My Chemical Romance and Avenged Sevenfold and others.

CHARITY CONCERT APPEARENCES

In recent years, Linkin Park have become known for their philanthropic work, especially concerning their own charity organisation Music For Relief. What follows is a small list of some of the charity concerts they have taken part in. The author has listed them in chronological order.

TRINITYKIDS CARE *(2002)*
Linkin Park played a charity show on 4th March, 2002 for the Los Angeles first paediatric hospice TrinityKids Care. The gig was held at the legendary House Of Blues in West Hollywood; 800 fans attended and the band raised around $85,000. The hospice is for terminally ill children. Only 11 to 15 year olds could attend with an $85 dollar ticket while parents and fans over 21 years old had to purchase a ticket worth $250.

TSUNAMI BENEFIT *(2005)*
On 18th February, 2005, Linkin Park (featuring Jay-Z) joined several other artists for a tsunami benefit concert at the Arrowhead Pond arena in Anaheim, CA with profits going to aid victims of the tsunami in South Asia. This was in conjunction with Linkin Park's charity Music For Relief. The event also featured No Doubt, Ozzy Osbourne and Blink 182.

LIVE 8 *(2005)*
Live 8 was organised by Sir Bob Geldof and Midge Ure, both of whom co-organised the 1985 charity concerts Live Aid (held in London and Philadelphia). This time around, Live 8 was arranged to coincide with the G8 Summit Conference in Scotland on 6th, 7th and 8th July, 2005. Live 8 was basically a set of concerts that took place on 2nd July in the G8 States (i.e. London, Paris, Rome, Berlin, Philadelphia, Moscow, Cornwall, Edinburgh, Chiba and Barrie) and Johannesburg in South Africa. In terms of the performances, aside from Pink Floyd reforming to play

Live 8

the London show, nothing special happened on the day.

Linkin Park performed at the Philadelphia show (with Jay-Z), which also featured over 20 diverse acts, including Stevie Wonder, Alicia Keyes, Def Leppard, Bon Jovi, Destiny's Child and Maroon 5.

Live Earth

LIVE EARTH JAPAN *(2006)*
Held at Makuhari Messe in Tokyo Japan on 7th July, 2006, Live Earth was a one day charity concert founded by ex-United States Vice President Al Gore and Kevin Wall. Linkin Park was on the bill alongside Rihanna and Xzibit, amongst others. The audience were that enthralled by Linkin Park they broke down the barrier and two songs in the show had to be stopped to calm every one down and secure the perimeter. Bennington even had a go at telling the audience in Japanese:

"Show me you can make a difference and thank you for supporting the cause."

Their set-list ran: 'One Step Closer', 'Lying From You', 'Somewhere I Belong', 'No More Sorrow', 'Paper Cut', 'From The Inside', 'Numb', 'Pushing Me Away', 'Breaking The Habit', 'Crawling', 'In The End', 'Bleed It Out', 'The Little Things

Give You Away', 'What I've Done' and 'Faint'.

A NIGHT FOR THE VETS: AN MTV CONCERT FOR THE BRAVE *(2008)*
Evidently organised by the music station MTV, a concert took place at the Nokia Theater in New York on 23rd October, 2008 in aid of the BRAVE: the Bill of Rights for American Veterans. It was a tribute to the men and women of the American armed forces. Linkin Park took part, but as they were on tour at the time, did so through a recorded performance shown at the concert, which included live sets by 50 Cent, Ludacris, Hinder and O.A.R.

MUSIC FOR RELIEF *(2008)*
Music For Relief is Linkin Park's own charity which they founded (with the American Red Cross) in 2004 to aid victims of natural disasters. On 12th October, 2008, they

Shanghai

played a concert at the 80,000-capacity Shanghai Stadium; and on 19th October they played a show at the 72,000-seat Beijing Worker's Stadium with all proceeds going to Music For Relief. Those shows were apparently the largest concerts staged in the region for over a decade. They also featured Chinese bands on the bill.

The band has also played several other shows in aid of Music For Relief, including a large gig at the Impact Arena in Bangkok in 2004.

Brad Delson told *vh1.com*:

"We played what was the largest Thai concert in the past 10 years. It was an amazing show, and I carry with me the hospitality of the Thai people and the people of southern Asia... And having been there, I can just say that people there were so welcoming to us, and I really hope that through this effort we can help in some small way."

In 2008, the band had to cancel Music For Relief shows in mainland China – Macau and Taipei – because Chester Bennington suffered severe back pains. The concerts were arranged to benefit Sichuan in Western China, which suffered a major earthquake in May 2008.

MEMORABLE GIGS /TOURS AROUND THE GLOBE

Obviously Linkin Park are American, and while much of their success is concentrated in Europe and North America, they have a loyal and growing following across the globe and have committed themselves to charity work in Asia. They have played some truly memorable gigs around the world so here is a brief list of shows that have certainly helped boost their global career. The author has listed them in chronological order.

KUALA LUMPUR, MALAYSIA *(2003)*

Linkin Park's debut gig in South East Asia was at the Stadium Merdeka in Kuala Lumpur in front of 28,000 fans in October 2003. Of course, given the political situation in Asia, the band was given strict rules and regulations. They played 'Don't Say', 'Somewhere I Belong', 'Faint', 'Numb', 'Crawling', 'Points Of Authority', 'P5hng Me A*wy' and 'Wth>You' and the encore consisted of 'In The End' and 'One Step Closer'.

SAO PAULO, BRAZIL *(2004)*

On 11th September, 2004 at the close of the mammoth *Meteora World Tour*, Linkin Park played to over 50,000 fans. At the time it was their biggest ever headlining show.

AUSTRALIAN TOUR *(2007)*

In 2007, Linkin Park embarked on their third Australian road jaunt. The tour was in support of the mega-selling *Minutes To Midnight* and they were supported by ex-Soundgarden and Audioslave frontman Chris Cornell.

TOUR DATES

12th October, Auckland, New Zealand (Vector Arena); 14th October, Melbourne (Rod Laver Arena); 16th October, Adelaide (Entertainment Centre); 18th October, Perth (Burswood Dome); 20th October, Sydney (Entertainment Centre) and 22nd October, Brisbane (Entertainment Centre).

MEMORABLE NORTH AMERICAN GIGS

For whatever reasons there have been certain concerts the band has played, which have become particularly cherished memories for fans. What follows is a brief list of some of the most memorable US and UK concerts. The author has listed them in chronological order.

HORSESHOE TAVERN, TORONTO *(2000)*

Linkin Park staged their first Toronto show at the Horseshoe Tavern in December 2000, prior to the release of *Hybrid Theory*. In a relatively short space of time, their fanbase grew in Canada and only three years later they began playing the likes of the Air Canada Centre, a 20,000-capacity venue.

KROQ ALMOST ACOUSTIC CHRISTMAS, LOS ANGELES *(2007)*

As the title suggests, this annual California concert is not quite devoid of electric guitars. It was created in 1990 by the LA based station KROQ and is held in December with Christmas just around the corner.

Linkin Park performed on both nights (Saturday 8th and Sunday

9th December, 2001) as headliners and returned in 2003 to play on Saturday 13th December. They came back again in 2007, playing on Saturday 8th December.

MADISON SQUARE GARDEN, NEW YORK *(2008)*

In February 2008, Linkin Park played a gig to a sold out crowd at New York's massive Madison Square Garden. Just as the band were about to close the gig with 'Numb', rapper Jay-Z came on stage to perform it with them and then play 'Jigga Who, Jigga What' from *Collision Course*.

Madison Square Garden

MEMORABLE UK GIGS

KING'S COLLEGE *(2001)*

On a quick-fire promotional tour of the UK and Europe, Linkin Park performed their first ever gig in Britain at King's College, the University of London on 11th January, 2001.

SET-LIST

'A Place For My Head' / 'Forgotten' / 'Papercut' / 'By Myself' / 'Points Of Authority' / 'And One' / 'In The End' / 'With You' / 'Runaway' / 'One Step Closer'

NOTTINGHAM ROCK CITY *(2003)*

An exclusive Radio One performance at the legendary Nottingham Rock City in the English Midlands, this sold out show cemented their reputation in the UK as a top live band. The gig was basically a showcase for their then upcoming release *Meteora*.

One reviewer wrote on *bbc.co.uk/Nottingham*:

"It might not be very trendy but this was a seriously polished performance with great sound made all the better by the fact it was in the cosy surroundings of Rock City and not some big arena."

O2 ARENA, LONDON *(2008)*

In January 2008, Linkin Park played two sold out shows at London's O2 Arena, the biggest venue in the UK. They played for 90 minutes and the set-list included 'Faint', 'Points Of Authority', 'Somewhere I Belong' and 'Wake' / 'Given Up'.

Lisa Verrico wrote in *The Times*:

O2 Arena

"Variously labelled rock-rap, nu-metal and rock-pop, Linkin Park proved to be a bit of all three at a riotous London show that barely paused for breath and often felt like a competition between band and fans as to which could make more noise."

NATIONAL BOWL, MILTON KEYNES (2008)

This gig was filmed and recorded for the 2008 release, *Road To Revolution: Live At Milton Keynes*. Held on 29th June at the out-door venue National Bowl in Milton Keynes, the show featured headliners Linkin Park with the following acts also on the bill: Jay-Z, Pendulum, N*E*R*D, Enter Shikari, The Bravery and Innerpartysystem. The show was staged (boldly) at the same time as the hugely popular Glastonbury Festival annual three day event. Jay-Z (who also headlined Glastonbury) joined Linkin Park on stage to perform 'Jigga What/Faint' and 'Numb/Encore' from *Collision Course*. One reviewer wrote on the popular online music magazine *Thrash Hits*:

"Chester Bennington was on firey form while Mike Shinoda did his best to continue the hip hop-based shenanigans. However, he did look far more comfortable when reciting more familiar lyrics or when sitting behind his piano."

National Bowl, Milton Keynes

They played the following songs in this order:
'One Step Closer' / 'Lying From You' / 'Somewhere I Belong' / 'No More Sorrow' / 'Papercut' / 'Points Of Authority' / 'Wake 2.0′ / 'Given Up' / 'From The Inside' / 'Leave Out All The Rest' / 'Numb' / 'The Little Things Give You Away' / 'Breaking The Habit' / 'Shadow Of The Day' / 'Crawling' / 'In The End' (*Encore*): 'Pushing Me Away' / 'What I've Done' *(Encore II)* 'Numb/Encore' *(feat. Jay-Z)* / 'Jigga What/Faint' *(feat. Jay-Z)* / 'Bleed It Out'

MEMORABLE TV APPEARANCES

Linkin Park have obviously appeared on television many times, for interviews, for awards and to promote their work or charity organisation Music For Relief. Some bands have broken the mold and changed the way we view television appearances, either because of controversy or the sheer brilliance of the performance. While Linkin Park have not performed on TV as memorably as, say, Nirvana, they have made some pretty spectacular one-off appearances. The author has listed them in alphabetical order.

AOL SESSIONS *(US)*
A music TV show from the United States, first aired in 2002. Over the years a host of popular artists have appeared, including Tori Amos, Snow Patrol and Jack Johnson. Linkin Park was in one episode in 2007 and Fort Minor actually appeared in one edition back in 2005.

GONNA MEET A ROCK STAR *(US)*
An American reality TV series from 2001, created by directors John Marshall and Guy O' Sullivan. Linkin Park made an appearance on the show as did Limp Bizkit, Incubus and Barenaked Ladies, amongst others.

JIMMY KIMMEL *(US)*
Jimmy Kimmel is a talk show host in America. The show first aired in 2003 and has won two Primetime Emmy's. Linkin Park appeared on the show on 19th May, 2007.

This little transcription is from the show:

Jimmy Kimmel: Didn't you get bit by a spider or something?

Chester Bennington: Yes, I got bit on my ass by a spider. And I thought that I had cancer but...

Jimmy Kimmel: ...it turns out you have super powers!

Chester Bennington: It turns out now that I can climb buildings, and save people from criminal acts

LIVE AT THE ROCK & ROLL HALL OF FAME *(US)*

An American TV series that ran from 2001 to 2003. It featured a host of popular artists, including Linkin Park (in 2001), P.O.D., The Vines and John Mayer, amongst others. It was direct by Liz Patrick.

GRAMMY AWARDS *(US)*

Held at Staples Centre in Los Angeles, Linkin Park performed 'Numb/Encore' at the 2006 Grammy Awards. They picked up the gong for 'Best Rap/Sung Collaboration'.

ROCKPALAST *(Germany)*

A very successful and long-running German rock show that dates back to 1974. Linkin Park performed on the show in 2004.

SATURDAY NIGHT LIVE *(US)*

Probably the most successful American comedy show of all time. It features sketches, stand-up gigs and music performances. Lots of successful comedians started on *Saturday Night Live*, including, Mike Myers, Bill Murray and Dan Ackroyd. Linkin Park appeared on the show as musical guests in 2007.

The band made memorable appearances at the following awards ceremonies which were aired on TV:

MTV Video Music Awards 2001
MTV Video Music Awards 2002
2003 Radio Music Awards
MTV Europe Music Awards 2004
MTV Video Music Awards 2007
MTV VMA Pre Show Royale 2007
MTV Europe Music Awards 2007

THE TOM GREEN SHOW *(US)*

Tom Green is an American comedian and said show is based on a

AOL Sessions

series of comedy sketches starring Green and is co-hosted by Glenn Humplik and Phil Giroux. Linkin Park appeared on the show in the US on 1st July, 2003.

TOP OF THE POPS *(UK)*
The iconic and once hugely enjoyed BBC music programme *Top Of The Pops* attracted artists of every genre of popular music. No longer on the air, *TOTP* is still remembered with reverence. Linkin Park appeared on the show a few times, live and with pre-recorded performances. But in 2001, when the band released *Hybrid Theory*, they made an impact with separate performances of 'Crawling' and 'Papercut'.

WHAT IS NU-METAL?

Nu-metal is basically a style that merged rap, metal and alternative rock; many of the bands were based in California. Traits of the genre include screaming vocals (as well, obviously, as rap vocals), repetitive but not melodic riffs; lack of central guitar solos, fast and heavy bass and bursts of drums. Of course, early rap-rock collaborations like Aerosmith with Run DMC and Anthrax with Public Enemy had a profound impact on the genre, as did the alternative metal bands. Another big influence on the genre was Faith No More, who merged all kinds of musical trends (punk, funk, progressive, thrash and rap) into one melting pot.

The genre started in the nineties (post-grunge) and seemed to have peaked around 2000-2003, but since then it has been ridiculed by the critics and is increasingly unpopular with music lovers. Linkin Park's *Minutes To Midnight* is far removed from the nu-metal sounds of *Hybrid Theory* and *Meteora*. Some of the bands to have emerged from the genre include Korn (*Issues*), Staind (*Break The Cycle*), Limp Bizkit (*Chocolate Starfish And The Hot Dog Flavoured Water*), Deftones (*White Pony*), Coal Chamber (*Dark Days*) and Papa Roach (*Lovehatetragedy*). Like any genre, the boundaries of what actually defines a nu-metal band are debatable; some say System Of A Down are nu-metal but others will argue against such a claim. Some of the bands, like Korn, formed before nu-metal kicked in, while others, like Linkin Park, released their debut albums during its peak years. But superficially, at least, all of them share similar musical traits.

Speaking before the release of *Minutes To Midnight,* Chester Bennington spoke to MTV:

"We're going for the music that inspired us, rather than the nu-metal type of sound... We're straying away from a lot of the predictable sounds we've had in the past, but there's no question in your mind when you hear it that it's Linkin Park. We've always said we write the music we write so that we can spread our wings as far as we want and try new things and go anywhere. I think we're really going to prove that with this new record."

CHAPTER 13

BITS & PIECES

SELECTIVE LIST OF AWARDS

Like most successful bands Linkin Park have won a fair few awards. It would be futile to try and list every one here simply because they've won so many of them. From the most obscure magazine gongs to the most famous American awards, Linkin Park are popular worldwide, and not just in English speaking terrortries. They themselves are probably not even aware of

every award or nomination they have received! The following list tells a story in itself, from 'Best Newcomer' to 'Best Band.' It didn't take long for Linkin Park to reach the top.

AWARDS WON (SELECTIVE LIST)

Best Foreign Artist Of The Year – *Emma Award (Finland)* – 2001

Best International Newcomer – *Kerrang! Award* – 2001

World's Best-Selling Rock Group – *World Music Award* – 2002

Best Foreign Rock Act – *Swedish Hit Music Award* – 2002

Best Rock Video ('In The End') – *MTV Video Music Award* – 2002

Best Hard Rock Performance ('Crawling') – *Grammy Award* – 2002

International Nu-Metal/Alternative Artist –*Echo Award (Germany)* – 2002

Best Hard Rock – *MTV Europe Music Award* – 2002

Best Group – *MTV Europe Music Award* – 2002

Best Rock Video MTV Video Music Awards 2008

Favourite Alternative Artist – *American Music Award* – 2003

Best Rock Group – *World Music Award* – 2003

Best International Band – *Kerrang! Award* – 2003

Best Rock Video ('Somewhere I Belong') – *MTV Video Music Award* – 2003

Favourite Alternative Artist – *American Music Award* – 2004

Viewer's Choice Award ('Breaking The Habit') – *MTV Video Music Award* – 2004

Best Rock Act – *MTV Europe Music Award* – 2004

Song Of The Year (Rock Alternative Radio – 'Numb') – *Radio Music Award* – 2004

Artist Of The Year (Rock Radio) – *Radio Music Award* – 2004

Best Album (*Meteora*) – *Fuse Rockzilla Award* – 2004

Best Video ('Faint') – *Fuse Rockzilla Award* – 2004

Best International Band – *NRJ Music Awards (France)* – 2004

Best Rap/Sung Collaboration ('Numb/Encore' with Jay-Z) – *Grammy Award* – 2006

World's Best Selling Rock Group – *World Music Award* – 2007

Favourite Alternative Artist – *American Music Award* – 2007

Favourite Pop/Rock Band/Duo/Group – *American Music Award* – 2007

Best Band – *MTV Europe Music Award* – 2007

Best Rock Video ('Shadow Of The Day') – *MTV Video Music Award* – 2008

Bring Da House Down – *MTV Asia Award* – 2008

Favourite Alternative Artist – *American Music Award* – 2008

Best International Video: Group – *MuchMusic Video Award (Germany)* – 2008

(After winning the American Music Award in 2008 the band posted a message on **linkinpark.com***. It read:*

*American Music Awards
November 24, 2008
LPN,*

Thank you SO much for your continued support of our band. We've been making music as Linkin Park for almost a decade, and, in that time, your collective dedication has never waned. We're so honored to have won an American Music Award last night, and are incredibly grateful to everyone who voted for us online. We worked for a year and a half to make Minutes To Midnight, *and spent an additional eighteen months on tour supporting it. I hope you enjoy the album as much as I still do.*
Happy Thanksgiving and Happy Holidays.
BBB)

NOMINATIONS (SELECTIVE LIST)

Best Band In The World – *Kerrang!* Award – 2001

Best Direction In A Video ('Crawling') – *MTV Video Music Award* – 2001

Best Rock Video ('Crawling') – *MTV Video Music Award* – 2001

Video Of The Year ('In The End') – *MTV Video Music Award* – 2002

Best Group Video ('In The End') – *MTV Video Music Award* – 2002

Favourite Breakthrough Artist – *MTV Asia Award* – 2002

Best International Newcomer – *Brit Award* – 2002

Best Rock Album (*Hybrid Theory*) – *Grammy Award* – 2002

Best New Artist – *Grammy Award* – 2002

Outstanding Hard Rock/Alternative Album (*Reanimation*) – *California Music Award* – 2003

Best Rock Instrumental Performance ('Session') – Grammy Award – 2003

Favourite Alternative Artist – *American Music Award* – 2003

Favourite Pop/Rock Band/Duo/Group – *American Music Award* – 2003

Favourite Video ('Pts.OF.Athrt') – *MTV Asia Award* – 2003

Favourite Alternative Artist – *MTV Asia Award* – 2003

Best Rock Act – *MTV Europe Music Award* – 2003

Best Single ('Faint') – *Kerrang! Award* – 2003

Best Single ('Breaking The Habit') – *Kerrang! Award* – 2004

Best Rock Instrumental ('Session') – *Grammy Award* – 2004

Best Rock Video ('Breaking The Habit') – *MTV Asia Award* – 2004

Favourite Rock Act – *MTV Asia Award* – 2004

Duo/Group Artist Of The Year – *Billboard Music Award* – 2004

Best Special Effects ('Somewhere I Belong') – *Fuse Rockzilla Awards* – 2004

Best Alternative/Rock Dance ('Numb/Encore' with Jay-Z) – *International Dance Music Award* – 2005

Artist Of The Year (Alternative/Active Rock Radio) – *Radio Music Award* – 2005

Best Video ('What I've Done') – *Kerrang! Award* – 2007

Favourite Pop/Rock Band/Duo/Group – *American Music Award* – 2007

Favourite Album (*Minutes To Midnight*) – *American Music Award* – 2007

Best International Album (*Minutes To Midnight*) – *Belgian TMF (The Music Factory) Award* – 2007

Best International Rock Act – *Belgian TMF (The Music Factory) Award* – 2007

Editing In A Video ('What I've Done') – *MTV Video Music Award* – 2007

Best Director ('What I've Done') – *MTV Video Music Award* – 2007

Best Group – *MTV Video Music Award* – 2007

Best Album (*Minutes To Midnight*) – *MTV Europe Music Award* – 2007

Rock Out – *MTV Europe Music Award* – 2007

The Good Woodie ('Music For Relief') – *mtvU Woodie Award* – 2007

Viral Woodie ('What I've Done') – *mtvU Woodie Award* – 2007

Choice Music: Rock Group – *Teen Choice Award* – 2007

Choice Music: Rock Track ('What I've Done') – *Teen Choice Award* – 2007

Best Direction In A Video ('Shadow Of The Day') – *MTV Video Music Award* – 2008

Best Special Effects In A Video ('Bleed It Out') – *MTV Video Music Award* – 2008

Favourite International Artist Of Asia – *MTV Asia Award* – 2008

Rock Out – *MTV Europe Music Award* – 2008

Headliner – *MTV Europe Music Award* – 2008

Best Video From A Film ('What I've Done' for *Transformers*) – *MTV Video Music Award Japan* – 2008

Best Rock Video ('What I've Done') – *MTV Video Music Award Japan* – 2008

Best International Video: Group ('Bleed It Out') – *Much Music Award* – 2008

National/International Album Of The Year (*Minutes To Midnight*) – *Echo Award (Germany)* – 2008

Favourite Music Group – *Blimb Award (Nickelodeon Kids' Choice Award)* – 2008

International Group/Duo Of The Year – *NRJ Music Award* – 2008

Favourite Song From A Soundtrack ('What I've Done' from *Transformers*) – *People's Choice Award, USA* – 2008

Choice Music: Rock Group – *Teen Choice Award* – 2008

Choice Music: Rock Track ('Shadow Of The Day') – *Teen Choice Award* – 2008

POLLS /END OF YEAR LISTS

Linkin Park and their albums have been named in various end of year polls and different types of lists since Hybrid Theory *was released in 2000. Here are some of those titles and entries:*

In December 2001, *Billboard* named Linkin Park 'Top Modern Rock Artist'; fourth 'Best Mainstream Rock Artist' and 'In The End' was named the fifth 'Best Modern Rock Track'.

In December 2002, ARC named Linkin Park twenty-fifth in 'Singles Artist Of The Year'.

In 2003, 'In The End' was named the third most played song on the radio in the US.

In January 2003, Linkin Park was named the fourth 'Best Band' in the *Kerrang! Reader's Poll.*

In January 2003, *Hybrid Theory* was named one of the '100 Greatest Albums Of All Time' by *Q* magazine.

TRANSFORMERS

Joe Hahn is the band's resident expert on all things related to *Transformers,* the famed eighties cartoon. In fact, Hahn is such a fan that he has been seen wearing *Transformers* T-shirts, and on stage his turntables occasionally have *Transformers* designs on them. The band famously contributed to the soundtrack of the 2007 live action Hollywood film (produced by Steven Spielberg) as well as the 2009 sequel. *Transformers* were initially a series of toys released in 1984 by Hasbro but produced and created by a Japanese company called Takara-Tomy. An animated series was created based on the toy concept and Marvel comic books were also released. They became hugely successful and acquired a cult fanbase over the years. The basic premise is that the Decepticons are the "baddie" robots and the Autobots are the "goodies." Famous characters include Optimus Prime, Bumblebee, Starscream, Megatron and Jazz. Visit *hasbro.com*

In July 2003, Linkin Park was placed number one band in *Hit Parader's* 'Top 10 Current Rock Artists' poll.

In September 2003, MTV 2 named Linkin Park the sixth 'Greatest Band Of All Time'.

In November 2003, MTV 2 called *Hybrid Theory* the tenth 'Greatest Album Of All Time'.

In December 2003, *Rolling Stone* rated *Meteora* as one of the 'Top 50 Albums Of 2003'.

In December 2003, *MuchMusic* named 'Numb' the 'Favourite Video Of 2003'. They also named 'Somewhere I Belong' the fourth favourite video and 'Faint' the seventh favourite video.

In December 2003, America's top rock radio station *KROCK* ran their annual 'Top 92 Most Played Songs Of The Year' poll which put 'Faint' at number four; 'Somewhere I Belong' at number 16; 'Numb' at number 25 and 'From The Inside' at number 30.

In 2005, *Q* magazine rated Linkin Park number nine in the '25 Most Pathetic Rock Stars Ever!' poll.

In 2005, *Classic Rock* placed *Hybrid Theory* at number 65 in their list of 'The Greatest Rock Albums Of All Time.'

In November 2006, Chester Bennington was pinned to number 46 in the poll 'Heavy Metal's All-Time Top 100 Vocalists' by *Hit Parader.* Mike Shinoda was ranked at number 72.

In 2006, the French magazine *Rock Sound* polled *Hybrid Theory* at number 46 in 'Les 150 Albums De La Génération' which in English is 'Top 150 Albums Of Our Lifetime'.

Hybrid Theory is listed in the 2006 publication *1001 Albums You Must Hear Before You Die* (edited by Robert Dimery).

In 2007, *Minutes To Midnight* was ranked as the twenty-fifth album in *Rolling Stone's* 'Top 50 Albums Of 2007'.

ROAD TO REVOLUTION: THE CRITICS RESPONSE TO LINKIN PARK'S MUSIC

Linkin Park – hell, most metal bands – have never been darlings of the critics. Of course, there is a fine divide between what's printed in the metal/rock press and what's printed in the mainstream music press. Here's a broad selection of quotes from published reviews, showing the vast range of responses Linkin Park continually receive from music critics. Given the sheer wealth of amateur online reviewers, the author has chosen to reference professional reviewers only. However, following the published quotes are some thoughts on the band from a number of writers and online reviewers the author has contacted for the specific purpose of this book.

QUOTES:

"We don't need to ask 'Are Linkin Park manufactured?', but rather could they have been? The only possible answer is, yes. Linkin Park's 'High Voltage', a B-side which they play tonight, ends with the words 'You can't put a label on a lifestyle.' Oh, but you can. Nu-Metal (or Sports Metal, as it is more accurately named, in recognition of the steroid-skulled jocks who have now colonised alternative music) is a world of strict rituals and codified clichés."
(**Simon Price**, *Independent*, London Arena gig review, 2001)

"Rap metal is dead. Linkin Park are not, because they were al-

ways more than the meager sum of that combination – more pop and classic rock in their riffs, hooks and drive."
(**David Fricke**, *Rolling Stone*, *Minutes To Midnight* review, 2007)

"...the group does stand apart from the pack by having the foresight to smash all nu-metal trademarks – buzzing guitars, lumbering rhythms, angsty screaming, buried scratching, rapped verses..."
(**Stephen Thomas Erlewine**, *All Music Guide*, *Meteora* review, 2003)

"If young rock acts are struggling to sell albums, someone forgot to tell Linkin Park. Seven years since their debut, Hybrid Theory, won a Grammy, the Californian sextet have shifted more than 50 million copies of just three studio albums..."
(**Lisa Verrico, *The Times***, O2 Arena gig review, 2008)

"Those against Linkin Park say they're more brand than band... Linkin Park are better placed than most of their peers, mind, mainly because they've solved their biggest problem – how do you follow up a multi-million selling debut LP? – In typically sensible Linkin style."

(**Michael Lane,** *NME*,
London gig review, 2003)

"...Linkin Park's first album hasn't exactly stood the test of time, but that's because it did exactly what rock was originally supposed to do. It provided a loud, bratty and thoroughly modern-sounding encapsulation of the frustrations of adolescence."
(**Trevor Baker,** *Guardian Online/Blog*,
Why It's Worth Celebrating Nu-metal's Anniversary, 2008)

SOME FURTHER THOUGHTS ON THE BAND

Carl Begai
(*Brave Words & Bloody Knuckles*)
"When Hybrid Theory *surfaced in 2000 the whole rap metal / crossover movement was tired and old, offering up nothing new within the done to death shotgun verses and crunch grooves. Linkin Park turned the genre on its ear through ridiculously simple song arrangements and, ironically, the singing talents of vocalist Chester Bennington. Expectations were painfully low given the hype surrounding kiddie skate-punk wannabe bad-asses Limp Bizkit, but that first spin through 'One Step Closer' was more than enough* to rewire the brain, with Bennington's "Shut up when I'm talking to you!" delivery powerful enough to take up forced residence for a week. The hits that followed in 'Papercut' and 'Crawling' continued the trend, but it was 'In The End' that cemented* Hybrid Theory*'s future status as a classic album. Not since Faith No More's 'Epic' had a song captured hearts and minds within rap metal fandom so completely. Buried treasures are to be had, however, in stellar full metal tracks 'Forgotten' and 'A Place For My Head' and the eloquent 'My December', all three ranking up there with the airwave hits. Sadly, the band hasn't been able to match the magic of* Hybrid Theory *over the last several years beyond a few intermittent sparks. A crying shame, actually, because beneath the video mega-budgets and million dollar studio productions lurks a band loaded with raw talent."*

Malcolm Dome
(*Classic Rock/Total Rock*)
"Linkin Park have smoothly become one of the most despised bands of the modern era – and it's hard to understand why. It seemed to start when they first appeared, with suggestions they were nothing more than a 'manufactured boy band with guitars.' Quite why there's been this antip-

athy is hard to fathom. In reality, they are a very good modern pop-rock band. The band write good, accessible songs and deliver them well. So, where's the problem? It must be said there's little obvious personality within the Park ranks, but their music is strong enough to stand on its own merits. It's interesting to note that early albums sidestepped anything controversial – even the language was clean, ensuring its appeal to a broad audience. Now, they've become a little more adult in style. But the essential plank of their success remains the ability to come up with hummable songs. Doubtless, they won't be remembered as pioneers, but I don't believe that was ever their ambition. They deserve respect for what they're good at, not opprobrium for what is meaningless in the Linkin Park world."

D.X. Ferris
(author of *Slayer's Reign
In Blood 33 1/3*)
"I'm all about the rap-rock, but I was never a fan of Linkin Park – before or after their rap era. That said, I respect them. On the early albums, here's what made them stand out the most: Unlike many rap-rock artists (and fans), they never thought they were Method Man or Eminem. It showed in how they rhymed, talked, and dressed.

Sure, they wore askew ballcaps from time to time. But Linkin Park wasn't full of yahoos who had listened to The Chronic one time too many and decided it was time to start spouting bullshit like, 'Step up and catch a beat-down from the ill player rhyme-sayers.' I never looked at the group at thought, 'Psah – frontin' white kids!' Unlike many of Linkin's contemporaries from that day, they never sounded like a bunch of douchebags who were just aping Rage Against The Machine or Limp Bizkit. And regardless of how you assign them to a genre – rap-rock, rap-metal, nu-metal – the group's staying power is unmatched. Linkin Park's heavy music was authentic and honest. It wasn't, strictly speaking, aggressive. In songs like 'One Step Closer'

and 'Somewhere I Belong', they're not summoning up some fake pro-wrestler rage against a perceived slight; they're representing suburban guys whose feelings are hurt – and they're appropriately pissed. (And they're not whining with that sissy-fied helplessness that would become so popular in the emo genres). Maybe something like 'Numb' is an overreaction, but that's what raging hormones are about; you hear similar gripes from The Cure to Metallica. After Incubus, Linkin Park is probably the most musical of the DJ-packing rock bands. You could tell they'd listened to different music like Depeche Mode and Nine Inch Nails – and they were trying to create their own thing. I'm not a fan of their post-rap material either, but it's pure. They're not chasing somebody else's ideas. Their sound is their own."

Lonn Friend
(author of *Life On Planet Rock*)
"[When I saw Linkin Park in 2003] Chester and DJ/MC Mike Shinoda stalked the stage and touched the children, the screamer and the rapper in breathtaking balance. The material was so strong, it resonated within the DNA of every fan, kicking them back into the cathartic electric chairs that'd been charged and juiced for their temporary salvation. 'Faint', 'Numb', 'Crawling', 'In The End', 'My December', 'Pushing Me Away', 'A Place For My Head', 'One Step Closer' – essential hymns for a population on the brink."

Mark Hoaksey
(Powerplay magazine)

"Interestingly, despite falling outside of the core of our editorial style at Powerplay, our one and only Linkin Park front cover, published during the promotional period for the band's debut album, was one of our biggest selling issues to date – a testament to the buzz the band was creating at the time. Though hardly pioneers, their melding of catchy metal riffs and vocals with electro and rap struck a cord with a generation growing up at the tail end of the misery-loaded grunge era. An album that was maligned as much as it was adored, and still a personal favourite of mine, that debut is a striking example of a young band stumbling upon a winning formula just at a time when the world needed something different. Unfortunately, nothing on successive albums came close to matching the energy and vitality of the debut. Sophomore offering Meteora *was patchy at best with only two or three quality rock songs, and the supremely disappointing third album* Minutes To Midnight *wouldn't even have registered a blip on the metal radar had it not been for the band's earlier work. Whether this change in style is down to the band members' own musical preferences, pressure from their record label, or simply a cynical search for greater revenue, it's impossible to say but if the band continues down its current creative path, then it will certainly alienate much of its existing fan base and in the current climate, it's unclear where replacements would be found. Despite this three-album slide from red hot to barely lukewarm, the band's excellent live shows still retain the raw metallic edge of the early days and have helped Linkin Park to retain credibility and maintain their popularity, however tours alongside bands from outside of metal music, such as rap artist Jay-Z, have further tarnished the band's image, adding to the confusion of fans and reinforcing the belief that the band wishes to eschew its metal roots completely in favour of pop mediocrity."*

Anthony Morgan
(*Lucem Fero.com*)

"My initial brush with metal music came in late 2000, a time when nu-metal experienced sunnier days. Several nu-metal records gained mainstream attention during that year, particularly; Chocolate Starfish And The Hot Dog Flavored Water *(Limp Bizkit),* Infest *(Papa Roach),* The Sickness *(Disturbed) and* Hybrid Theory *(Linkin Park). Though metal's Internet community will likely snigger, I'll just*

plead guilty, and admit to the fact that all of those albums were purchases I personally made. Nu-metal's time has since passed, though several years on, Linkin Park's third album Minutes To Midnight *figured amongst the top five on several charts worldwide. Certain quarters love the group, whilst others loathe the group with a passion. Are Linkin Park all that bad? Chester Bennington, particularly, boasts a voice whose versatility is likely the envy of many, and can execute an array of vocal styles, whether they be heavier, or more tender. More importantly though, acts like Linkin Park serve an extremely important purpose. Further investigation on my part led me to discover Metallica, and the rest, as they say, is history. Since then, I've discovered a variety of metal acts who're lesser known than Linkin Park, and others who're mainstays of the genre. Also, I ventured into the world of metal journalism. Without more commercially led acts like Linkin Park, where would I have been, and others like myself? Linkin Park are a flagbearer on behalf of metal, and attract the curiosity of unknowing listeners. Some of these listeners will be discouraged by these less commercial groups, while others will become lifelong metal fanatics like I did. Without the likes of Linkin Park, there's little hope of attracting the metal fanatics of tomorrow, and new fans are what will keep metal alive in years to come. I'm all for Linkin Park, and hope more commercially laden metal/hard rock acts like them make a firm dent in mainstream music."*

Jason Ritchie
(Get Ready To Rock.com)
"Linkin Park for me are a success due to two things – first their videos which mix the standard band performance with some almost Hollywood like fantasy film sequences. Many videos made today have little thought going into them but the Linkin Park ones really do stand up to repeated views. Secondly, of all the nu-metal bands Linkin Park are one of the few that have transcended the genre and found fans across the musical spectrum. Normally when a metal fan sees/hears mixing desks they run for the hills, but Linkin Park meld the mixing element so seamlessly into their music you hardly notice it. Every musical genre has a few bands that have the longevity and the talent to succeed, Linkin Park are one such band and will be played long after most nu-metal bands are found residing in the 'Where are they now?' files."

Joe Shooman
(author of *Trivium: The Mark Of Perseverance*)
"There's one thing you can say about Linkin Park and that's that everyone has an opinion on them. Many metallers of the traditional kind were first confused, then annoyed, then perhaps a little intrigued by the fusion of rap and metal purveyed by LP and others, but Chester Bennington et al had a little more in their locker than that. Although the first forays of Hybrid Theory *and* Meteora *were certainly good examples of what became known as nu-metal and placed the band central to that movement, subsequent work has shown that the group are more than prepared to express themselves in more ways than the template would indicate. It's interesting that nu-metal has/had become so derided – the musical landscape was crying out for something interesting in the void left by grunge – but its speed and beat always had in it an inbuilt obsolescence that meant it'd date very badly, very quickly. The challenge for groups like LP is to develop into equally artistic but more contemporarily-palatable sounds and it seems they're up for the challenge. It wasn't to everyone's tastes, but you couldn't ignore it, and any band that has the ability to polarise opinion must necessarily therefore also have something about them worth investigating."*

LINKIN PARK IN THEIR OWN WORDS

"Hip-hop right now is mostly based on keyboard music. One of my goals of the Fort Minor album was to keep the big sound of a hip hop album, but make it using live instruments and hand-played keyboard parts. It's an organic hip-hop album. When you hear a tambourine, bass, or guitar, it's played by hand."
Mike Shinoda
(*antimusic.com*, 2005)

*"With a lot of the textures in the past I didn't really have any solos as I thought that they just sounded somewhat clichéd in rock songs. And I felt that, at least in my tastes, popular alternative music has clearly come around full circle today and that in the case of this record [*Minutes To Midnight*] some of the solos on the record really I think, made the song that so much more special."*
Brad Delson
(*ultimate-guitar.com*, 2007)

"Today, so far, I've gone to the gym, I've gone to eat, I bought a CD, and I sat in my hotel room and watched television. Later, I'll go to the venue, eat, play some vid-

eo games, play a show, play some more video games and go to sleep – the best part of the day being the show. The rest of the stuff – you're waiting for that time."
Mike Shinoda
(*USA Weekend*, 2003)

"When Mike and I sat down and wrote the lyrics [for Hybrid Theory] we wanted to be as honest and open as we could. We wanted something people could connect with, not just vulgarity and violence. We didn't want to make a big point of not cussing, but we don't have to hide behind anything to show how tough we can be."
Chester Bennington
(*Rolling Stone*, 2001)

"It's been such a ride, when we put out that album [Minutes To Midnight], we had been gone for a few years and we didn't know what the fans would think of the new direction, and now looking at this whole thing, it has spawned more singles than any other album, and it's just great to look back at it and say, 'Okay, we took a huge risk, and luckily the fans are still with us.' "
Mike Shinoda
(*Winnipeg Sun*, 2008)

"Chester's the emotional leader – he brings a real fire to everything that goes on... Mike and Joe are the creative forces in the band. Rob and Brad handle the business stuff. I'm the one who doesn't have a talent."
David Farrell
(*Blender*, 2002)

"When people ask I tell them that I'm the lead emcee and I'm the backup vocalist for Chester. He's doing the harmonies when I'm rapping so we're patting each other's backs."
Mike Shinoda
(*shoutweb.com*, 2000)

"There were many inspirations. The main ones being the world itself. I tried the best I could to make this video ['What I've Done'] a mirror to the world. The imagery used was carefully selected to show the dynamic contrast between the accomplishment of man and the demise of man. We have been blessed to live a life with many luxuries that have been discovered throughout history. At the same time, it is not all fun and games. There is a fine balance in the world that can be tipped at any point in time and some may argue that it is being tipped. We as a civilization can only maintain that balance with responsibility."
Joe Hahn
(*lpassociation.com*, 2007)

"The American middle class is probably the hardest working class of people in the country. It's not like we have things handed to us on a silver platter... It's turned into a f**king rags to riches story. Whatever. "I'm not a loser."

Chester Beinnington
(*Q Magazine*, 2003)

"First, MTV called Jay [-Z] and told him they wanted to do a live mash-up performance. They wanted to know who he would like to do it with. He called us."

Mike Shinoda
(*soundslam.com*, 2004)

"Going back to Linkin Park is like going back home. I always joke that I came into hip-hop through the back door, because people know me from Linkin Park, first and foremost. And so when they hear my album, they go, 'Oh, there's the Linkin Park guy.' When I was putting together the Fort Minor record, it probably would've been easier to put my name on the front of it or to make songs that sounded like Linkin Park. But it's all about making something that's honest."

Mike Shinoda
(*MTV*, 2007)

"I also think ▓▓▓▓ a really solid fan base out the▓▓ too, that went out and got the reco▓▓ Min-

utes To Midnight], since we've been around for a little while now. We had our 10 year anniversary as a band and we spent a lot of time touring and on the road, really connecting with our fan base. I think that had something to do with the numbers also."

Rob Bourdon
(*Live Daily*, 2007)

"I think the VMAs [MTV Video Music Awards] have completely lost touch with a broad scope of music. It was very bubble gum and Disney, which is why bands like Foo Fighters, and everybody else in my group weren't there. Honestly I didn't think we were going to win, because we literally felt like we were too old."

Chester Bennington (*Entertainment Weekly*, 2008)

"When we make music, we're not thinking of being part of any genre. I think most people can tell the obvious differences between Red Hot Chili Peppers, Rage Against The Machine, Limp Bizkit and us. There are similar elements, obviously, but when you break it down to the things that give each band their own sound, it's pretty easy and simple to tell each band apart."

Mike Shinoda
(*Sydney Morning Herald*, 2003)

"I guess there is less stress for me actually in the studio and it takes less time because of all the work that goes on before. Before we enter the studio is when all the pressure is on me to get everything up to speed or up to where it needs to be for the actual recording. Probably about three months before we started recording I was working on my parts and working on the parts and getting all that stuff together."*

Rob Bourdon
(*shoutweb.com*, 2003)

ART CENTRE COLLEGE OF DESIGN

Founded in 1930 in Los Angeles, the college moved to Pasadena in 1976 and opened a second campus in 2004. It's a private institution and apparently one of the world's leading colleges for the study art and design.

A first thought would be that this institution has nothing to do with Linkin Park. However, the college boasts a long list of notable artists amongst its former students, including the film director Michael Bay (*Bad Boys*), film director Zack Synder (*Watchmen*), screenwriter Roger Avary (*Pulp Fiction*) and Joe Hahn and Mike Shinoda. Indeed, it was here that Shinoda and Hahn first met, although Joe Hahn didn't graduate from the Art Centre College Of Design. Shinoda was studying graphic design and illustration; he graduated in 1998 as the youngest in his class, earning a Bachelor of Arts (BA) in Illustration. In 2004,

Shinoda returned to the college to found the Michael K. Shinoda Endowed Scholarship, which was first awarded in 2006. Like all scholarships, it was created for those who are exceptionally talented but need financial assistance. Shinoda funds the scholarship programme by selling his artwork and illustrations on his website *mikeshinoda.com* and at exhibitions.

Speaking at an exhibition in November 2006, Shinoda told reporters (*artisannews.com*):

"The intention of the art show, besides my effort to put some of this stuff that I've done in the past few years up on display, is I wanted to give some of the proceeds to my scholarship at Art Centre, that's a college of design and illustration scholarship. With the stuff selling online, it's done really well. I don't have a bottom line figure for how much we made for the scholarship yet, that actually comes at the end of this first quarter, however the stuff is still up at mikeshinoda.com. So, if you want to check out the art or if you want to support some young aspiring artist who can't afford college then check that out."

Visit *artcenter.edu*

"The way we write is to bring in something that either one or two guys have been working on and develop it together."
Dave Farrell (*bassguitarmagazine.com*, 2007)

RANDOM TRIVIA

Some of the following little anecdotes are repeated elsewhere in the book; however, it is always handy to have a list of trivia on a band just in case you should need it in a pub quiz! Everybody loves trivia...

Linkin Park have toured with an array of different artists, including Cypress Hill, Adema, DJ Z-Trip, Xzibit, Mudvayne, Slipknot, Marilyn Manson, Limp Bizkit, Snoop Dogg, Papa Roach and Blindside.

Mike Shinoda is an accomplished graphic illustrator and artist. He has exhibited his art at galleries in

Los Angeles and started a scholarship in 2004 at California's Art Centre College of Design to benefit aspiring artists.

The band purposely misspelled 'Pancake' on the DVD *Frat Party At The Pankake Festival.*

In December 2008, it was announced that Linkin Park are the most popular band on online social networking sites like Facebook. Over four million fans added the band to their profiles via this link: *iLike.com/linkinpark*.

Collision Course was a number one hit in the American *Billboard 200* but failed to make the top 10 in the UK in 2004.

In December 2008, Linkin Park's music (along with all other artists on the Warner Music Group label) was taken off YouTube because of a dispute between Warner and Google, the company that owns YouTube.

Their debut album *Hybrid Theory* garnered the band three prestigious Grammy awards: 'Best New Artist' and 'Best Rock Album' and for the single 'Crawling' they bagged a nomination for 'Best Hard Rock Performance.'

Before settling with 'Linkin Park', the band played under the monikers 'Xero' and 'Hybrid Theory.'

Linkin Park have their own record label: Machine Shop Recordings.

Meteora is named after the famous rock pillars in Greece which house six monasteries.

In 2002, the band created an annual festival called Projekt Revolution.

Linkin Park "went green" in 2007 by declaring that $1 from every ticket sold on the Projekt Revolution festival would go to American Forests.

Guitarist Brad Delson was an extra in the 1991 Hollywood film *Bill & Ted's Bogus Journey.*

The song 'What I've Done' from *Minutes To Midnight* features on *Guitar Hero World Tour.*

Joe Hahn opened a retail concept store called Suru (in Melrose Avenue, LA) in 2005.

Jay-Z features on the 2008 live album/DVD *Road To Revolution: Live At Milton Keynes.*

Fort Minor is the name of the side-project of Mike Shinoda. Their album *The Rising Tied* was released in 2005 through Machine Shop/Warner.

Joe Hahn had a small acting role in the short film *Little Pony*, directed by Filip Engstrom.

Minutes To Midnight is a direct reference to the Doomsday Clock. The Bulletin of the Atomic Scientists (basically, a board of directors) at the University of Chicago created the symbolic clock in 1947 during the Cold War as a way to say the human race is only minutes to midnight when Doomsday (the end of the world) would happen.

Brad Delson and Rob Bourdon are both of the Jewish faith.

Linkin Park fuse alternative rock, metal and hip-hop, which creates a nightmare for High Street record stores that categorise artists by genre.

SURU

SURU is the name of a small clothing store Joe Hahn owns in Los Angeles. As well as selling clothes, the store has held exhibitions and art shows. On 15th November, 2008, SURU held one by the artist Axis; the show was called 'Welcome To My Nightmare.'

The SURU official website states:

'SURU (which means 'hand printed' or 'print by hand' in Japanese) is a concept retail store and brand. The vision is simple: combine the world of art and fashion into a retail store that caters to today's ever growing demand for high-end street wear and fashion forward consumers. Like art, the focus is on exclusivity and rarity where limited edition apparel, vinyl toys and books are the focus of the retail space. Since its inception, SURU has gained worldwide recognition due to its affiliations with Joe Hahn, who is co-owner of the brand and a member of the rock band Linkin Park. Situated on the infamous Melrose Strip, the SURU retail experience is innovative and minimalistic in design, with a conveyor belt revolving around the store showcasing its T-shirts.'

Mike Shinoda designed the album cover for Styles Of Beyond's debut album *2000 Fold*.

Like many rock/metal stars Chester Bennington has lots of tattoos and has even worked with Club Tattoo in Arizona.

Linkin Park have released the same amount of live CD and DVDs (inc. *Frat Party*) as they have original studio albums.

Chris Cornell features on the 2008 EP *Songs From The Un-*

derground. He can be heard on 'Crawling.'

The youngest member of Linkin Park is Rob Bourdon, born 20th January, 1979.

As well as a Linkin Park song, 'Leave Out All The Rest' is the title of a 2008 episode of the hit US crime show *CSI*. After striking a deal with broadcasters CBS, the song features in said episode. It also features in the vampire fantasy film *Twilight* and was used on a UK TV promotional ad for *Law And Order*.

Chester Bennington was bitten by a recluse spider during the 2001 Ozzfest tour of the States.

Joe Hahn has directed music videos for Static X, Story Of The Year, Xzibit, Alkaline Trio and The X-Ecutioners.

OFFICIAL LINKIN PARK BOOKS

From The Inside: Linkin Park's Meteora (2004/05)

Linkin Park's first (and so far only) officially released book is a look behind the scenes of the band's second studio album *Mete-*ora. It was published in the US in 2004 and the UK in 2005 by Hal Leonard/Bradson Press. The text was written by Steve Baltin and it is complimented by the photography of Gregg Watermann. The book also has an introduction by David Fricke, the Senior Editor at *Rolling Stone* magazine.

The book's press release says,

"Since emerging on the music scene with their multi-platinum debut release, Hybrid Theory *in 2000, Linkin Park has established themselves as not only one of the most compelling recording artists of a generation, but one of the most versatile as well. Through the release of two studio albums and various remix and live projects, the band has continually delivered their music packaged in exciting ways, most recently with* MTV Ultimate Mash-Ups Presents – Jay-Z/Linkin Park: Collision Course *with rapper Jay-Z, which entered the* Billboard 200 *album chart this week in the number one position (please see separate release). Known for their unwavering commitment to their fans worldwide, Linkin Park has created a benchmark of sorts in fan relations that other artists can only ever hope to achieve. To show appreciation for their passionate legion of fans,*

Linkin Park has decided to give something back: a behind-the-scenes look into the experience of creating and performing their second album, Meteora. *Pho-tographer Greg Watermann was brought in to document their lives on and off the stage during their 2003-2004 world tour and the results come alive in* From The In-

TATTOOS

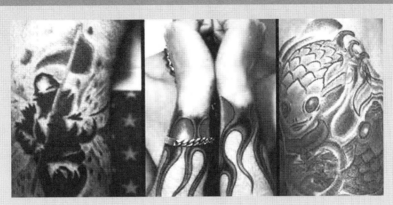

Frontman Chester Bennington is what you could call a "tattoo enthusiast." He got his first tat aged 18. Many rock stars have an abundance of tattoos – most famously Ozzy Osbourne, Tommy Lee and Lemmy – but for Bennington, it's not just about appearance but art and meaning: the tattoos have to mean something to him on a personal level. Bennington is also involved in the "tattoo community" and in March 2009 it was announced that he was teaming up with Club Tattoo owners Thora and Sean Dowdell to open a Club Tattoo in Planet Hollywood at the Miracle Mile Shops, Las Vegas. Bennington also has a personal connection to Club Tattoo in Tempe, Arizona, where he had some of his older tattoos done. Bennington's body art includes a Japanese Coi Fish, Pisces, a *Hybrid Theory* sol-dier, flames and a dragon, amongst other things.

Bennington told *vegasdeluxe.com*:

"Sean [Dowdell] and I met when I was just getting into high school, and he was pretty close to getting out of high school. We started a band, Grey Daze, based out of Phoenix. We were in a band for probably six years during that time. We did well for ourselves. There was a really great club that we would play at all the time, and Sean decided he wanted to open the first Club Tattoo right next to it. That was the first one, 14 years ago. Sean was solo at that time, and I was working at Burger King and riding my skateboard back then. But I laid the tiles and did the painting, and that's how it all started."

Visit *clubtattoo.com*

side: Linkin Park's Meteora. *This fully authorised tome – the band's first ever – provides an intimate behind-the-scenes look at the musicians during their tour. The book furnishes readers with eyewitness accounts of the good times, bad days and bunches of random events that happened to Mike, Rob, Phoenix, Brad, Mr. Hahn and Chester during their travels throughout Europe, North America, Southeast Asia, Australia and Japan.*

From The Inside *also gives fans the opportunity to go beyond the security gates and onto the tour bus, offering a personal view of Linkin Park's everyday lives. The book includes candid captions written by the members themselves and is filled with more than 200 exclusive never-before-seen colour and black-and-white pho-tographs by Watermann on premium paper that capture the essence of what life was like for the group, from writing and recording songs in the studio, to playing shows on stage. In addition,* From The Inside *includes a special sixteen page section that contains photos from the making of the five music videos from* Meteora.

From The Inside: Linkin Park's Meteora *is for anyone interested in knowing how six widely different young men stay grounded amid the pressure and pace of fame and adoration. It presents a glimpse of the group behind the songs and into the unbelievable phenomenon that is Linkin Park."*

UNOFFICIAL LINKIN PARK BOOKS

Linkin Park – The Unauthorised Biography In Words And Pictures (2001)

This slim full colour unofficial biography of the band was published in 2001 by Chrome Dreams. It was written by Ben Graham and edited by Billy Dancer. It was the first biography of the band and it's an easy read with plenty of photographs and a fluent writing style.

The book's press release says:

"With rock and metal acts now forming the largest chunk of the pie chart we more commonly know as 'The Music Business', and 'Nu Metal' bands (rock/rap crossover artists) representing the lion's share, Linkin Park are truly a band whose time is now. By somehow managing to attract fans of metal, rap and to some extent, boy bands, they are without a doubt the most successful rock act to hit the scene since Korn and Limp Bizkit started the whole thing. Having sold over three million albums since the release of their stunning debut Hybrid Theory *just six months ago, making it one of the longest staying albums currently gracing the UK's top 20 (a rare feat for a rock record in today's fickle market) and recently being exposed to over two million hungry metal fans through their in-clusion on the prestigious Ozzfest tour, this Californian six piece have already hit the big time and still have so much to achieve.* Linkin Park – The Unauthorised Biography In Words And Pictures, *picks up the threads and tells the tale. Superbly presented with the target audience of 13 - 25 year olds in mind, offering equal parts stunning photography and intelligent text, and a pocket money sized price tag to boot, this first available biography on the hottest new band around is certain to appeal to their millions of fans."*

UNOFFICIAL LINKIN PARK DVDS

Linkin Park – Conspiracy Theory (2007)
A documentary charting the band's rise to global fame. This 86 minute documentary was released on DVD in 2007 via Chrome Dreams.

The press release says,

"Linkin Park are a phenomenon of their generation, mixing a metal sound with rap and rock beats that has created a sensation worldwide. But who are they really? Get beyond the hype and get the real story with this in-depth

documentary that delves into the history of the band and the individuals who comprise it, exploring the reasons for their spectacular success. Featuring exclusive interviews with the band and those closest to them, Conspiracy Theory *is an unprecedented opportunity for fans to get to know this award-winning band whose*

Linkin Park – From Whisper To A Scream (2008)

Released in 2008 by Plastic Head, this 62 minute long documentary does not examine the making of *Minutes To Midnight*, only the albums that came before (most-

innovative, creative approach to making music has made them one of the most popular groups of their time."

Linkin Park Unauthorized (2007)

An unofficial documentary on the band released in 2007, after the huge success of *Minutes To Midnight*. It was issued by Whe Europe Limited.

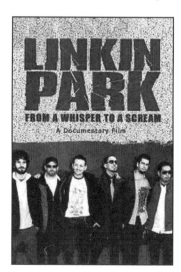

ly *Hybrid Theory* and *Meteora*). Like other documentaries of its ilk it is lightweight with no revelations and input from the band.

UNOFFICIAL CD / AUDIO BOOKS ABOUT LINKIN PARK

Maximum Linkin Park – The Unauthorised Biography (2001)

This was the first ever audio biography of the band. Released in 2001 by Chrome Dreams, it includes comments and interview footage from the band themselves as well as a fold-out poster and an eight page illustrated booklet.

Linkin Park X-Posed – The Interview (2007)

Released in 2007 by Chrome Dreams, *X-Posed* is a fascinating collection of interviews with the members of Linkin Park.

The press release says,

"Linkin Park X-Posed *offers the opportunity to hear this top selling artist in their own words – get the low-down straight from the horse's mouth! The disc provides up-to-the-minute interview material from a wide variety of sources, and is entertaining as well as being highly informative. Fans can finally hear what motivates, inspires and amuses their favourite artist, with countless recollections painting a fascinating insight that is otherwise unobtainable elsewhere.*"

Linkin Park – The Document (2007)

An audio documentary on the making of Linkin Park's music including *Minutes To Midnight*. It was released in 2007 by Chrome Dreams.

The press release says,

"*Over 50 minutes of in-depth interviews with members of Linkin Park in which they talk about the making of their latest album. The*

band discusses the background to many of the songs, and explains the entire process of putting the record together, from production to finance and promotion. A detailed and intriguing look at Linkin Park and the making of Minutes To Midnight, *this documentary film goes behind the scenes and tells the Linkin Park story in its entirety. Includes rare footage, exclusive interviews, location shots, comment and criticism from rock's finest commentators and many other features. 'Extras' include interactive quiz and digital discography."*

WEBSITES – LINKIN PARK IN CYBERSPACE

Linkin park are literally all over the web. Just type their name into Google and you'll get page after page of news and information relating to the band. For general news on the group it is worth looking at websites like **blabbermouth.net, mtv.com** *and* **artistdirect.com.** *Magazine sites like* **classicrockmagazine.com, rollingstone.com, nme.com** *and* **bravewords.com** *are regularly updated and contain the latest news on the rock and metal scene. And for biographies and music videos the following websites are also useful:* **mp3.com, youtube.com** *and* **allmusicguide. com.** *Alternatively, search for information on the band yourself by typing their name into a search engine like Yahoo or Google. Here is a list of the good (and not so good) Linkin Park websites, including the ones that are not endorsed by the band.*

BAND

linkinpark.com

The band's official website includes a section called 'LPTV' which has promo clips from the 2008 Projekt Revolution tour, and various odds and ends such as personal messages from the band. Fans can become part of the network and make comments through a special 'Fans' section where you can join the forum and chat with other LP fans. You can also download music and photos and look at up-to-date tour photos. All of this is on the 'Home' page. The 'Band' section includes a sub-section for each member: you can read the band's biography and read their blogs while the 'Live' section includes past and present tour dates. The 'Music' section includes videos and the band's discography. Fans can also buy the official Linkin Park merchandise in the 'Shop'.

myspace.com/linkinpark

Linkin Park's official MySpace page has the usual information, such as a blog, a biography, a shop and music videos. Fans can also download some of their songs and buy their latest release, *Road To Revolution: Live At Milton Keynes.*

facebook.com

Like most major artists Linkin Park are also on the hugely successful social networking site Facebook. You can become a 'Fan' of the band at this link: *facebook.com/pages/Linkin-Park/8210451787* At the time of writing in early 2009

the band had a total fan count over of 4,000,000.

linkinparkmerch.com

The *Linkin Park Online Store* is linked to their official website. It sells CDs, DVDs, t-shirts, posters, banners and various other types of merchandise for all fans.

linkin-park.com

linkin-park.com has a lot of substance and is apparently 'The Most Popular Linkin Park Fan Site.' It has all the obvious material like a biography, discography, tour dates, a gallery and a forum, but also a section that includes a display of posters, video clips, greeting cards, ring tones, stickers and t-shirts which fans can buy through the site. There's even a page that includes song lyrics. If this site doesn't have what you need there is a link directly to Google.

lpamerican.com

This is a fansite run by Brazilian fans; you can view the text in English or Portuguese. It is bang up to date and contains an archive of interviews and biographies. It's well worth a visit.

lptimes.com

This website has the usual batch of biographies, images, articles and links. There's also a section that has downloads for videos and band interviews. There's a store that sells merchandise and a home page containing the latest news on Linkin Park. The home page has a link to YouTube, which is useful (mostly for past and recent interviews with the band). This is a neatly maintained archive site.

lpassociation.com

The *Linkin Park Association* website is a visually appealing one. It has the following sections: 'News', 'Band', 'Music', 'Images', 'Tours', 'Downloads' and 'Forums.' There is also a 'Contact Us' page. It is regularly updated with the latest news on Linkin Park projects.

linkinparkforums.com

This features forums where fans can chat online about the band and their music.

linkinparksource.com

This (long neglected) website includes links to interviews with the band and articles in magazines like *Rolling Stone* and *Rock Sound*. This site doesn't even include information on *Minutes To Midnight* and it needs updating as those articles only date from 2000-01, but it is useful for information on the band's genesis. *Linkin Park Source* has the following sections: 'Articles/Bio', 'Discography', 'Lyrics', 'Tours', 'Pics', 'Forum' and 'Links.'

linkinparkwallpaper.net

This neatly designed site is updated as far as 2007's *Minutes To Midnight* and has sections called 'Gallery', 'Projects', 'Trivia', 'Quotes' and 'Fansites.'

Other Linkin Park related websites:

lpjz.com
linkin-park-lyrics.com

linkinpark.co.uk
urtone.warnerbrosrecords.com/
linkinpark
linkinpark.warnerreprise.com
lpstreetteam.com
lpfuse.co.uk

PERSONNEL

mikeshinoda.com

The official solo website of Mike Shinoda includes a blog, a display of Shinoda's artwork, photos of Shinoda, videos (no music videos but personal ones) and a store that sells Shinoda's official merchandise.

cbennington.com

This is the official website of Chester Bennington. It's basically a blog but also includes photos, links and a message board. Fans can receive the latest news on Bennington and Linkin Park by email.

robbourdonfansite.blogspot.com

An unofficial website featuring up to date news about Rob Bourdon and Linkin Park. It's basically a blog that's been online since 2007, which also features pictures of Bourdon and a forum where fans can chat online with each other. The webmaster is Tamara (female-metalzombie.blogspot.com).

delsononline.blogspot.com

A fansite dedicated to Brad Delson, it features the following sections: 'Bio/Facts', 'Interviews', 'Media', 'Blog Posts', 'Quotes' and 'Contact Us.' It is regularly updated.

joehahn.org
A regularly updated fansite dedicated to Linkin Park DJ Joe Hahn. There's not a great deal of substance; it's basically a blog with news updates.

bassslut.com
This is the official website of former Linkin Park bass player Scott Koziol. At the time of writing this site is under construction.

Other solo websites:

mikesonline.blogspot.com
chesterbeinnington.co.uk
chester-land.net
scottkoziol.com

OTHER

fortminor.com

This is the official website for Fort Minor, Mike Shinoda's hip-hop side-project. The site has the following sections: 'Bio', 'Media', 'Shots', 'Live', 'Community', 'MySpace', 'FM Militia', 'Street Team', 'Gear' and 'Links.'

fortminormilitia.com

The official fan club website for Fort Minor. You have to be a member to enter the website but you can browse the 'About FM Militia' page.

Other websites of interest:

myspace.com/fortminor
fortminor.co.uk

LINKIN PARK
IN SHOWBIZ

The following websites add a different view on the members of Linkin Park. As a successful American metal band with a broad audience they are often covered in the celebrity online press.

CelebrityOnlineNews.com
celebrityonlinenews.com/Celebrities/Linkin-Park

WhosDatedWho.com
whosdatedwho.com/topic/6371/linkin-park.htm

Askmen.com
askmen.com/men/entertainment_150/196_linkin_park.html

CelebrityPhotoz.com
celebrityphotoz.com/Linkin_Park

Celebs Quotes
celebsquotes.com/l/linkin-park

SNEAKERS

As well as being an artist and a musician, Mike Shinoda is a sneaker (trainers in Britain) designer. In 2008, he teamed up with DC Shoes and designed two pairs, called the MSDC Xander and the MSDC Pride. They featured Japanese and Koi designs on the sides and insoles. DC Shoes and Shinoda had previously worked together on a much smaller production. *"The first one was fun,"* Shinoda told *sneakerfreaker.com*,

"I considered it a bit of an experiment. I designed the packaging and the insole, and remixed the colours. I look at it like a prelude to this shoe."

The MSDC Xander and the MSDC Pride were given a limited release in August 2008 and were made available on *mikeshinoda.com*.

In May 2009, it was announced that Shinoda had re-teamed with DC Shoes for their third sneaker design together as part of the DC Remix series. This particular sneaker was named Xander Remix. It was inspired by his Japanese heritage and proceeds from sales went to the Michael K. Shinoda Endowed Scholarship at the Art Centre College of Design in Southern California. Speaking about the sneaker on *blabbermouth.net*, Shinoda enthused:

"We got an incredible response to the Xander Remix, a shoe I designed last year... I felt that a 'summer version' would be exciting; it's new, with lighter colours and patterns, but retains the comfort and durability of the last shoe. I wanted them to be worn every day yet still look and feel great, so I tested them personally. I wore them while on tour, in countries all around the world and they performed great... As a kid, I used to fold paper samurai helmets as part of the tradition for Japanese Boys' Day, a national Japanese holiday that falls in early May and celebrates children... It's kinda funny that the holiday coincides with the release of the shoe, which has origami-inspired patterns."

TIMELINE – SOME IMPORTANT DATES

What follows is a basic potted timeline of the band's career so far. Where possible exact dates have been referenced but in some cases day and month information is not available, only the year in question. But it still serves as a reliable timeline. If anything these dates show just how successful the band became in a relatively short period of time – by music business standards anyway.

1976

20th March
Chester Bennington was born on this day

1977

8th February
David Farrell was born on this day

11th February
Mike Shinoda was born on this day

15th March
Joseph Hahn was born on this day

1st December
Brad Delson was born on this day

1979

20th January
Rob Bourdon was born on this day

1995

Exact date unknown
Brad Delson and Mike Shinoda formed Xero (soon to be joined by Joe Hahn)

1996

Exact date unknown
The initial line-up of Xero was completed as Mark Wakefield and Dave Farrell joined the camp

31st October
Chester Bennington married his first wife Samantha

1997

Exact date unknown
The self-titled EP *Xero* was released (featuring Mike Shinoda, Brad Delson and vocalist Mark Wakefield)

1998

Exact date unknown
Chester Bennington left
Grey Daze

1999

March
Arizona based singer Chester
Bennington joined Xero (soon
to be re-named Hybrid Theory)
after a successful audition in
California

May
The self-titled EP *Hybrid Theory*
was released (featuring Shinoda,
Delson, Bennington, Rob Bour-
don, Kyle Christener and
Joe Hahn)

Exact date unknown
Hybrid Theory became Linkin
Park

2000

August
'One Step Closer' was released
on radio

October
The video for 'One Step Closer'
was premiered

24th October
Linkin Park's debut album *Hy-
brid Theory* was released in the
States

28th November
'One Step Closer' was released
in the States

2001

20th January
Hybrid Theory was released in
the UK

27th January
'One Step Closer' was released
in the UK

17th April
'Crawling' was released
in the States

21st April
'Crawling' was released
in the UK

30th June
'Papercut' was released
in the UK

25th September
'Papercut' was released
in the States

16th October
'In The End' was released
in the States

20th October
'Papercut' was released
in the UK

August
Linkin Park won 'Best Interna-
tional Newcomer' at the *Kerrang!*
Awards

October
Linkin Park performed 'One Step
Closer' at the VMA's with The X-
Ecutioners

19th November
The band's fan club Linkin Park
Underground was formed.
The club sent members the re-
mastered version of the *Hybrid
Theory EP* (the initial 500
copies were signed by all
band members)

20th November
Linkin Park's first DVD *Frat
Party At The Pankake Festival*
(aka *Frat Party*) was released

2002

February
'Crawling' won 'Best Hard Rock
Performance' at the Grammy
Awards

11th March
A 'Special Edition' version of
Hybrid Theory was released
in Japan

7th May
The Japanese only release *In The
End: Live & Rare* went on sale

15th July
'H! Vltg3/Pts.OF.Athrty' was released in the States

Exact date unknown
'Enth E Nd / Frgt/10' was
released in the States

30th July
Reanimation was released
in the States

3rd August
'H! Vltg3/Pts.OF.Athrty' was
released in the UK

10th August
Reanimation was released
in the UK

December
Linkin Park announced plans for
a new studio album (*Meteora*)

December
Joe Hahn directed the music
video 'Symphony In Major X'
for Xzibit

2003

February
Linkin Park won 'Best Rock
Act' and 'Best Video' for 'Pts.
Of.Athrty' at the MTV Asia
Awards

February
linkinpark.com went online

March
Linkin Park were named *launch.
com*'s 'Artist Of The Month'

17th March
'Somewhere I belong' was released in the States

25th March
Meteora was released in the
States

29th March
'Somewhere I Belong' was released in the UK

5th April
Meteora was released in the UK

April
Meteora went Platinum

May
Guitar World magazine put
Linkin Park on their May issue

10th May
Mike Shinoda married Anna
Hillinger

10th June
'Faint' was released in the States

21st June
'Faint' was released in the UK

August
'Somewhere I Belong' won 'Best
Video' at the VMA's

August
Linkin Park performed live and won 'Best International Act' at the *Kerrang!* Awards

2nd August
Linkin Park performed at the Reliant Stadium in Houston, Texas (this was recorded for the CD/DVD *Live In Texas*)

3rd August
Linkin Park performed at the Texas Stadium in Irving, Texas (this was recorded for the CD/DVD *Live In Texas*)

2nd September
Frat Party was reissued in CD size case

20th September
'Numb' was released in the UK

14th October
'Numb' was released in the States and the official guitar tab book hit stores

November
Chester Bennington and David Farrell attended the American Music Awards where they were guest presenters

18th November
Live In Texas was released in the States

6th December
Live In Texas was released in the UK

December
Live In Texas was certified Gold

2004

12th January
'From The Inside' was released in the States

March
Linkin Park donated $75,000 to the Special Operations Warrior Foundation

February
'Lying From You' hit the US airwaves

23rd March
'Lying From You' was released in the States

3rd June
Linkin Park headlined the second day of the Download festival at the Glasgow Green (Scotland)

5th June
Linkin Park headlined the first day of the Download festival at Donnington (England)

22ⁿᵈ June
'Breaking The Habit' was released in the States

29ᵗʰ June
The 'Tour Edition' version of *Meteora* was released

18ᵗʰ July
Linkin Park and Jay-Z performed at The Roxy Theatre in LA; the performance is featured in the CD/DVD set *Collision Course*

August
'Enjoy The Silence' by Depeche Mode was remixed by Chester Bennington

16ᵗʰ November
'Numb/Encore' was released in the States

30ᵗʰ November
Collision Course was released in the States. Also, the official book *From The Inside: Linkin Park's Meteora* was published in hardcover in the States

4ᵗʰ December
'Numb/Encore' was released in the UK

11ᵗʰ December
Collision Course was released in the UK

2005

1ˢᵗ June
From The Inside: Linkin Park's Meteora was published in hardcover in the UK

2ⁿᵈ July
Linkin Park performed at Live 8 (in Philadelphia)

10ᵗʰ September
Chester Bennington performed 'Let Down' at ReAct Now: Music & Relief benefit concert; he was joined by Julien-K

22ⁿᵈ November
Fort Minor's *The Rising Tied* was released in the States

2006

1ˢᵗ January
'Dirt Off Your Shoulder/Lying From You' was released worldwide (with video)

8th February
Linkin Park performed with Jay-Z at the American Grammy Awards in LA. (They picked up 'Best Rap/Sung Collaboration')

10th April
The Fort Minor single 'Where'd You Go' (produced by Brad Delson) was released in the States

28th July
The big screen adaption of *Miami Vice* was released in the States: Linkin Park contributed to the soundtrack

August
Linkin Park had accrued around 50 songs for what would become *Minutes To Midnight*

12th-13th August
The band performed at the two day festival Summer Sonic in Japan

1st September
The film *Crank* was released in the States: it features a cameo by Chester Bennington

2007

10ᵗʰ April
'What I've Done' was released in the States

5ᵗʰ May
Live versions of 'Given Up', 'What I've Done' and 'No More Sorrow' were made available on *Sessions@AOL*

7ᵗʰ May
'What I've Done' was released in the UK

9ᵗʰ – 18ᵗʰ May
Minutes To Midnight was released around the world

12ᵗʰ May
Linkin Park performed 'Bleed It Out' and 'What I've Done' on *Saturday Night Live* in the States

9ᵗʰ June
Linkin Park headlined the famed Download festival at Donnington (England) on the second day (Saturday)

7ᵗʰ July
Linkin Park performed at the charity festival Live Earth Japan

10ᵗʰ July
Rock Phenomenon Mixtape CD (hosted by Mike Shinoda) was reissued with a new album cover.

27ᵗʰ July
Linkin Park performed 'Shadow Of The Day' for the first time live in Auburn, Washington

20ᵗʰ August
'Bleed It Out' was released in the UK

16ᵗʰ October
'Shadow Of The Day' was released in the States

12ᵗʰ November
'Shadow Of The Day' was released in the UK

20ᵗʰ December
'What I've Done' was made available as a playable song on the interactive game *Guitar Hero III: Legends Of Rock*

2008

16ᵗʰ January
Linkin Park performed 'Valentine's Day' for the first time at a show in Hanover, Germany

17ᵗʰ February
'Given Up' was released as a download single in the UK

3ʳᵈ March
'Given Up' was released as a download single in the States

March
Joe Hahn released his short film *The Seed*, which premiered at Pusan International Film Festival

29ᵗʰ June
Linkin Park played a sold out show at Milton Keynes Bowl, England (this was filmed for the CD/DVD *Road To Revolution*)

11ᵗʰ July
The second public art gallery by Mike Shinoda – called 'Glorious Access (BORN)' was pre-

miered at the Japanese American National Museum in LA

14th July
'Leave Out All The Rest' was released in the UK

15th July
'Leave Out All The Rest' was released in the US

24th November
Road To Revolution: Live At Milton Keynes (CD/DVD) was released in the UK
28th November

Songs From The Underground EP was released

2009

9th February
It was announced that Linkin Park would play on the new touring festival (of the UK and Europe) called Sonisphere with Metallica

11th February
Tickets for Linkin Park's headlining gig at Knebworth on 1st August as part of the

JAPANESE AMERICAN NATIONAL MUSEUM

From 12th July to 3rd August, 2008, the Japanese American National Museum – based in Little Tokyo, LA – staged the first of a two-part exhibition created by Mike Shinoda. Dubbed 'Glorious Excess (Born)', it was a blend of paintings, illustrations and digital works that fused pop culture commentary with classical influences. Proceeds from the exhibition were donated to Shinoda's scholarship programme, Michael K. Shinoda Endowed Scholarship.
Shinoda told reporters (*mtnops.com*):

"I believe in the work of the Japanese American National Museum and we have had a great relationship for the past few years. I'm proud to share the debut of this new series with the Japanese American National Museum."

Visit *janm.org*